D0143790

Asking Questions

Questions

A Rhetoric for the Intellectual Life

LEX RUNCIMAN
Linfield College

CHRIS ANDERSON
Oregon State University

Allyn and Bacon
Boston • London • Toronto • Sydney • Tokyo • Singapore

Vice President: Eben W. Ludlow
Series editorial assistant: Grace Trudo
Executive marketing manager: Lisa Kimball
Composition and prepress buyer: Linda Cox
Manufacturing buyer: Suzanne Lareau
Cover administrator: Linda Knowles
Editorial-production service: Shepherd, Inc.
Electronic composition: Shepherd, Inc.

Copyright © 2000 by Allyn & Bacon
A Pearson Education Company
Needham Heights, Massachusetts 02494

Internet: www.abacon.com

All rights reserved. No part of the material protected by this copyright notice may be reproduced or utilized in any form or by any means, electronic or mechanical, including photocopying, recording, or by any information storage and retrieval system, without the written permission of the copyright owner.

Library of Congress Cataloging-in-Publication Data

Runciman, Lex.
    Asking questions: a rhetoric for the intellectual life/by Lex Runciman and Chris Anderson.
        p. cm.
    Includes bibliographical references.
    ISBN 0-205-27828-0
    1. English language--Rhetoric. 2. Academic writing--Problems, exercises, etc. 3. Critical thinking--Problems, exercises, etc. 4. College readers. I. Anderson, Chris, 1955- II. Title.

PE1408.R855 1999
808'.042--dc21

99-042044

Printed in the United States of America

10 9 8 7 6 5 4 3 2 1   04 03 02 01 00 99

Credits begin on p. 223, which constitutes a continuation of this copyright page.

Table of Contents

Preface to Students

We want to start by affirming some things about students. We believe you're intelligent and thoughtful people, anxious to learn and already capable of high-order thinking. You want and should be taken seriously. We also know from experience that all of us are conditioned by a commercial culture that often replaces the complexity of the world as it really is with sound bites and sitcom stereotypes. It's only natural that many people in our classrooms are uneasy about the challenges of the intellectual life.

This book wants to help you meet those challenges. It wants to give you a clear sense of what defines the intellectual life, why such a life matters, and how such a life may be lived in a practical way.

This book is a collection of things to do. We don't lecture. We don't rehearse all the lessons about the writing process and the rhetorical situations that all of you have heard for years already—however valuable these lessons are. We ask questions, and break up our discussions into dozens of group and solo activities. We say, imagine that you're in this situation with this information—How would you think? What would you do? Take this reading and look at it from this angle—what do you see? And these activities, in turn, are grounded in each chapter by a set of writing topics for longer, academic essays—challenging topics—topics we hope will engage you in the ideas and methods of the book. To put this another way, the various classroom activities are meant to train you for the writing and rewriting of the papers.

Both the activities and the paper topics are the "Qs" of the QEC (Question, Exploration, Conclusion) method that we describe in Chapter 1. Your responses in class and at home are the "exploration."

The conclusion is, in part, the instructor's responsibility—through lectures or comments in the margins—though in another way it's finally your own responsibility to come to your conclusions as you decide what is possible, reasonable, worthwhile.

Our emphasis throughout this book is on what we regard as the "essential moves" of academic thinking and writing, the basic acts required in any piece of discourse in any discipline—making and supporting claims, stating an idea and then illustrating that idea. This, we want to show you, is the key to the university.

Chapter 1 invites you to resist clichés, and to recognize the need for concreteness that structures all academic writing right down to the shape of paragraphs. Chapter 2 introduces methods of analyzing and summarizing hard, demanding reading, methods that depend on understanding just this ebbing and flowing from the general to the particular. Chapter 3 takes critical reading a step further by demonstrating the need to "read between the lines," not just in literary texts but in all texts. Chapter 4 translates this method of deep analysis to the consideration of causes and effects. Chapter 5 brings forward all the work of the previous chapters and applies it to the making of decent and coherent public arguments. Finally, in Chapter 6, we suggest that many of our most important problems can't be reduced to the affirmative or the negative but exist in a kind of creative tension.

We propose simplified formulas—from QEC:CS to a "Revision Checklist," to something we call "TRIAC" (Topic, Restriction, Illustration, Analysis, Closure)—for helping you begin. Our strategy is to keep testing these simplifications against the complexities of difficult writing assignments. We want to say, don't panic—when in doubt, fall back on these schemes. But on the other hand, jump in. This is supposed to be hard. Get lost—you have many resources to help you find your way again.

Because what it comes down to, in any course at the university, is the need to engage complexity. What it comes down to, as the poet William Stafford once put it, are the very terms of the "intellectual way":

> Suppose you start to write for some cause you believe in, and suddenly you're smitten with the recollection or a realization that there's something in that cause or some recent thing that's been done by people in that cause that would spoil your case. So you suppress it. That would be one way. It wouldn't be my way. I feel that the university way, the intellectual way, the way I want to promote here, is to face all the complexities of your thought as you go along.[1]

We want to promote this way as well—not the suppressing of struggle and uncertainty but the expressing of it, the accepting of it, because the acceptance of tension and messiness is exactly the way of the intellectual, the way of the university. Stafford also said:

> As an intellectual I speak to you in a university. So let me appeal to you. What we have, the glimmer we have in front of us, is the possibility that if we all key ourselves up enough and are alert enough, and are not satisfied with partial truths, partial information, we may find our way to some kind of betterment.[1]

We, too, are speaking from universities, and what we believe is that in every classroom there are many glimmers of truth. What this book tries to offer are projects and activities and writing topics that will help you key yourself up enough, become alert enough, to recognize the nature of these partial truths, these partial answers, and to move beyond them to some kind of real and lasting betterment.

---

[1]From *Crossing Unmarked Snow: Further Views on the Writer's Vocation,* edited by Paul Merchant and Vincent Wixon, University of Michigan Press, 1998.

A Note to Instructors

We think this ancient truism applies for our postmodern students: learning comes from doing—and from serious doing, from activities and topics that complicate and challenge.

For our colleagues, we intend this book to be practical and useable. None of us need a text that does our theorizing for us. We all know what to say. What most of us need on Monday morning is another activity for class—something that will grab students' attention and actually work. *Asking Questions* tries to provide so many of these exercises that planning a course is a simple matter of selecting and sequencing what seems the most workable. The book offers a long menu from which to choose—some activities for one term and others for the next, in whatever order makes sense for that group of students.

Chapter 1 is essential—it lays out the ideas and methods that structure the rest of the book. After that, it's possible to leave out chapters or take them up in different sequences.

In this sense, the whole course is supplied—not just the prompts to get students started, but the in-class work to help them get the papers done. There's even an underlying theme for a quarter or semester—in the readings and in the invitations to self-reflection: education itself, and what it means to learn and grow. In a way, *Asking Questions* really asks students just one question, over and over: Why are you here in a college or university?

The classroom activities in each chapter are also general enough to apply to any of the old reliable paper topics that teachers always have on file.

But in focusing on what we call "the essential moves" of making and supporting claims, we've left out many important issues. For example, the chapters are not sequenced by genre or discipline. Though we're conscious of these divisions and often call attention to them, our effort is to identify what they share: a thoughtful skepticism; a grasp of what has already been researched and said; an ability to interrogate what's said by looking past the surface; an awareness of the complexities of causation; a recognition of common methods of persuasion; and an understanding that most truly difficult problems *are* difficult precisely because of the contradictions and tensions they evoke.

We don't say, here's how you write this kind of paper in this field or that field. We assume that later courses will address such specifics. Though it's essential that students come to understand how language adapts to the demands of audience, and though the Essay Options in this book specify readers, audience has not been our primary emphasis. We talk, only in passing, about style and voice. What we've done is narrowed our focus and simplified our claim for all the reasons that teachers always simplify: to exaggerate what seems most important, to make it obvious, to hammer it home.

The idea that an essay supplies evidence for a thesis is so basic as to be a truism, but it's exactly this truism that we believe our students most need to understand and adapt as a new situation or new problem requires. The process revolution has finally finished its work in elementary, middle, and high school. Almost everyone comes to the university knowing how to freewrite, journal, draft, and revise—good things, very good things. It wasn't always so. When students had to spend twelve years being indoctrinated in the five-paragraph theme—twelve years cut away from their imagination and intuition, as they did a generation ago—it was necessary to take up the first year of college composition in various acts of resistance and liberation. But the situation is reversed now. Many students come to the university no longer knowing how to do what John Bean calls "thesis-supporting" writing. Many students no longer know how to make a claim, support that claim, and support that claim in a coherent way. And as many of us who were trained in the process approach have rediscovered through the experience of our teaching, making and supporting claims is something we value very much, something we can't give up. It's the work of the university.

Yet we don't ignore writing-process questions. Each chapter includes a section titled "Essay Options: Getting Started." Each section offers a variety of activities aimed at giving students at least one process to follow, one set of activities and concerns they can fall back on if they need to as they write.

In the end, the six chapters that follow ask students not to do six different things but to do this one basic thing six different times—this act of supporting a thesis—and in six different situations, with six different sets of complex variables, gaining skill with each iteration.

It's practice in this intellectual work, we believe, that best teaches us to enlarge our various truths.

Finally, we would be remiss if we failed to acknowledge the useful reviews by L. Bensel-Meyers (University of Tennessee at Knoxville), Carol Rutz (Carleton College), Linda Woodson (University of Texas at San Antonio) and James C. McDonald (University of Louisiana at Lafayette). Their comments helped us fashion a better book. Lastly, thanks to our families, who generously tolerated our rants and frustrations.

Acknowledgments

Whatever virtues this book reflects are due in large part to the education our students have given us over the years. We would particularly like to thank Shelley Fickes, Scott Gallagher, Kate Lamont, Tanya Williams, Sarah Breeze, Anne Zimmerman, and Krista Peterson who wrote essays that appear here or in the Instructor's Manual.

Chapter 1:
Challenging Commonplaces

Think of a group you belong to that is often described in a sort of easy shorthand—all women in their twenties; all men in their twenties; all college students; all people who bowl in leagues; all city people; all truck drivers; all teachers. You've likely heard comments about such groups—usually judgmental and often negative, such as "All men in their twenties are bad drivers," or "All college students are binge drinkers."

We rely on generalizations to support the arguments we make; it would be inefficient to cite statistics and use examples every time we want to make a point. But generalizations can slide quickly into stereotypes, and the problem with stereotypes is that they are always untrue in particular cases and often in most cases. *All* college students aren't binge drinkers; some don't drink at all. *All* men aren't better with tools than *all* women. And which tools specifically do you mean? Just think about your own brothers and sisters or parents. Look in a mirror.

❖ *Solo Activity 1.1* Freewrite a portrait of a student you know, a friend, or acquaintance. Use this portrait to support or deny the following generalization about the current generation of college students from an essay by University of Virginia teacher, Mark Edmunson. Or you can freewrite a quick story from your own student experience as a way of interrogating Edmunson's claim. In other words, support it or call it into question with a particular example:

> "Most of my students seem desperate to blend in, to look right, not to make a spectacle of themselves. The specter of the uncool creates a subtle tyranny. It's apparently an easy standard to subscribe to, this Letterman-like, Tarantino-like cool, but once committed to it, you discover that matters are rather different. You're inhibited, except on ordained occasions, from showing emotion, stifled from trying to achieve anything original. You're made to feel that even the slightest departure from the reigning code will get you genially ostracized. This is a culture tensely committed to a laid-back norm."

Note: "Freewrite" means to write freely, getting down on paper your first thoughts without worrying about how clear they are or how correct or accurately spelled your prose might be. Just think in words on the page; write as quickly as you think. ❖

❖ *Group Activity 1.2* Go around the group, with each of you reading what you wrote for Activity 1.1. Based on this evidence from your group members, what claim would your group want to make about Edmunson's view? What conclusion is actually supported by the evidence from your group? ❖

Of course, we've taken Edmunson's comment out of the context of the examples and particulars he goes on to use. But that makes a point: When we read generalizations like this—generalizations that probably get our blood temperature a little higher and push us out of whatever "laid-back" norm may exist—we immediately want to see what justifies such claims. Generalizations raise the expectation of support. You say this—but is it true?

❖ *Group Activity 1.3* Work together to think about the purpose of a college education. Why do you need these classes and learning experiences? Why do you want such things? What's the use or value of spending more time in the effort to learn how to think? With all this in mind, write a paragraph that explains why it makes sense to begin this book with a chapter titled "Challenging Commonplaces." Why start the whole effort with this? ❖

❖ *Group/Solo Activity 1.4* Make a list of various ways you could do research to support or disprove the generalizations by Mark Edmunson above. What kinds of statistics would you need, for example, and where you would find them? What sort of experts would need to be consulted? Don't actually do the research project, just outline it. ❖

❖ *Group/Solo Activity 1.5* Consider the likely context of the rest of Edmunson's article. What sorts of things would he have to do to demonstrate the claim he's just made? What evidence would you expect as you read further? What would the essay need to do in order to change your mind—to move you away from whatever position you already hold? ❖

❖ *Group/Solo Activity 1.6* Based on clues in the language of this brief passage, speculate about Edmunson's audience and purpose. Is he addressing college students? Who might be open to claims such as his? Granted, you have little evidence to go on—that Edmunson is a teacher, who seems to be painting an unflattering portrait of his students. But what might be his agenda? ❖

The intellectual work you're doing here is fundamental to what college courses ask us to do. And the focus on specifics—on evidence and careful evaluation of that evidence—forms the basis of clear communication on paper. Good thinking and good writing depend on evidence, details, examples, specifics—and on the ability to stand back and make accurate generalizations, accurate assertions. Both moves are necessary for the intellectual life. They complement each other. In a way, a good thesis statement or conclusion is a generalization that actually fits the facts. A stereotype is a false or lazy generalization—a conclusion or label that's gotten detached from the particulars and even covers them up.

The Edmundson quotation is, in effect, a generalized assertion. What it finally does is stimulate our interest in the essay and its evidence. If generalizations were enough, we could just turn in the topic sentences of paragraphs without the paragraphs themselves. We wouldn't need essays, just outlines.

INTELLECTUAL LIFE

We started this book with an example that focuses on college students partly because we want to emphasize the ways that all intellectual life actually exists inside individual people. As useful as it may be to try and separate classroom thinking from what goes on outside the classroom, we want to assert that it's often just as crucial to recognize that all thinking—and all academic conclusions—come from human beings. An intellectual life is not separate from the "real." The trick is to integrate and act—as individuals and as communities—on all we know.

❖ *Group/Solo Activity 1.7* Using experience, observation, or common sense reasoning, complicate any of the following clichés. Start by choosing one from the list below (or, if you prefer, work from a commonplace you identify yourselves). Make three lists. First, make a list of several reasons to doubt this conclusion, to think that maybe it's not universally true; second, make a list of several factors that might lead a person to think this commonplace is true; and third, make a list of several qualities or details that might describe a person for whom this truism simply wouldn't be true—age, gender, place of birth, and so on.

- It's better to give than to receive.
- Haste makes waste.
- Just do it.
- It's better to have loved and lost than never to have loved at all.
- Honesty is the best policy.
- Hard work is always rewarded.
- Cleanliness is next to godliness.
- Good things come to those who wait.
- Strike while the iron is hot.

Then turn around the situation. Using experience, observation, or common sense reasoning, *support* the cliché you've just doubted. After all, just because they're clichés doesn't mean they're *not* true.

Or begin with something you've always taken for granted—Sunny weather is better than rainy. Traveling is better than staying put. ❖

THE CULTURE OF CLICHÉS

The effort to challenge clichés and commonplaces—to ask for compelling evidence—means making various kinds of intellectual efforts that actually run counter to much that we see everyday. Just consider the number of commercial messages we receive from television, billboards, newspapers, radio, magazines, bus placards, and so on. None of these commercial messages really wants us to think carefully. They seek mere assent. They want us to accept their messages without any challenge or analysis—and then to act on this acceptance (usually by spending our money). Some good can come from this, but we want to suggest the huge difference in expectation between a commercial message and an intellectual life. Whatever its product, the commercial message says, "Don't think, just accept." An intellectual life affirms that individual freedom and identity rest on the effort to recognize, consider, and reconsider our choices.

Look carefully at the Isuzu ad on pages 6 and 7 for clues about contemporary attitudes toward work, leisure, the individual, and society. On the left are blurry, treeless hills. On the right is a large, blocky Isuzu Trooper. The road is hardly visible, and that suggests the contradiction. Without roads, machinery, and other products of "civilization," none of us could get anywhere—but because sport utility vehicles are already clogging the landscape, there's little nature left.

The ad, however, doesn't want us to think about such contradictions. It wants us to buy this vehicle, and so it disguises complexity—the man is alone; the vehicle is alone—hoping to tap into our deep, American desire for independence and solitude. The value of "outrunning civilization" is a powerful commonplace in our culture (a remnant of our frontier history), an unexamined assumption of enormous influence.

❖ *Group/Solo Activity 1.8* First, imagine an advertisement for your college or university and write a paragraph that describes its key images. Develop a caption similar in length and structure to the Isuzu ad's "Outrun Civilization."

Now compare your ad to the Isuzu ad. What are the crucial differences between the two products being sold?

Next, put yourself in the place of a teacher preparing to meet a class of students who have been bombarded all their lives with images like the Isuzu ad. Make one list of the skills and attitudes that these students bring to the classroom and another list of the new skills and attitudes that your students will need to succeed at the university.

Finally, how will you teach these new ideas? ❖

❖ *Group Activity 1.9*
Consider the following description of an advertisement. Imagine the ad, then work together and write two paragraphs responding to the following questions. What messages does this ad send about the values and qualities of success? Would you argue that it sends differing messages to women and to men? And finally, given the ad as you understand it, what roles do intellect, concentration, independence, self-motivation and choice play?

Here is the description of the advertisement which ran for three consecutive September Sundays in the fashion section of several large metropolitan newspapers. It features a tall, blonde, white, blue-eyed, 20-something woman standing in the doorway of a chic apartment.

The door itself—large, painted black, with a large brass knocker—is open. The doorway features intricate molding. The floor of the apartment appears to be made of black and white marble laid in a diamond pattern. In the distance, and slightly out of focus, one can see part of a gold, gilt-edged mirror and the back of what looks like an overstuffed brown leather chair or sofa. The woman's hair falls to her shoulders and partly obscures one eye. Her chin is down; her eyes appear to be looking slightly up at the camera. She wears nothing but a deeply black, soft, luxurious fur coat. This coat is closed loosely under her chin, and it falls well above her knees. She leans against the doorframe, her hands in the pockets of the coat, one bare foot crossed casually in front of the other. The fine print at the bottom of the ad indicates any brand name or store name. The ad features this phrase in rather large print: Open the door. ❖

Media stereotypes are hardly limited to commercial messages. By watching any amount of network television, you know that most, though not all, weekly series are built around characters who present exaggerated stereotypes—often for comic effect. Typically, the comedy urges a kind of subversion: we're not meant to take the stereotypes too seriously. Still, if we watch, we're exposed.

❖ **Solo Activity 1.10** Watch an evening of television, and make a list of all the stereotypical people you see—the geek, the absent-minded professor, the dumb blonde, the southern bigot, the hunk, the tough cop, and so on. Then write a paragraph that describes the overall effect of watching and keeping these notes. Has this kind of watching changed your views about television stereotypes at all, or have your earlier views only been confirmed? ❖

ASSUMPTIONS AND THE UNIVERSITY

Our point is not to say that television is horrible—that may qualify as a commonplace itself. Nor do we want to condemn the desire to escape the stresses of daily life or suggest that physical appearance and money are irrelevant. The point is that all of us are conditioned by a culture that makes us unconsciously resistant to the values and ways of thinking that go into the academic enterprise.

Parker Palmer said, "If things were as they seem, education would not be necessary." The assumption of the university is that things are not always as they seem. The assumption is always of complexity.

As soon as you begin to engage that complexity, you are no longer so easily manipulated. College offers a world of ideas, meanings, and processes that can give you even greater freedom and success than the man in the Trooper or the woman in the window. As a full participant in the world of ideas, you're able to declare yourself. And whatever has already been thought, seen, or felt becomes available to your curiosity and wonder.

❖ *Group Activity 1.11*   Read the poem "Theme for English B," and then respond to the questions that follow.

LANGSTON HUGHES
Theme for English B

The instructor said,
    Go home and write
    a page tonight.
    And let that page come out of you—
    Then, it will be true.
I wonder if it's that simple?
I am twenty-two, colored, born in Winston-Salem.
I went to school there, then Durham, then here
to this college on the hill above Harlem.
I am the only colored student in my class.
The steps from the hill lead down to Harlem,
through a park, then I cross St. Nicholas,
Eighth Avenue, Seventh, and I come to the Y,
the Harlem branch Y, where I take the elevator
to my room, sit down, write this page:

It's not easy to know what is true for you or me
at twenty-two, my age. But I guess I'm what
I feel and see and hear, Harlem, I hear you:
hear you, hear me—we two—you, me, talk on this page.
(I hear New York, too.) Me—who?
Well, I like to eat, sleep, drink, and be in love.
I like to work, read, learn, and understand life.
I like a pipe for a Christmas present,
or records—Bessie, bop, or Bach.

I guess being colored doesn't make me *not* like
the same things other folks like who are other races.
So will my page be colored that I write?
Being me, it will not be white.
But it will be
a part of you, instructor.
You are white—
yet a part of me, as I am a part of you.
That's American.
Sometimes perhaps you don't want to be a part of me.
Nor do I often want to be a part of you.
But we are, that's true!
As I learn from you,
I guess you learn from me—
although you're older—and white—
and somewhat more free.

This is my page for English B.

Why does Hughes resist his teacher's instruction to write a page that "comes out of you"? According to the poem, how does the poet's cultural context—where he lives, how he lives, the color of his skin—influence who he is? Is Hughes attacking his instructor for being white? To what extent—or not—does this poem seem dated? ❖

By emphasizing the personal and specific, "Theme for English B" underscores what we're saying about stereotypes, commonplaces, and unexamined assumptions. We'd like you to do the same in Essay Option 1A.

Essay Option 1A

Write a three- to five-page essay that, like Langston Hughes' poem, describes "where you have come from" to get to this class. Include not only your dorm, sorority, or apartment, but also your hometown, family, and background in general. Also explain your hopes or expectations for your college courses and your own intellectual life.

As you explain all this, call readers' attention to commonplaces and unexamined assumptions—both those your experience supports and those your experience contradicts. Think of the class as your audience, both the students and the instructor.

UNDERSTANDING INTELLECTUAL LIFE AS A QEC PATTERN OF THINKING

So far, this chapter has encouraged you to examine and be thoughtful about assumptions, rather than to accept them at face value. Now we want to show you a method you can often adapt to interrogate and explore any commonplace—or new situation—that arises in your classes or elsewhere. For convenience, we call this method QEC, which stands for question, examine, conclude. It is, in fact, a method you already practice, though you may not know it.

Say it's a weekday morning. You wake in a somewhat befuddled, dreamy condition. You climb out of bed and make your way to the closet. You stand there looking at whatever hangs from a hanger or sits lumpy on the floor. Eventually you decide what clothes to wear, get them in hand, and head for the shower.

You've just followed the QEC pattern: question, examine, conclude. When you moved to the closet, you had a question in mind: What will I wear today? When you peered into the closet, that was an effort of examination—(even if it was cursory and not so wide-awake). And by the time you had clothes in hand and were on your way to the bathroom, you'd made a conclusion: I'll wear these.

With such a relatively simple question, the QEC pattern stays uncomplicated and direct. But in life and in college courses, the questions tend to get complicated quickly. In fact, the QEC pattern usually gets repeated in a number of small ways before we can confidently arrive at the conclusion to our original question.

Consider the example, "Should I rent this apartment?" In the effort to examine this question, the major question becomes a series of subquestions: What does it cost? How large is it? "How close is it to the locations—like work or school or childcare—I need? Each of these questions (and there are probably several others just as important) generates an effort to examine evidence. And eventually these examinations give us a fuller factual picture. Only then can we come to an informed and thoughtful conclusion: rent this apartment or continue looking.

We could chart it this way:

> Question = Should I rent this apartment?
> Examination = Raise and answer these subquestions:
>> Q: What does it cost?
>> E: The newspaper ad says the rent is $XXX per month, plus a deposit.

C: "That's a lot." or "That's reasonable." or "That's less than I anticipated."

Q: How large is it?

E: XXXX square feet, X bedrooms, X bathroom(s)

C: "That's pretty small." or "That's ok." or "That's larger than I/we need."

Q: How close is it to locations I need?

E: 10-minute walk to school, 15 minutes by bus to work, childcare available upstairs

C: The location is great.

Conclusion = How do the facts and judgments add up now?

❖ *Solo Activity 1.12*   Think about an important decision you made recently—perhaps a significant purchase; a decision to come back to school or to attend *this* school; or a choice about where you should live, what your diet should or shouldn't be, and so on. These are just examples, so don't feel limited by them. Whatever decision you focus on, chart it as we've done in the previous example. Be sure your chart reflects how your decision-making actually worked. If the entire description runs more than a page, show only part of the process.

Once you've made your chart, ask yourself how deliberate and careful you were with this decision. Write a paragraph to describe this.

Note, we don't want to suggest that all impulsive decisions are wrong or necessarily mistaken. We do want to suggest, however, that thoughtfulness is often preferable. ❖

QEC AND ACADEMIC THINKING AND WRITING

Most academic thinking and writing follows the same basic QEC pattern, though academic questions are rarely direct, their answers rarely simple. Here are some examples of how the pattern could work in a variety of settings:

Question = Does industrial pollution contribute to global warming?

Examination = Research and experiments, surveys of existing research showing the data for climate change, and the scientific efforts to understand the reasons for that data. Much debate about how to collect that data and about how to interpret it once it's collected.

Conclusion = Yes, these particular industrial pollutants have been shown to contribute, in this measure, to the warming of the planet. Or no, they have not. Or whatever other conclusion seems warranted by the evidence.

Another example:

Question = What affect does television have on the way we think?

Examination = Reading books by media experts, education experts, and cognitive psychologists, and doing research in the effort to test hypotheses. Debate about how much weight to put on various opinions and studies.

Conclusion = Television tends to have the effect that makes us both passive and disjunctive thinkers, but that's ok (or not) . . .

❖ *Group Activity 1.13* Think of the other courses in which you're currently enrolled or already have finished, and identify three academic questions that you gave considerable attention.

Following the previous format, chart the QEC pattern for each question. ❖

FROM THE PERSONAL TO THE PUBLIC: EXTENDING QEC TO QEC:CS

When you think about and then decide to rent an apartment, you generally can go ahead and act on your decision. Although others might want to know more about it or even question it, the choice is yours. If you want to explain, you can, but allowing for a few exceptions, you're generally not obliged to. The situation is quite different in academic settings.

In college courses and in academic research, the effort is often to argue for truths larger than individual ones. As an example, you may choose to smoke in private. But as a matter of policy—a general truth—you may be prohibited from smoking in many public places.

That policy stems from a general, well-documented truth—that cigarette smoke is addictive and harmful. This general truth has been established not on the basis of individual opinion or individual decision-making, but rather on the basis of extensive evidence. Once the evidence was gathered, an argument was made based on what the evidence said. We could chart it this way:

Question = What are the effects of cigarette smoke?

Examination = Many tests designed to answer questions such as "What is the composition of cigarette smoke?" and "What are the effects of various levels of cigarette smoke on the lungs of children, women, men, and the elderly?" and "How much exposure to cigarette smoke is harmful?" and "To what extent should manufacturers be held responsible for the use of the products they make, advertise, and sell?" Each of these many questions generates its own limited answer.

Conclusion = The conclusion here rests on how a person adds up the answers to each of the questions examined. One possible example is that cigarette smoking constitutes significant danger to non-smokers who are exposed to the smoke.

That's the QEC pattern as we've already seen it. But no policy decisions have resulted yet. That takes extending the QEC pattern two more steps, to the act of making a *claim* (or claims) and then offering convincing *support*. Those are the last two steps in QEC:CS, claim and support. Notice how a claim follows from the conclusion. And the supporting evidence gets drawn from the results of the earlier effort to examine the original question.

Claim = Cigarette smoking should be banned in most public areas.

Support = Scientific evidence of the danger of cigarette smoke to non-smokers, and a belief that public agencies have a duty to protect the public they serve.

In college classes, the claim and the support of those claims typically get most of our attention. The QEC part of the pattern helps us think hard, while the CS part of the pattern helps us determine what we actually want to say to others. In fact, the claim and support parts of QEC:CS force us to think about our audience, who we're talking to, and what they already think or know.

So if QEC represents the process of thinking in academic life (and all conscious life), CS represents the form of presentation. Think about it: Doesn't virtually every course ask you to make a claim (or several claims) and then show your reasons? Even a mathematics course does this—you're asked for an answer to a problem (i.e., the claim), and you're also asked to "show your work" (i.e., to show your teacher the support for your claim). In classes like math that don't involve objective tests—those with true/false or multiple choice questions—if you're not given homework, then you're asked to write papers.

❖ *Group Activity 1.14* Based on Group Activity 1.13, extend each of the QEC charts you made so they now include two more steps: claims and supports. Hint: Think about what was presented as true (the claims) and how it was shown to be true (supports). ❖

QEC AND COLLEGE WRITING

When you write an academic paper, you take the C, your conclusion, from the QEC process and use it as a thesis, supporting it with details from your exploration. It's QEC upside down.

> C (Conclusion) is now phrased as a claim. The support for the claim is drawn from everything you discovered in the process of E (examination and exploration).

Thus if we studied television and its effects on viewers, that effort would take us through the QEC process. If we then decided to write about what we'd learned, we would be making claims and offering supports:

> C (claim) = Television tends to make us passive and disjunctive thinkers.
>
> S (support) = Studies, examples, statistics, and all that you turned up in your examination (the E in QEC) of the issue

In the end, the essential moves of the intellectual life are not difficult to understand. They all come down to making and supporting claims—explaining a hunch, backing an intuition, justifying a decision. You *say* this is a good used car, but can I take it to my mechanic before I decide to buy it? You *say* this guy you want to fix me up with is funny and smart, but I'd like to take a look at him first. Our whole life can be seen as a succession of efforts to find support for the claims we come to. Is there a God? Is cheating really wrong? Should I become an engineer?

USING DETAIL, POINTING TO SPECIFICS

If commonplaces or unexamined assumptions are generalizations without support, then the way to challenge commonplaces is to emphasize the E part of QEC by seeking out and looking hard for evidence. Looking for evidence means examining cases, paying attention to detail, and searching for the hard data.

The intellectual demand for detail and support is obvious when it comes to science. If you *say* you have proof that life exists on other planets, you'd better deliver the evidence. If you *say* you can double the efficiency of an electric motor, you'd better be able to demonstrate both the process and the results. Otherwise, there's no press conference, no funding, and no credibility.

It may be less obvious that other kinds of arguments require support. But the demand is the same. If you insist that Hamlet is gay, the professor will expect to see the passages from the play that support this claim. If you argue that women think differently than men, then you need to cite the studies or make the observations that have led you to this conclusion.

When it comes to challenging a commonplace, the need for detail and evidence is especially great and can even have moral force. Isn't racism a matter of commonplaces that have gone unchallenged—all people of color are _____ ? Doesn't all sexism follow the same pattern? Don't all -isms run that same risk?. In a sense, institutions that protect the rights of individuals are trying to protect society from commonplaces—trying to insist on the free play of particulars.

Social reforms are only possible when someone gets underneath the commonplaces into the wonderful and messy particulars of how real life is lived. We're not talking about a whole race anymore, but this particular individual with this particular face. We're not talking about a whole gender, but rather your own mother standing at the sink or leaning over the hood of your Chevy, peering at the manifold, her face all covered with grease.

When we challenge a commonplace, we're probing all the complexity and nuance behind it. We're working to bring that complexity into the open—into the discussion, where all the details can be heard and considered. In this sense, challenging a commonplace depends to some considerable degree on the same kind of effort involved in reading literature. Both invite a looking past surfaces to an involvement with the fascinating and often contradictory nature of lived life as it is closely observed.

This emphasis on the varieties of example, on particulars, and on the attention that particulars require has always been the work of the university—to challenge the easy, thoughtless stereotypes that dominate popular consciousness through the slow, careful, in-depth probing of complex, shifting, situated data.

Essay Option 1B

Drawing on experience, observation, research, or reading, write an essay with the following thesis:

Everyone says _____ .
But in my experience [observation, research, reading]
I have found _____ .

Make sure your essay carefully establishes the truth—or lack of it—in the commonplace (what everyone says). And clearly present your own experience, observation, research, or reading. Readers should understand your experience and be able to see how the essay applies your experience to the original commonplace. Hint: Continue to read this chapter for more information on ways to structure your essay with claims and supports. Again, think of your classmates and your instructor as the audience.

RHETORICAL DIAGRAMMING

In its effort to challenge commonplaces and replace the so-called truth with something more thoughtful and accurate, good academic writing tends to ebb and flow between assertion (claim) and specific evidence (support). Generalizations get support, every claim has details underneath, and every paragraph is made up of examples and analysis. In other words, basic paragraphing strategies act out the important intellectual work that we've discussed so far.

One way to illustrate this is with a technique called rhetorical diagramming. Simply indent a sentence farther to the right if it's more particular than the one before it—if it gives details or analysis of the previous sentence. The rhetorical diagram of a successful paragraph may show a lot of back and forth movement. Some sentences may move back out to a higher level of generalization, but there is always significant movement to the right—to the level of the particular.

Here's a rhetorical diagram of the beginning of an essay:

ELLEN GOODMAN
In the Male Direction

There was a time in my life, I confess, when I thought that the only inherent differences between men and women were the obvious ones.

> In my callous youth, I scoffed at the mental gymnastics of sociobiologists who leaped to conclusions about men and women from long years spent studying bugs.

> I suspected the motives of brain researchers who split the world of the sexes into left and right hemispheres.

But now, in my midlife, I can no longer deny the evidence of my senses or experiences.

> Like virtually every woman in America who has spent time beside a man behind a wheel, like every woman in America who has ever been a lost passenger outward bound with a male driver, I know that there is one way in which the male sex is innately different from the female: Men are by their very nature congenitally unable to ask directions.

The historical record of their unwillingness was always clear.

> Consider, for example, the valiant 600 cavalrymen who plunged into the Valley of Death . . . because they refused to ask if there wasn't some other way around the cannons.

> Consider the entire wagon train that drove into the Donner Pass . . . because the wagon master wouldn't stop at the station marked Last Gas before Disaster. . .

Whatever seems most general goes against the left margin. Anything that gives specific evidence slides to the right. Thus, CS is visually represented—the rightward movement is the work of the "S."

Use rhetorical diagramming particularly in these two situations: as a way to understand what you're reading (by helping you distinguish the assertions and claims from the supporting evidence) and also as a way to test your own prose to see whether you're giving readers the specific examples they need in order to see the truth of your assertions.

❖   *Group/Solo Activity 1.15*   Rhetorically diagram each of the following passages. Based on your diagrams, explain why you'd assert that one passage is more fully developed than the other. Finally, decide as a group whether the evidence offered in the *Reviving Ophelia* passage tends to convince you or not. If it does, what works? If it doesn't, what more do you need to find in the discussion?

Early draft (unrevised)
Education faces serious challenges. Some people argue that public schools spend too much on administrative costs. And students sometimes don't know how to learn. Parents play a role, too. And class size can be important to the academic atmosphere. Often, students arrive at school without having had enough sleep. Sometimes they haven't even eaten any breakfast.

From *Reviving Ophelia* by Mary Pipher:
Schools have always treated girls and boys differently. What is new in the nineties is that we have much more documentation of this phenomenon. Public awareness of the discrimination is increasing. This is due in part to the American Association of University Women which released a study in 1992 entitled "How Schools Shortchange Girls."

   In classes, boys are twice as likely to be seen as role models, five times as likely to receive teachers' attention and twelve times as likely to speak up in class. In textbooks, one-seventh of all illustrations of children are of girls. Teachers chose many more classroom activities that appeal to boys than to girls. Girls are exposed to almost three times as many boy-centered stories as girl-centered stories. Boys tend to be portrayed as clever, brave, creative and resourceful, while girls are depicted as kind, dependent and docile. Girls read six times as many biographies of males as of females. Even in animal stories the animals are twice as likely to be males. (I know of one teacher who, when she reads to her classes, routinely changes the sex of the characters in the stories so that girls will have stronger role models.)

Note: Pipher's explanation goes on for several more paragraphs of detail and explanation under the topic sentence stated in the opening paragraph included here. ❖

CONSIDERING THESIS STATEMENTS AND THE EFFORT TO CHALLENGE COMMONPLACES

Let's go back to the claim part—or thesis statement—of the CS pattern, since it is this part that controls the ebbing and flowing of detail. The ebbing and flowing is, in a sense, "underneath" that controlling idea.

Thesis statements get bad press. The association is always with boring and uninteresting writing, as if a thesis statement always has to be about something unimportant and unexciting. For example, Florida is warm and lovely place to visit in the winter. It is, of course, but does anyone need to write about this? Commonplaces tend to be bad thesis statements, because they're too general to apply in any particular case.

Consider the commonplace, "Those who do, do; those who can't, teach." In a less abbreviated form as a thesis statement, it may go like this: "People who are adept at doing something just do it, while those who can't really do it well end up teaching it instead." This thesis statement offers such a broad generalization that readers won't take very long to find a contradictory example in their own range of knowledge or experience. What about the boat owner who loves to teach others to sail? What about the accomplished cook who routinely gives others recipes and a set of detailed instructions? What about the auto mechanic or accountant who teaches a night class at the local community college?

❖ *Group Activity 1.16* Revise the previous weak, general thesis statement into a more supportable claim. Write a paragraph that explains why you think your revision is better. If you can't revise it, explain why you can't. Either way, write a paragraph of at least five sentences explaining your thinking.

Here's a similar example to the one above of a commonplace disguised as a thesis statement: Acupuncture can be very helpful for many people. Now, here's an improved revision: Acupuncture seems weird to a lot of people, but I found that it actually helped me with my back problem. ❖

A good thesis statement should express the really good idea you had—the idea that made you want to write the paper in the first place and that may make somebody else want to read it. A good thesis statement should tell readers what you want to claim. Follow these guidelines to develop a good thesis statement:

- It should be particular, focused (i.e., *not* a commonplace).
- It should be an answer to some sort of limited question—unless you're writing a book.
- It should be important to the writer and the readers.
- It should predict all particulars that follow it.

Finally, recognize that thesis statements don't always need to be statements. They can sometimes be questions. That is, sometimes you'll be able to reproduce part of the QEC thinking process on the page as a way of leading readers forward. Thus, a not very successful thesis statement such as:

> Bicameral legislatures have been very important in the American system of government.

could become:

> I didn't think visiting the state legislature would be very interesting. But I was impressed with how empty all the seats were in the main hall, and I'm wondering if we're really represented at all. Who does the work?

A thesis statement such as this is really a collection of sentences that combine to work together.

❖ *Group/Solo Activity 1.17* Consider these thesis statements. For each one, predict the content of the paper that would follow it.

- Acupuncture seems weird to a lot of people, but I've found it actually helped me with my back problem.
- I didn't think visiting the state legislature would be very interesting. But I was impressed with how empty all the seats were in the main hall, and I'm wondering if we're really represented at all. Who does the work? ❖

A CHECKLIST

Finally, just as something such as QEC:CS is underneath all intellectual work, the end result of that work can be judged by several basic standards. In school, you produce pieces of writing, and those pieces of writing are usually judged. One definition of school is "the place where you are constantly graded."

Here is a checklist for evaluating all the writing assignments in this book, as well as all the writing you do at the university for whatever class and in whatever discipline. Think of it as a way to explain and assess just what happens in the "CS" part of our acronym:

- The paper has a thesis—a single, clear idea stated somewhere in the essay—usually at the beginning.
- The paper shows some understanding of the ideas in the chapter and the discussions in class. It reflects conscientious involvement in the intellectual work of the class.
- The idea is illustrated with concrete detail that is then analyzed—the idea is supported with facts, personal experience, or common sense reasoning, and the details fit the claim being made.
- Everything in the paper is related to the main idea, but the details remain subordinate to it. The essay is more than a listing of separate ideas. The logical connections are clearly evident.
- Word choices are accurate. Sentences are straightforward and reasonably varied.
- There are no significant grammar, punctuation, or proofing mistakes.
- In addition, the paper shows some effort to comment on the significance of the idea, for you and for someone else. Why does it matter?

Of course, many more qualities than just these go into good writing—qualities that matter to both readers and writers, such as an engaging voice or genuine interpretative insight. But the ones listed are the central—qualities that best define the academic enterprise.

If you can put a check in the margin by each of these criteria, you've met the minimal standard for college-level work in virtually any discipline.

THE ESSAY OPTIONS: GETTING STARTED

So far, this chapter has presented two essay options; others are found at the end of the chapter. They all have one thing in common: They ask you to draw on your own experience as a way to help you and your readers understand the dangers (and sometimes the truths) of commonplaces. This chapter also has presented a variety of tools—or ways of thinking—to help you in this effort, especially with QEC:CS.

When you use QEC:CS to write an essay, you start by identifying the main questions posed by the assignment. With the questions in mind, you then should be able to consider how you want to explore and examine them—the "E" part of QEC. For the essay options in this chapter, you'll probably draw on your own experience, select parts of it, and tell small stories in an effort to illuminate or clarify the parts of your experience that help you understand those main questions. At that point, you should be able to ask yourself how the stories add up and then determine what conclusions you can come to.

We've presented QEC as a *thinking* process, and it is. But it also can be a *writing* process, a set of questions for brainstorming on the page. Your writing can be aimed at helping you think more clearly and completely.

This kind of prewriting isn't always necessary. With any project, there's an important stage of not writing, when you turn the idea over in your mind, walk around with it, and let your unconscious work. Some of us clean house, replenish the bird feeder, or sharpen every pencil in the neighborhood before we ever put our fingers on the keyboard. Maybe these are simply ways of waiting and trusting.

What you're watching for includes two things: (1) the idea you really want to write about—the one that really excites you; and (2) failing that, the idea that's most possible, the one you actually have words for. In fact, the second possibility is usually the key to starting. What's most enabling in the process of writing is finding something small enough to be doable. For example, it's not necessary to detail my whole relationship with my father, but rather, how every time I visit, we always end up making dinner together.

While it's true that the process of writing is mysterious and intuitive, explicit and guided prewriting techniques can sometimes help writers discover and develop their hunches. Often thinking *in* writing is the best way to arrive at a thesis, and QEC can be one useful way to stimulate that thinking.

❖ *Solo Activity 1.18* Write a paragraph that describes your personal rituals for writing—from the clothes you wear to the room you write in to the paper you use. Think about the deeper intellectual processes at work here. Do you outline? Do you write more than one draft? How do you know when you're ready to write? What exactly do you do when you revise? What prewriting and invention strategies have you learned in the past, such as freewriting, looping, clustering? And how useful have you found them? ❖

❖ *Solo Activity 1.19* Develop a QEC chart similar to the one that precedes Solo Activity 1.10 for your own essay. If you have trouble fitting your ideas into this format, then simply write them down on paper. Either way, your QEC chart or your notes should fill about a page. Go for that level of detail. ❖

❖ *Group Activity 1.20* Working either in pairs or trios, help each other refine and add to whatever each of you has developed for Solo Activity 1.19. If you have a QEC chart, explain it and listen to the responses it provokes. What's in your head that's not yet on paper? Add it to your chart wherever it belongs—probably under either E for evidence/examples or under C for conclusion. If you can't figure out how to fit your notes into a QEC chart, ask for help from fellow classmates. ❖

Moving from QEC to CS

As you thought about your own experience, you probably recalled several stories or memories that could be used for your essay. But how can you choose among those materials? How can you decide what should go into your essay and what might not fit? Actually, you can't answer these questions until you move to claim and support—you have to first ask yourself what you want to say to other people: what claim or claims do you want to make based on your experiences?

If you're working on Essay Option 1A, for example, you're explaining where you have come from and how you see your college education as important to you. You're also considering your own background in terms of whatever commonplaces it involves, either because it confirms a commonplace or because it contradicts or revises one. So part of your claim may be "This is who I am," or "Here's what I think my education is for," or "Here's what I'm hoping from my education." Part of it also may be "As a result of thinking about all this, I see how some commonplaces hold a grain of truth, while others seem clearly false."

The audience is fundamental at this and at every stage of your thinking. You'll share some information with a friend that you wouldn't feel comfortable sharing with your parents. You know intuitively that the president of the university should be addressed more formally (in most situations) than your roommate. What prompts Langston Hughes' "Theme for English B" are questions about the nature of his audience—his reader is white, and in a position of power, and may not really want to know who the poet is or be open to the poet's "real" voice.

In fact, the issue of audience explains the demand for detail in the first place. With a close friend or family member, there's no need to explain certain experiences. You've shared them. A hint such as "Remember that time at Black Lake?" is enough, and suddenly all the memories and sensations flood back just by mentioning the place. But other people are outsiders. The hint is merely a phrase for them. It stays unintelligible without the fuller context.

The whole point of writing a paper like this is to tell where the lake is, what it looks like, and exactly what happened there in sufficient detail that outsiders can become insiders. The paper is trying to enable *us* to share the experience.

❖ *Solo Activity 1.21*   Write a paragraph of your essay as a letter to a brother, sister, or close friend. Then rewrite the same paragraph as part of a writing assignment to be graded by a writing instructor. How does the image of your audience influence the style and content of what you write? How does that image affect your writing process?

We don't want to put words in your mouth; rather, we want to point out that until you know your claim and who your audience is, you won't know which parts of your experience really should become part of your essay. ❖

❖ *Solo Activity 1.22*   Based on the thinking you've done so far about the assignment and about your own experience, make a chart that shows the claims ("C") you want your essay to make and the supports ("S") you could use to show readers why your claims seem true to you. You should write at least half a page. ❖

❖ *Group Activity 1.23*   Based on your work from Solo Activity 1.22, explain to your group what your claims could be and how you could support them. Listen to them as they react, as they ask you questions to understand your plans more fully, or as they ask you for explanations about how you plan to support your claim(s). The questions your group members ask are probably the same questions the readers of your essay will have. ❖

❖ *Solo Activity 1.24*   Try writing a thesis statement—up to three sentences long—that could form the core of your essay. ❖

❖ *Solo Activity 1.25*   Write the first paragraph for your essay, and then use rhetorical diagramming to see if it moves beyond the level of mere generalization. ❖

❖ *Solo Activity 1.26* Write a paragraph of your essay using the following pattern:

- Write down a sentence quickly—without worrying about its elegance—that states your main idea (T = theme, thesis, topic).
- Write the phrase, What I mean is,
- Follow this phrase with a restatement of your first sentence—a resaying of it in somewhat different and more particular terms (R = refinement, restatement, reinforcement).
- Write the phrase, For example,
- Follow this with two or three sentences that describe, in detail, particulars that illustrate your claim (I = illustration, example).
- Write the phrase, This is how my example fits the claim I am making:
- Follow the colon with two sentences that link the example with your first sentence, and show how the details demonstrate your point (A = analysis).
- Write the phrase, In conclusion,
- Follow this with a sentence that suggests the implications and importance of what you've said (C = conclusion, closure).

This method won't give you the kind of smooth prose you may want for a final draft. Think of it as a guided meditation—a rough and ready way to write a brief version of your whole paper that can be used as a kind of outline.

We'll talk more about the logic of this TRIAC pattern in Chapter 2. ❖

Essay Option 1C

Use several examples to extend Solo Activity 1.1 to essay length—roughly five pages. Choose your examples so they accurately support whatever claim your experience tells you is truthful. Do you agree with Edmunson's characterizations, disagree, or find them partially true and partially false? Whatever your claim, your examples should illustrate and support it.

Essay Option 1D

Extend Group/Solo Activity 1.7 by drawing on examples from your own experience. As stated in Essay Option 1C, choose your examples so they accurately support whatever claim your experience tells you is truthful. Do you find the commonplace you selected for discussion true in your experience, or false, or partly or sometimes true and partly or sometimes false? Whatever your claim, your examples should illustrate and support it.

Essay Option 1E

Extend Group/Solo Activity 1.8 or Group Activity 1.9 into a two- to four-page essay.

Essay Option 1F

Imagine a poster that depicts a beautiful stream surrounded by trees with the following caption from Thoreau: "In wildness is the preservation of the world." Write an essay that describes an experience you've had in the natural world, such as on a camping trip. Describe the experience as accurately as you can, measuring those concrete details against the easy clichés of much nature writing. Is backpacking always such a wonderful experience? Do people who go into the wilderness always come back full of spiritual insight? (Sometimes, of course, they do, as maybe you have.) In light of this, explain what the quote from Thoreau may mean.

SAMPLE STUDENT ESSAY, OPTION 1B

As you work on your own essay for this chapter, consider the strengths and weaknesses of the following student essay. Does it follow the directions? Does it communicate clearly? Use the checklist in this chapter as a guide while you read and evaluate.

SCOTT GALLAGHER

Address Unknown

"You've got mail," pipes the tinny voice of my computer. I Obediently double-click my virtual mailbox to find sixty-plus E-mails awaiting my perusal. During my Christmas break, I had fallen behind in my ongoing race to keep up with this technological marvel of modern communication. An hour-and-a-half later, after wading through it all, I realized that this blessed medium for conveying messages had become a convenient curse that is slowly driving me insane.

I'll be the first one to admit that I was initially very excited about getting an E-mail address and conversing on the world-wide-web. I got on-line when I started college last fall. I sent my first tentative messages to friends back home. They were long and carefully proofread for spelling errors and readability. The next day, I couldn't believe how excited I was when I logged on to find that I had received my first E-mail! Two clicks later I discovered that I had been chosen for a **Golden Business Opportunity** and, for a mere $30 (Visa, Mastercard, or Discover), I could become a millionaire at home in my spare time! You can imagine my excitement. I later realized that, in the jargon of the internet, I had been "spammed".

Spamming is when businesses, large and small, send out hundreds of thousands of unsolicited E-mails as a way of marketing their product. I've received messages offering Incredible FREE offers like FREE CD's, FREE software, FREE porn, and, my all-time favorite, a FREE juicer with an order of sixty dollars or more of frozen meat. It seems the infromercial has hit the virtual airwaves. Meanwhile, I waste a lot of my time pushing the delete button whenever I see a message with the word FREE, multiple dollar signs, or more than one "X" attached to it. However, it's not always that easy. The marketing gurus have found ways to trick you into opening and reading their advertisements. One of my professors told me she had received trick E-mails with subject lines that read "Re: Your Question Answered," "Here's the information you requested!" and "Returned mail: cannot send message." The most irritating trick I encountered was the one the read "Attn: about your paper," which, having just turned one in that morning in my English class, I immediately opened to find an offer to buy a Virtual Girl-friend on disk. The ad said she'd "give me a reason to procrasti-nate." Don't these people know I'm a student and that I don't have any money?

When I finally did receive a reply from an actual person, I dis-covered another danger of this technological miracle, the more you E-mail, the more illiterate you become. One friend responded to the long, carefully prepared message I had sent him about my first week in college with, "Snds great dude don't forget study." Even though I understood his minimal reply, it angered me that he didn't even take the time to check his spelling or respond with at least a few more sentences. It seems that with the advent of E-mail, cap-tions have replaced letters as the norm, and this informal message system is fast becoming illegible.

As well as being informal it is also impersonal. More and more communication between people seems to be occurring via E-mail. You no longer have to speak with other people in person. That form of communicating became unnecessary with the introduction of automated message response systems, those annoying computer voice recordings telling you to choose from an endless menu of options before finally talking to a human. Now that, too, is increasingly becoming unnecessary. Progress has removed the need to listen and talk by creating a purely textual medium where you can complain and get your questions answered electronically! You don't even have to open your mouth. How convenient!

Today's society is becoming more and more dependent on this fast, cheap technology. According to Time magazine "in 1994, 776 billion E-mail messages moved through U.S.-based computer networks. This year that number is expected to more than triple, to 2.6 trillion and, by the year 2000, is expected to triple again to 6.6 trillion." We can't escape it. Everything is going to E-mail, even signing up for financial-aid and scheduling classes for the fall term. Because of this, I have resolved to retain my E-mail address. I really don't have a choice if I want to function efficiently in our increasingly computer oriented society. Regardless of how much I hate it, I must continue to put up with an infuriating medium that sends annoying Mailer-Daemon's to taunt and frustrate me as I reluctantly check my mailbox, but which, in the end, reminds me whom the evil being was who probably thought this whole thing up.

Chapter 2:
Listening to Others:
Reading and Summarizing
What You Read

E-mail and postcards, letters from friends, notes on your door or refrigerator, voice messages on your answering machine at home or at work, letters to the editors in your local paper, the words on the pages of this or any other book—what do they all have in common? They're all substitutes for actual human voices; they're replacements (though not always satisfactory ones) for face-to-face conversation. Sometimes the voices are actually recorded, as in voicemail messages or those on an answering machine. Sometimes they're in print, in language on a printed page or on a computer screen. Sometimes they sound absolutely contemporary, while other times they sound old and distant. Still, you're "hearing" a human being. Even when an organization (say a political party or a bank or a group like Mothers Against Drunk Driving) writes to you, even when a textbook sounds depersonalized in its steady focus on facts and information—these messages come from people. The interchange is always human: for it to work you need to listen.

Why listen? If you do, you can take advantage of other's experiences; you can avoid mistakes they made and share their insight without doing any work but reading.

❖   *Solo Activity 2.1*   Scan your memory, and see if you can recall three recent occasions when you followed written or printed directions and thereby successfully accomplished some task. In each case, what was the task? Could you have finished it successfully without the directions? Write a paragraph that answers these questions. ❖

❖   *Group Activity 2.2*   Assume that you cannot read any words in any language. What effects would this inability have had on your actual day today or yesterday? As a group, compile a list of things that would have been much harder—or impossible—if you could not read at all. ❖

Contemporary culture offers us more reading opportunities than we know what to do with. We can log on to the internet and spend all morning looking at the pixels that make up the web sites on our screens. We can read major newspapers online. We can go to a library and feel overwhelmed by all the choices on the shelves. We can go downtown and read every neon sign, street sign, poster, billboard, bus placard, and bumper sticker. Each word represents some piece of information. Most of these words come at us and disappear so quickly we barely even register them.

❖   *Solo Activity 2.3*   Take exactly six minutes, and make a list as long as you can that includes all the things you read today and yesterday, including any words on paper, billboards, a computer screen, on the side of a bus, on your refrigerator, on your desk—everything). Whether you read it entirely or partially doesn't matter—include it on your list. List these individually rather than by groups; for example, instead of "menus" (a group) write the menu at 3rd Street Pizza, the menu in the Student Union coffee shop, and so on. If you still have time, list all the human voices you heard today and yesterday in a recording (not in person). Don't list singing voices, but include every other recorded speaking voice you've heard. ❖

❖   *Group Activity 2.4*   Compare your lists from Solo Activity 2.3. As a group, construct a single list of everything that was read or listened to—other than music—for more than fifteen minutes at one time. From that list, identify the things that were read or listened to for more than thirty consecutive minutes. Based on your group's lists, what would your group say about how often you get practice maintaining your focus on reading or hearing a single text or single recorded source for thirty minutes or more? ❖

COLLEGE READING AND CONTEMPORARY CULTURE

It's easy to bring television expectations to reading. We expect flash and dazzle, the quick cuts to new images. But maybe even more importantly, we *don't* expect any of it to really mean much. The situation comedy glosses over the real complications of dating or family life, and the video game lets us endlessly start over. It's all good fun in its way, but it's not true that if you design a building and it falls down, you can simply start over without penalty. Nor are human relationships as simple as laugh tracks and mood music. Television is not life, and we know that. But it's easy to be conditioned, and it's particularly easy to bring our television expectations to reading and to thought in general.

❖   *Solo Activity 2.5*   Begin this activity by watching thirty minutes of television. Have a sheet of paper in front of you as you watch, and make a check mark every time the screen images switch from one context to another (i.e., from show to commercial, from commercial to commercial, from commercial to newsbreak, and so on). Once you've finished watching, write at least one paragraph that addresses these questions: How would you describe this half hour of your life? What happened? What did you do? Was it enjoyable? What made it a good or bad experience? Did it encourage you to think about anything? If yes, how did it do this, and what did you think about? Finally, why did this thirty minutes of television entertain you (or not)? As a group follow-up, discuss the results of this activity by using this question as your springboard: What does this activity tell you about the ease or difficulty of watching television and studying for college courses? ❖

LEARNING TO ASK QUESTIONS, LEARNING (AGAIN) TO READ

In the next couple sections, we aim to give you a cornucopia of reading tips—more than you can use. Your job is two-fold: Read every tip and every explanation, and then identify the three tips you think will be most useful to you. Take notes if necessary—which also is one of the tips. There will be a test.

USING QEC:CS TO ASK QUESTIONS ABOUT WHAT YOU'RE READING

We introduced QEC:CS in Chapter 1. The letters, again, stand for Question, Examine (or Explore), Conclude: Claim and Support. The question-examine-conclude part refers to three major thinking activities, while the claim-support part refers to the thinking that results in communication to others. Broadly speaking, if we think by questioning, examining, and concluding, we communicate—at least in academic settings—by claiming something is true and then supporting our claim.

Often times, when a writer claims something, the readers can see at least some of the writer's thinking process on the page. We can often see the Questions the writer wants to investigate, the way the writer Explored and examined those questions, how the writer's Conclusions led directly to the writer's Claims, claims Supported by at least some of the evidence the writer discovered in the thinking process itself.

What does this mean for reading? It means that when you look at a text—some reading for a college class—for the first time, you can ask yourself these questions:

Q = What questions make up the focus and provoke the discussion here? Example: If you're reading a weather forecast in the paper, you can readily determine the question on the forecaster's mind—what will the weather be tomorrow? The question may not be stated directly—but if you look for it, you can find it.

E = What examining, exploring, or investigating did this writer do? The weather forecast may not show any evidence of this at all; but the weather page may show a satellite photo, and that's probably part of the evidence a forecaster uses. In an academic text, look for experiments, stories, or process descriptions that help answer these original questions.

C:CS = What conclusions has this writer come to based on the evidence? These conclusions will often be at least part—or perhaps all—of the claim the writer makes. In the weather forecast, each part of it is a claim— the predicted high, predicted low, and predicted amount of sunshine, cloud cover, or precipitation, including the form the precipitation may take. A typical weather forecast in a newspaper won't include supporting information—(it doesn't tell you how it examined or explored its original question either).

In academic reading, the claim—or "thesis"—can often come first, with the movement from claim to supporting reasons. But another common pattern starts with a wide-ranging discussion and gets more focused and specific as it goes along. This pattern begins with supports and ends with the claim that fits all the supporting information.

Suppose we take this tactic and apply it to some prose:

> Ten years ago, universities were churning out special-education teachers and school boards were racing to develop individualized communications programs and separate facilities for students needing extra help. But more recently, cash-strapped boards have retrenched, leaving parents of children with learning disabilities, attention deficit or emotional problems no alternative but to resort to the squeaky-wheel approach—or scramble for the growing number of private alternatives.[1]

Start by looking at this excerpt in a sentence-by-sentence approach, and ask yourself, "What question does this sentence answer?" If you can make a list of these questions, you'll see the writer's concerns:

- first sentence: What were universities doing to help address the problem of students who needed extra help?
- second sentence: What's happened more recently? How have parents had to react?

Clearly, you cannot do this kind of sentence-by-sentence analysis with long texts, but then again, this is rarely necessary. In general, what you read will focus on relatively few—but important—questions. And every large, important question will come with its own discussion and its own explanations, examples, or anecdotes about real people—all in the effort to show how the writer has, in fact, answered the large question. If you can see the question and how the writer answered it, then you're doing a good job reading. If you can do this the first time, you may avoid the frustration of not understanding what the text says.

❖ *Group Activity 2.6* Read the following passage, and then work together to identify the major questions *and* answers (i.e., the claims) *and* the reasons (i.e., the supports) for the answers that the writer makes. ❖

---

[1]From *"Why Kids Can't Read,"* by Robert Sheppard, *Maclean's,* September 7, 1998.

DEBORAH TANNEN
Intimacy and Independence

Intimacy is key in a world of connection where individuals negotiate complex networks of friendship, minimize differences, try to reach consensus, and avoid the appearance of superiority, which would highlight differences. In a world of status, *independence* is key, because a primary means of establishing status is to tell others what to do, and taking orders is a marker of low status. Though all humans need both intimacy and independence, women tend to focus on the first and men and on the second. It is as if their life-blood ran in different directions.

These differences can give women and men differing views of the same situation, as they did in the case of a couple I will call *Linda* and *Josh*. When Josh's old high-school chum called him at work and announced he'd be in town on business the following month, Josh invited him to stay for the weekend. That evening he informed Linda that they were going to have a houseguest, and that he and his chum would go out together the first night to shoot the breeze like old times. Linda was upset. She was going to be away on business the week before, and the Friday night when Josh would be out with his chum would be her first night home. But what upset her the most was that Josh had made these plans on his own and informed her of them, rather than discussing them with her before extending the invitation.

Linda would never make plans, for a weekend or an evening, without first checking with Josh. She can't understand why he doesn't show her the same courtesy and consideration that she shows him. But when she protests, Josh says, "I can't say to my friend, 'I have to ask my wife for permission'!"

To Josh, checking with his wife means seeking permission, which implies that he is not independent, not free to act on his own. It would make him feel like a child or an underling. To Linda, checking with her husband has nothing to do with permission. She assumes that spouses discuss their plans with each other because their lives are intertwined, so the actions of one have consequences for the other. Not only does Linda not mind telling someone, "I have to check with Josh"; quite the contrary—she likes it. It makes her feel good to know and show that she is involved with someone, that her like is bound up with someone else's.

Linda and Josh both felt more upset by this incident, and others like it, than seemed warranted, because it cut to the core of their primary concerns. Linda was hurt because she sensed a fail-ure of closeness in their relationship: He didn't care about her as much as she cared about him. And he was hurt because he felt she was trying to control him and limit his freedom.

A similar conflict exists between Louise and Howie, another couple, about spending money. Louise would never buy anything costing more than a hundred dollars without discussing it with Howie, but he goes out and buys whatever he wants and feels they can afford, like a table saw or a new power mower. Louise is dis-turbed, not because she disapproves of the purchases, but because she feels he is acting as if she were not in the picture.

Many women feel it is natural to consult with their partners at every turn, while many men automatically make more decisions without consulting their partners. This may reflect a broad differ-ence in conceptions of decision making. Women expect decisions to be discussed first and made by consensus. They appreciate the discussion itself as evidence of involvement and communication. But many men feel oppressed by lengthy discussions about what they see as minor decisions, and they feel hemmed in if they can't just act without talking first. When women try to initiate a free-wheeling discussion by asking, "What do you think?" men often think they are being asked to decide.

Communication is a continual balancing act, juggling the con-flicting needs for intimacy and independence. To survive in the world, we have to act in concert with others, but to survive as our-selves, rather than simply as cogs in a wheel, we have to act alone. In some ways, all people are the same: We all eat and sleep and drink and laugh and cough, and often we eat, and laugh at, the same things. But in some ways, each person is dif-ferent, and individuals' differing wants and preferences may con-flict with each other. Offered the same menu, people make differ-ent choices. And if there is cake for dessert, there is a chance one person may get a larger piece than another—and an even greater chance that one will *think* the other's piece is larger, whether it is or not.

❖ *Group/Solo Activity 2.7* Do this activity as a group, or read and do it alone overnight and then discuss it in your next class. Turn to "Pas-sion at Yale" on page 42, and read only the first two paragraphs. Based on only this much of the article, what would your group say is the major question—or set of major questions—that this article addresses so far? If you had to narrow your decision to a single question that captures the writer's concern in these two paragraphs, how would your group phrase that question? Make it as specific as possible but focus on only the first two paragraphs. Use QEC:CS as a method, and be ready to show how QEC:CS helped you arrive at your answers. ❖

THE PROBLEM OF NEW VOCABULARY

We don't want to proceed too far into this chapter without acknowledging one of the most common difficulties in reading texts for college classes—encountering words you've never seen before or finding familiar words used in very specific, esoteric ways. Learning new vocabulary can sometimes be the point of the course. Think of what happens in an anatomy class when students learn the names of parts of the body. Once you know the names of the bones in the human hand, for example, you can be precise about which particular bone is broken. Without such precision, you may not know how much or how little to immobilize that sore hand.

Can you still effectively read something that presents unfamiliar vocabulary? Yes. Or you can at least make a useful start. If you've read the discussion of using QEC:CS as a reading tool, then you're ready to try the next activity.

❖ *Group/Solo Activity 2.8* Read the following two passages. Use what you know about QEC:CS to identify the writer's main questions—the main interests or main concerns. Make a note of the sentence(s) that show you these questions or concerns. Be ready to identify sentences that either support, illustrate, or explain those main interests. Finally, make a list of the unfamiliar words you encountered. What made it possible for you to locate the writer's main interest even though you didn't understand every word of the passage? ❖

ELLIOT A. NORSE
Ancient Forests of the Pacific Northwest

As they age, trees acquire more nonphotosynthetic tissue that must be "fed" by photosynthesis. Their respiration increases while photosynthesis remains roughly constant. Hence, the amount of photosynthate they allocate to net growth gradually decreases. In the period from thirty years until rotation (say, eighty years), a young stand undoubtedly accumulates more wood than an old one; Dean DeBell and Jerry Franklin (1987) suggest about twice as much. Ecosystem ecologists would say that their gross production is about the same but that net production in the young forest is higher. But . . . looking only at rates of wood growth is wrong for several reasons. One is that foresters measure only changes in above ground biomass because they are most concerned with usable wood production. But as mentioned earlier, belowground production in a Douglas-fir stand equals aboveground production. Unfortunately, we know far less about belowground than aboveground patterns of production. Carbon accumulation may reach its maximum much faster or much slower. Because belowground production is so large and so dynamic, it should not be ignored in examining the ecosystem's C uptake.

ALISON KING

Inquiry as a Tool of Critical Thinking

The hallmark of a critical thinker is an inquiring mind. Good thinkers are good questioners. A broad definition of critical thinking includes not only knowledge construction of the creation of meaning but also the ability to search for and use meaning (Beyer, 1987). Critical thinkers are constantly analyzing new situations, searching for complexity and ambiguity, looking for and making connections among aspects of a situation, speculating, searching for evidence, seeking links between a particular situation and their prior knowledge and experience. Good thinkers are always asking, "What does this mean?" "Is there another way to look at this?" "Why is this happening?" "What is the evidence for this?" and "How can I be sure?" Formulating questions such as these and using them to make meaning is what characterizes good thinking. Isidor Rabi, the 1944 Nobel Prize winner in physics, learned to be a questioner very early in life. He recalls that when he was a child, every day when he returned home from school his mother, instead of asking him what he had learned in school that day (as most other mothers did), asked him what good questions he had asked. Rabi claims that his mother's daily greeting on his return from school had a strong influence on the development of his inquiring mind.

The level of thinking that occurs in a college classroom is influenced by the level of questions asked. Particular questions can be used to activate the specific thinking processes and skills we wish students to engage in. For example, when questions are merely factual, only facts are recalled; however, when questions are at higher cognitive levels, requiring inferences and analysis, evaluation, and integration of information, critical thinking is more likely to occur. Unfortunately, research shows that fewer than 5 percent of teacher questions are high-level cognitive ones (Dillon, 1988; Kerry, 1987), which suggests that professors may not be asking the kinds of questions likely to induce critical thinking in their students. Furthermore, the frequency of student-generated questions in the classroom is very low, averaging .11 per hour per student in classrooms in several countries; of these, most are factual questions rather than high-level thought-provoking ones (Dillon, 1988; Kerry, 1987). Neither of these statistics is surprising, because most college professors have not been taught how to use questioning in the classroom.

USING TRIAC TO MAKE SENSE OF WHAT YOU READ

By now this much should be clear—reading is an active effort to make sense out of words. TRIAC is another way to structure that effort. It's another acronym—like QEC:CS—but it takes those essential moves a little further. Think of it as a more detailed version of the claim and support part—a way of getting inside what it means to make and support a claim.

The letters TRIAC stand for Topic/thesis, Restatement, Illustration, Analysis, and Conclusion. You can use TRIAC to create a series of blanks to fill in as you read. This gives you something concrete to do as a reader (rather than simply letting someone else's words wash over you). The reading process feels productive—because it is—and taking such notes makes it much easier for you to reacquaint yourself with the reading later.

All this can be done on a computer, or you can do it using paper. On a computer, begin by typing each of these questions, and leave yourself room to enter answers:

- What's the topic here, and where is it most clearly announced?
- Is the topic restated or revised as the essay goes on? Where in the reading does this happen?
- What illustrations, examples, stories, or proofs are offered to make the topic clearer or to prove the thesis? List each new one as it appears.

- What analysis or interpretation does the essay give in order to clarify its points?
- What conclusion does this writing come to? Does it simply restate its original thesis? Does it come to a conclusion you couldn't have seen when you first began to read? How do the illustrations and analyses add up to yield that conclusion?

Typing all this information may seem cumbersome at first, but soon these questions become a normal part of your reading and note-taking process. And by responding to these questions—either on a computer or paper—you start to build your own understanding of the reading itself.

❖   *Group Activity 2.9*   Assuming you're working in a five-person group, assign each person a letter in TRIAC. One person is responsible for T, another for R, and so on. Once each letter is assigned, silently read the following passage. As you read, look for the part(s) of the passage that do what your letter stands for. Each sentence in the passage is numbered so you can easily refer to each one. If your letter is A, then you're looking for sentences that analyze or offer interpretation. Once everyone has finished reading and has found their part of the passage, discuss the passage together. Decide which sentences fall under each letter. You can group sentences together—not every sentence has to be assigned to a different TRIAC slot. ❖

Helena Curtis and N. Sue Barnes

Biology

Most people have a limited awareness of the natural world and are concerned chiefly with the organisms that influence their own lives (1). For example, gauchos, the cowboys of Argentina, who are famous for their horsemanship, have some 200 names for different colors of horses but generally divide plants into four groups: *pasto*, or fodder; *paja*, bedding; *cardo*, wood; and *yuyos*, everything else (2).

Most of us are like the gauchos (3). Once beyond the range of common plants and animals, and perhaps a few uncommon ones that are of special interest to us, we usually run out of names and categories (4). Biologists, however, face the task of systematically identifying, studying, and exchanging information about the vast diversity of organisms—more than 5 million different species—with which we relative newcomers share this planet (5). In order to do this, they must have a system for naming all these organisms and for grouping them together in orderly and logical ways (6). The problems of developing such a system are immensely complicated and begin with the basic unit of biological classification, the species (7).

Species in Latin means "kind," and so species, in the simplest sense, are different kinds of organisms (8). A more rigorous definition of species was set forth by Ernst Mayr of Harvard University, who said that species are "groups of actually or potentially interbreeding natural populations which are reproductively isolated from other groups" (9). The phrase "actually or potentially" allows for the fact that although members of the human population of Greenland are not likely to interbreed with those of Patagonia, they are still members of the human species; similarly, transporting a group of insects to some remote island does not automatically make them members of another species (10). The words "groups" and "populations" are important in this definition also (11). The possibility that single individuals of a different species may have occasional offspring—such as by the crossing of lions and tigers in a zoo—is unimportant in terms of the group (12). Mayr's definition conforms to common sense: if members of one species freely exchanged genes with members of another species, they could no longer retain those unique characteristics that identify them as different kinds of organisms (13).

❖ *Group/Solo Activity 2.10* Read "Passion at Yale." See if you can use TRIAC to classify each paragraph in this article according to what the paragraph does. If it offers a new topic or thesis, it gets classified as T. If it restates or focuses that original topic/thesis in a sharper or more precise way, it gets classified as R, and so on. With seven paragraphs, you should come up with seven classifications. ❖

DAVID DENBY

Passion at Yale

Does the Constitution care about coed dorms?

As college students gather in the opening weeks of a new semester, there is, we hear, a scandal brewing, a dirty secret spreading its stain through the like of undergraduates, whose like is conducted, at many campuses, in coed dormitories. The secret (which, of course, is not very new and not entirely secret) is that there isn't very much sex going on. There's *some,* of course: some students are very active sexually (and become either famous or notorious for it), and a few may even have the grace or the misfortune to experience what would have been known in another era as passion. But many students "hook up" only now and then, and others may be defiantly chaste, or perhaps lonely or indifferent, and spend the best part of four years in a state of bluesy sexual withdrawal, rarely experiencing so much as the dip of a window shade.

All this serves as the necessary ironic background for the recent announcement by a group of five Yale freshmen and sophomores of the Orthodox Jewish faith that they may begin a lawsuit against the university in order to fight the requirement that they spend their first two years at Yale living in coed dormitories. (At Yale, freshmen generally live on all-male or all-female floors but share some bathrooms; sophomores live in single-sex suites joined by bathrooms. It may, on occasion, by necessary to knock.) Such a residence requirement, the students declare, contradicts religious rules that demand privacy and modesty as well as sexual abstinence prior to marriage. So far, Yale has refused to waive its requirement that the students live in the dormitories, and, in response, the Yale Five (as they style themselves) have asked for the assistance of a prominent lawyer— Nathan Lewin, of Washington—who describes the affair as a constitutional issue in which the students' rights to free religious expression have been infringed. In the past, Mr. Lewin has successfully sued for the rights of Orthodox Jews in public jobs to maintain elements of religious observance—the right of an Air Force psychologist, say, to wear a yarmulke at work. But no one is prohibiting the exercise of religious observance at Yale, and the students can maintain a kosher diet in an off-campus dining hall. What's at stake for the Yale Five is the *atmosphere* of undergraduate life—the threat it poses to their purity of conduct. But temptations must surround the orthodox of any faith when they leave family and community and enter the world. Though the sensibilities of these students may be affronted, have their constitutional rights been abrogated?

One remains puzzled by the students' notion that dormitory life is a parade of licentious goings on—or, at least, a series of remorseless intrusions. "There is no way to keep female visitors away," one of the Five as quoted as saying. ("I should be so lucky," his dorm-mates may be thinking.) Yes, every dorm resident does have to put up with occasional annoyances—a floormate, say, who won't turn down a CD-player. But no one is forcing the students to do anything in particular. No one is requiring of them—as certain heretical Christian sects were accused of requiring of members—that they lie next to young virgins as a test of their resolve. One of the Five did complain that during freshman orientation he was subjected to a lecture on condoms. It strikes one as exceedingly curious, however, that any university student should be shocked by mere information. Furthermore, students need not avail themselves of the condoms that Yale—continuing to operate in loco parentis—offers to its charges to prevent the spread of sexually transmitted diseases and, of course, unwanted pregnancies. Doors can always be locked. It is hard to believe that if a student wants to live quietly and privately in a Yale dormitory others will not, after a while, respect the signals he is sending out.

In a *Times* Op-Ed piece that appeared last Tuesday, Elisha Dov Hack, one of the Yale Five, complained of a sign he spied during an orientation tour which touted "100 ways to make love without having sex." One of the advertised ways that offended Mr. Hack was "Take a nap together." The sign, of course, was a joking nudge to behave responsibly. Yet even the notion of a mere coed snooze strikes Mr. Hack as heresy. Unmarried intimacy of any kind—or even proximity—seems to be what disturbs the Yale Five. "We cannot, in good conscience," Mr. Hack writes, "live in a place where women are permitted to stay overnight in men's rooms." In that case, Mr. Hack should avoid living in big-city apartment buildings as well.

The students' grievance appears to be produced by a combination of harsh medieval ardor and culture-of-complaint hypersensitivity. If the students care so much for modesty and chastity, they could, of course, attend a seminary. But it's the Yale degree they want, and they can hardly accuse the university of false advertising. Living in a coed dorm for two years is now part of the known Yale experience, just as taking certain required courses, like the Literature Humanities and the Contemporary Civilization courses at Columbia, is part of the life of other schools.

No modern university can be asked to spare its observant students the chagrins of a secular existence, for almost every aspect of the curriculum itself has been formed by secular assumptions. In class, the students may hear religion discussed in historical, political, and military—rather than sacred—terms; they may even hear religion discussed as a system of illusion. In every discipline, the disenchanted modern world awaits them. One of the Yale Five is a biology major. The Hebrew Bible says nothing about evolution. Will the student boycott his courses? One thing that separates a faith community from a learning community is that in the latter one's preconceptions are constantly, and productively, under duress. The experience of confronting both new ideas and people who think differently from oneself has traditionally formed the heart of a liberal education.

It's bad enough that the dormitories at Berkeley are partly balkanized by special-interest groups and that at many universities African-Americans congregate at meals (often to the dismay of white students who would like to mingle with them and make friends). Such self-imposed separations attack the very idea of a university. By not giving in, Yale no doubt wants to avoid a situation in which separatist communities increase their demands on the university. And Yale is right. If universities continue to humor every group's sensitivities, then what is to stop blacks from demanding protection from exposure to white students, gays from exposure to straights, fundamentalist Christians from exposure to Jews and Muslims? In this society, existence is rarely free from jostling: we all, every day, find our deepest convictions offended, even traduced by *something*. In that respect, the Yale Five, whether they get their way or not, will have to take their chances along with the rest of us.

COLLEGE READING: OBSERVATIONS AND ADVICE

QEC:CS and TRIAC are useful tools. We want to also offer the following observations and bits of advice. Compare our list to what you already know and do, and adopt whatever looks useful.

1. *Read in a place where you can think clearly and focus your attention.* Maybe that's a quiet room or the middle of a coffee shop with music and loud talk. Wherever it is, read in a place where you can really *read*.

2. *Be interested.* Sometimes interest won't be a problem because you're already involved and curious. But when interest doesn't come naturally, invent it. Pretend if you must, but try to read with the engagement and openness of intellect that you need in order to pay full attention. Don't wait for the reading itself to entertain you; entertainment isn't the point, understanding is.

3. *Schedule enough time.* Academic reading isn't something you can do on the run or over Cheerios. You schedule other important things in your life—running, time with friends, the classes you're taking. If you schedule an hour or so of reading each afternoon, the slow and careful attention that academic texts demand isn't nearly as difficult to give. For many

people, scheduling an hour in the afternoon and another one in the evening turns out to be more productive than two hours at the same time.

4. *Don't lose heart.* If you find something difficult, assume others will, too. Many times, readings are assigned precisely because the teacher knows they will raise questions. Raising questions is the point. There's nothing wrong with you, and you're not stupid. You're just on a road and don't yet know where you're going. You wouldn't expect to breeze through your first game of golf. University-level reading is at least as intricate as golf, and some of the same patient effort is required to master its skills. Expect that you'll run into patches that seem incomprehensible or at least blurry.

5. *Remember that the process of academic reading requires community; you need other people.* You can read comics like Luann or Dilbert or Sylvia alone, without help. And while you may mention the punchline to someone in passing, you don't need to talk over the deeper meaning of the cartoon in order to understand the cartoonist's point. But with the sort of reading you do in school, you're reading the same thing as dozens of other people, and you're always meeting at intervals to talk about that reading together. In a way, that's what a university classroom is—a place where people come together to read the same thing at the same time. Someone says something; someone else says something else; and suddenly we see a point in the text we didn't see before. An idea comes clear.

The parallel with writing is strong. There's this false, romantic notion of the writer all alone in a garret and huddled near a candle. In fact, writers are always getting feedback and collaborating as they revise. That's how they revise. Reading isn't really a solitary act either. We need feedback on our first readings so we can go on to a second, fuller reading. And we need feedback on the second reading so we can go on to something even deeper.

That's where the teacher comes in, too. Students often approach us early in the term, worried that they come to a class not understanding the reading for that day. We hear, "I only get it after you've lectured about it," as if there's something wrong with that. Authority is part of the process. One way you navigate all these readings and rereadings is with the

help of an experienced reader who's been there before you—
a reader who was guided by an experienced reader before him
or her, and so on. You wouldn't expect to find your way
through a foreign country without a guide of some sort, or
without consulting a map or asking for directions. Teachers
have been in this territory before you. In some important
sense, they live in it.

The important question is what you understand at *the
end* of the class.

6. *Decide how to read based on your analysis of the reading itself.*
In general, narrative reading—or reading that tells a story—
is easier than reading based on ideas (rather than story). On
the other hand, stories can't be skimmed because you risk
missing some turn in the story, but a carefully organized, logical presentation can sometimes be skimmed precisely
because the logic is announced and obvious. Skimming will
rarely give you the depth of any discussion—that always takes
deliberation.

❖ *Group/Solo Activity 2.11* Read the following two examples. As
you read, take notes about their organization and the intentions of each
writer. Then write a paragraph that compares the two readings. What are
their similarities, and what are their differences? Assume you had the full
text of each reading. Would you follow the same reading process with
each one? If so, why? If not, how would you read each one?

Example 1

In the sagebrush to the north of the Mountains in central Mon-
tana, where the Judith River deepens its channel and threads a slow,
treacherous current between the cutbanks, a cottonwood log house still
stands. It is in sight of the highway, about a mile downriver on a gravel
road. From where I have turned off and stopped my car on the sunlit
shoulder of the highway, I can see the house, a distant and solitary dark
interruption of the sagebrush. I can even see the lone box elder tree, a
dusty green shade over what used to be the yard.

I know from experience that if I were to keep driving over the cat-
tle guard and follow the gravel road through the sage and alkali to the
log house, I would find the windows gone and the door sagging and the
floor rotting away. But from here the house looks hardly changed from
the summer of my earliest memories, the summer before I was three,

when I lived in that log house on the lower Judith with my mother and father and grandmother and grandmother's boyfriend, Bill.

Example 2

Wallace Stegner, the dean of western writers, identifies the West as "two long chains of mountain ranges with deserts and semi-deserts in their rain shadow" (Stegner, 1992, p. 46). Although there are different ideas about where the "American West" begins and ends, most writers on the West, like Stegner, focus on the contiguous region west of the 100th meridian.

In this paper I explore and develop three ideas: (1) that the aridity of western North America and its attendant characteristics have fundamentally shaped the work of western agricultural economists and encouraged some distinctive western contributions to the study of economics; (2) that, in our attempts to understand economic relationships that are critical to rural western economic development, we need to move beyond our standard equilibrium economic models and explore some emerging models of spatial development and institutional change in which the concept of "increasing returns" plays a key role; (3) that, given the urban concentrations and sparseness of settlement, the high degree of geographic mobility of people and capital in the western United States, the dominant and contested federal presence, and the region's natural amenities, this region provides a fine laboratory for testing these frameworks.

(Bruce Weber, opening to "Crossing the Next Meridian: The Economics of Rural-Urban Interdependence, Institutions and Income Distribution in the American West.") ❖

7. *Read with a highlighter.* You should highlight:
   - words or phrases that are new or that you don't understand
   - whole sentences that state a main or central point
   - whole sentences that summarize a main point; for example, sentences that begin with "In short . . . ." or "In other words"
   - transition words or phrases, such as "first . . . second," "in addition," "in contrast," "on the other hand," "similarly," and so on, that help you see the reading's structure
   - sentences posing major questions which the text will go on to answer

   Highlighting is better than simply sitting and letting your eyes move over text. When you read with a highlighter, you're aware that you're supposed to be looking for something to highlight, so you've given yourself something to do rather than merely listen.

8. *Write all over your textbooks.* We think that reading with a pencil in your hand (so you can revise or erase) is even more productive than reading with a highlighter. Why? Because most assigned college reading is complicated, and the danger is that it will simply seem discouraging. In fact, it's quite easy to operate according to the "I'm-lost-so-I-can-stop-now" principle. Once you realize the reading has confused you, you don't have to read anymore. This *is* an admission of defeat, (and no one particularly likes defeat); on the other hand, it's an admission that gets us off the hook. We can blame the reading—"It's too hard" or more commonly, "It's dull"—so we don't have to blame ourselves for stopping too quickly. At its worst, this leads to a depressing spiral—the reading is hard, so you don't read it; the next reading is hard too, so you read even less, and so on.

   We want you to mark up your books like crazy. Put "yes" or "wow" or "ok" in the margin when you agree with something. When you see how an example is connected to an earlier assertion, draw an arrow that takes your eyes back to the earlier assertion or write "see page . . ." in the margin. Develop your own shorthand—use wiggly lines for material that loses you and straight lines for material that seems particularly clear. Use stars, asterisks, or plus and minus signs— whatever makes sense to you. And above all else, write your comments in the margins so they reflect your own reading experience.

❖ *Solo Activity 2.12*   Annotate a section of this book—specified by your teacher—as we just suggested. Use any method, but make sure you indicate agreement and disagreement, link any examples to the generalizations they support, and underline or somehow emphasize what you think merits the emphasis. ❖

❖ *Group Activity 2.13*   In small groups in class, pass your own book to your left and get the book from whomever sits on your right. Look at how the other person annotated the same passage you did. What similarities and differences do you see in terms of what was important to you and what was important to this other reader? Continue passing books until you've seen the annotations of everyone in your group. Working as a group, write three sentences about what this activity says about academic reading and the practice of annotating texts. ❖

❖   *Solo Activity 2.14*   Earlier in the chapter, we promised a test, so here it is. The last several pages provided eight tips to becoming a better, more involved intellectual reader. If you apply even a few of them, we think you'll notice the following differences:

- Reading takes longer, but the time goes quickly.
- You end up with a variety of specific questions about what you've read.
- Reading becomes a judgmental activity—you begin to notice and judge the decisions made by the writers you're reading.
- Reading holds your attention longer because you're talking back to the voice on the page.

These are our predictions. Are they at all accurate? After employing some of the tips provided so far in this chapter, what changes do you notice in how you read and how well or poorly you understand? Write at least one paragraph of six sentences minimum that makes your claims for the changes you noticed as a result of using the information in this chapter. We recognize that you could claim all the tips were useless. Write a second paragraph that supports your claims and explains your reasons for making them. ❖

SKIMMING AND CLOSE READING

We're not too excited about mentioning skimming, not because we don't do it, but because it can too easily become an excuse to avoid the close reading that college courses often demand. On the other hand, it's often true that you may have more reading assigned than time you have to devote. Thus, you'll frequently have to decide how to proceed and make the best of this situation. First principle: Some familiarity and understanding is better than none. In fact, even fifteen minutes with a text might at least begin a process of understanding that you can build on later. Here are some general guidelines:

a. Literary genres like novels, plays, and poems resist skimming. Part of the artistry of literature lies in its compression—its exclusion of what's not central. This compression can seem almost breathtaking in poems, where clearly every word counts. In fiction or drama, that compression accounts for why people sometimes seem to eat only one meal a day, or don't seem to ever work, or never visit the bathroom. So it's probably not a good idea to try to skim literature. Plot summaries can help, but even they won't substitute for close reading. (Chapter 3 discusses literary reading.)

b. With non-literary reading, pay close attention to assertions, thesis statements, or early paragraphs that outline intentions to be followed later.

c. You may be able to skim lengthy examples or explanations. Such sections often make more sense once you have a clear overview.

d. Pay close attention to the inclusion of exceptions or counter-arguments. Noting them—even if you skim their substance—will give you a clearer view of what's central.

e. Don't assume that skimming is anything more than a temporary solution. Instead, plan to reread once your time or class discussion give you a better sense of the reading's content and importance to the course.

❖ *Solo Activity 2.15* Identify a somewhat lengthy reading you recently had to read for this or another course. Copy the first page if your teacher doesn't already have it. Then explain how you read it, whether or not you tried to skim it, whether or not you felt your reading was successful and time efficient, and how you would read such material next time. Overall, this assignment should give you about a full page of writing. It does not need to be revised, but it should be thoughtful. ❖

SUMMARIZING WHAT YOU READ

Summaries seem like they should be easy to write; after all, we compose summaries almost every day:

"How was your morning?"
"OK. I got up late, grabbed a bite to eat, and barely made my 10 o'clock class."

But you actually performed hundreds of individual actions—you just summarized them in a few words.

❖ *Solo Activity 2.16* Assume that you were the one who responded to the question, "How was your morning?" by saying "OK. I got up late, grabbed a bite to eat, and barely made my 10 o'clock class." Make a list of the details this summary would have left out. If you get stuck, think about everything you do between the time you open your eyes in the morning and when you arrive at a 10 o'clock class.

Once you have listed at least ten things you left out, write at least two sentences that discuss what this activity has shown you about summaries or the act of summarizing. ❖

Our everyday experience with summarizing suggests that writing summaries of written material ought to be easy. We informally summarize all the time and, unlike other writing projects, the content for a summary is already given. But writing summaries usually ends up taking more time and effort than planned. Why? Because, though the content is indeed given, there's also too much of it. Summarizing well asks writers to make a series of intellectual decisions about what's important enough to mention in the summary—and we've found no shortcuts.

❖   *Solo Activity 2.17*   Think of a game you know well (anything from checkers to gin rummy to lacrosse to Monopoly). Assume that you've mentioned this game to a friend who replied, "I'm sorry, I don't know anything about that game." Make a list of things this person needs to understand in order to see how the game works. Don't worry about any order to this list, just write down the things that seem important to understanding this game.

Once you have a list, what would you have to do next in order to make an intelligible written summary of this game? ❖

The act of summarizing is more than merely deciding what to mention. A summary requires some kind of form or structure, because without that, the summary won't make any sense. If you're trying to summarize a game, then you're really talking about a set of very particular objects—in checkers, a board and a number of flat, round, black and red disks—and a process or series of actions undertaken with those objects. In addition, those moves follow certain rules. And like all specialized knowledge, the game comes with its own vocabulary, such as "to jump," "to crown," or "to king".

Even so, it takes time and careful explaining before you can play a new game with a novice. And it takes patience and careful questioning before a novice feels confident about playing a new game according to the rules. This situation offers one advantage that reading a summary does not—if you're learning a new game and don't understand some aspect, you can ask questions and get answers. If you're reading a summary and you don't understand something, you'll simply have to guess at the answer. A successful summary shouldn't make you guess about points that matter.

SUMMARIZING IN COLLEGE CLASSES

Summaries quickly convey information to readers who need or want to know it. A menu is a summary; a baseball box score is a summary; a weather map is a visual summary.

In a college course, a summary may seem like little more than a useless exercise—since the teacher often knows the material you're summarizing. So why do it? Think of it in this way: writing a summary gives you the chance to get credit for intellectual work. Teachers assign summaries because the material is important enough to the course to merit the attention you'll have to give in order to summarize well.

The effort to summarize is really the effort to *understand,* and that understanding makes persuasive agreement or disagreement possible; it makes reasoned response possible. The ability to make an individual, reasoned response lies at the heart of this book. Summarizing is a process you use to internalize and take advantage of someone else's thinking. The act of understanding is an act of claiming, so what others think and say becomes available to you to keep, modify, or reject over something you know is better-reasoned. In fact, the whole point of formal education is to put you in touch with other people's thinking, so you know you're not alone and don't have to live as though you're the first thinking person on the planet.

This intellectual process starts with close examination and understanding. In college courses that often means it starts with summarizing.

READING TO SUMMARIZE

The fact that you plan to write a summary of what you're reading should change the way you go about reading it. For one thing, it should provoke a new sort of focused curiosity. Earlier sections of this chapter discussed two primary ways—QEC:CS and TRIAC—to help you interrogate and understand what you read. Use these tools, because the more you use them, the more you'll get out of them.

The following additional questions often prove useful:

- *How does this reading start?* If the material you plan to summarize begins with a story, then the story will likely lead readers to a particular conclusion—that is, the story is told for a reason. And that reason is likely to be *the* point or one of the main points of the reading. The writer probably starts with an example in order to generalize from it.

  If the reading begins with statistics or a hodge-podge of facts, pay attention to where they lead: chances are, these facts or statistics lead to one of the major assertions in the writing.

  If the reading begins with a straightforward assertion, pay attention to it and then how it is supported, explained, or argued. Watch where the assertion leads, since some writers begin with counter assertions or counter examples.

❖ *Solo Activity 2.18* Choosing from material for this or some other course, locate a reading that begins in one of the three ways we just mentioned. Make a photocopy of the reading so you can bring it to class. Write several sentences that explain how the beginning of this reading helps you understand the writer's point. Try to choose a reading that's difficult. Once you've written your sentences, staple them to the photocopy. ❖

- *How would you outline the progression the reading follows?* As a reader, you can follow the progression even if the particulars confuse you. For example, if a writer introduces an assertion and follows it with three reasons, you don't need to fully understand the assertion or the reasons to see the overall progression. In other words, you could sketch an outline even if you don't fully understand the specifics. In addition, if a writer starts with a story and then generalizes from it, you don't need to understand every part of the story to identify the generalization. It's like putting together a jigsaw puzzle—if you can see the big picture a reading makes, then you're halfway to making sense of the details.

  Also note the way the text uses any sort of graphic design to help you see its sections; for example, chapter titles often use larger print size than subheadings within the chapters. Paying attention to such cues can help you see the outline of a reading; sometimes this can be clear just from a detailed table of contents.

- *On what does this writer spend the most words?* As a general rule—just "allowing" for occasional exceptions—writers spend more words on important, complex areas of their discussion and fewer words on the obvious or unimportant ones. Noticing how much space is devoted to a particular topic or section can give you a rough idea about its importance. If you read a twelve-page chapter and seven of those pages are devoted to a single topic, you can bet that single topic is important. Your summary needs to reflect that importance.

❖ *Group/Solo Activity 2.19* Sketch an outline of the preface to this book. Pay attention to the way the material is organized and to the parts of the discussion that get the most space. Once you've compiled your outline, write a 250-word paragraph that discusses both the easy parts and the difficult parts of actually summarizing the preface. ❖

- *What is the tone of the writing, and how does tone reveal the writer's purpose?* Most factual writing has a relatively neutral tone; it doesn't lean on you too hard or ask for your agreement. In contrast, most persuasive writing wants to lean on you and ask for your agreement; therefore, persuasive writing typically carries a more insistent, intense tone. After all, it wants to change readers—either to change their minds or urge them to take action.

  Tone matters when you summarize because, while a good summary will certainly note the tone of the original, a summary itself typically seeks to maintain the neutrality of factual writing. This can be difficult if you're trying to summarize a frankly argumentative piece. The temptation is to agree (if you agree) or to argue (if you disagree). In summarizing, however, your own agreement or disagreement is not the issue—simple understanding is. If you aim to summarize, then you aim to reproduce the original in a shorter form, one that does justice to the original even as it condenses it.

  As you summarize, your goal is to understand. And this may mean putting aside your own positive or negative responses so you can maintain the neutral tone that a summary requires.

❖ *Solo Activity 2.20*   Choosing from material for this or some other course, identify a reading with a strongly insistent tone. Write a paragraph that identifies this reading, indicates its purpose and tone, identifies your own stance, and ends by explaining why you find it easy or difficult to actually write a formal summary of this reading. ❖

ESSAY OPTIONS 2A AND 2B

Essay Option 2A

Write a summary, maximum 750 words, of "Claiming an Education" (page 57 ff). Assume that you're writing this essay to a teacher to demonstrate that you've read and understand Rich's essay. By reading your summary, the teacher should see that you understand the author's logic and her major assertions. Focus your summary on the writer's points, and be a neutral reporter. Do not include your own opinions about what Rich says; instead, try to accurately and fairly reproduce the logic and emphasis of what you read.

Your summary also must include at least 25 words from the essay as part of the 750-word maximum. You may include more than 25 words, but you cannot exceed the 750-word limit. And you may use one long quotation or several shorter ones to reach the 25-word minimum.

Essay Option 2B

Write a summary of "Passion at Yale." Assume that you're writing this essay to a teacher to demonstrate that you've read and understand this essay. By reading your summary, the teacher should see that you understand Denby's logic and his major assertions. Focus your summary on the writer's points, and be a neutral reporter. Do not include your own opinions about what Denby says; instead, try to accurately and fairly reproduce the logic and emphasis of what you read.

Your summary also must include at least 25 words from the essay as part of the 750-word maximum. You may include more than 25 words, but you cannot exceed the 750-word limit. And you may use one long quotation or several shorter ones to reach the 25-word minimum.

ADRIENNE RICH

Claiming an Education

For this convocation, I planned to separate my remarks into two parts: some thoughts about you, the woman students here, and some thoughts about us who teach in a women's college. But ultimately, those two parts are indivisible. If university education means anything beyond the processing of human beings into expected roles, through credit hours, tests, and grades (and I believe that in a women's college especially it *might* mean much more), it implies an ethical and intellectual contract between teacher and student. This contract must remain intuitive, dynamic, unwritten; but we must turn to it again and again if learning is to be reclaimed from the depersonalizing and cheapening pressures of the present-day academic scene.

The first thing I want to say to you who are students, is that you cannot afford to think of being here to *receive* an education; you will do much better to think of yourselves as being here to *claim* one. One of the dictionary definitions of the verb "to claim" is: *to take as the rightful owner; to assert in the face of possible contradiction.* "To receive" is *to come into possession of; to act as receptacle or container for; to accept as authoritative or true.* The difference is that between acting and being acted-upon, and for women it can literally mean the difference between life and death.

One of the devastating weaknesses of university learning, of the store of knowledge and opinion that has been handed down through academic training, has been its almost total erasure of women's experience and thought from the curriculum, and its exclusion of women as members of the academic community. Today, with increasing numbers of women students in nearly every branch of higher learning, we still see very few women in the upper levels of faculty and administration in most institutions. Douglass College itself is a women's college in a university administered overwhelmingly by men, who in turn are answerable to the state legislature, again composed predominantly of men. But the most significant fact for you is that what you learn here, the very texts you read, the

This talk was given at the Douglass College Convocation, September 6, 1977, and first printed in *The Common Woman*, a feminist literary magazine founded by Rutgers University women in New Brunswick, New Jersey.

lectures you hear, the way your studies are divided into categories and fragmented one from the other—all this reflects, to a very large degree, neither objective reality, nor an accurate picture of the past, nor a group of rigorously tested observations about human behavior. What you can learn here (and I mean not only at Douglass but any college in any university) is how *men* have perceived and organized their experience, their history, their ideas of social relationships, good and evil, sickness and health, etc. When you read or hear about "great issues," "major texts," "the mainstream of Western thought," you are hearing about what men, above all white men, in their male subjectivity, have decided is important.

Black and other minority peoples have for some time recognized that their racial and ethnic experience was not accounted for in the studies broadly labeled human; and that even the sciences can be racist. For many reasons, it has been more difficult for women to comprehend our exclusion, and to realize that even the sciences can be sexist. For one thing, it is only within the last hundred years that higher education has grudgingly been opened up to women at all, even to white, middle-class women. And many of us have found ourselves poring eagerly over books with titles like: *The Descent of Man; Man and His Symbols; Irrational Man; The Phenomenon of Man; The Future of Man; Man and the Machine; From Man to Man; May Man Prevail?; Man, Science and Society;* or *One-Dimensional Man*—books pretending to describe a "human" reality that does not include over one-half the human species.

Less than a decade ago, with the rebirth of a feminist movement in this country, women students and teachers in a number of universities began to demand and set up women's studies courses—to *claim* a woman-directed education. And, despite the inevitable accusations of "unscholarly," "group therapy," "faddism," etc., despite backlash and budget cuts, women's studies are still growing, offering to more and more women a new intellectual grasp on their lives, new understanding of our history, a fresh vision of the human experience, and also a critical basis for evaluating what they hear and read in other courses, and in the society at large.

But my talk is not really about women's studies, much as I believe in their scholarly, scientific, and human necessity. While I think that any Douglass student has everything to gain by investigating and enrolling in women's studies courses, I want to suggest that there is a more essential experience that you owe yourselves, one which courses in women's studies can greatly enrich, but which finally depends on you, in all your interactions with yourself and your world. This is the experience of *taking responsibility toward yourselves.* Our upbringing as women has so often told us that this should come second to our relationships and responsibilities to other people. We have been offered ethical models of the self-denying wife and mother; intellectual models of the brilliant but slapdash dilettante who never commits herself to anything the whole way, or the intelligent woman who denies her intelligence in order to seem more "feminine," or who sits in passive silence even when she disagrees inwardly with everything that is being said around her.

Responsibility to yourself means refusing to let others do your thinking, talking, and naming for you; it means learning to respect and use your own brains and instincts; hence, grappling with hard work. It means that you do not treat your body as a commodity with which to purchase superficial intimacy or economic security; for our bodies and minds are inseparable in this life, and when we allow our bodies to be treated as objects, our minds are in mortal danger. It means insisting that those to whom you give your friendship and love are able to respect your mind. It means being able to say, with Charlotte Brontë's *Jane Eyre:* "I have an inward treasure born with me, which can keep me alive if all the extraneous delights should be withheld or offered only at a price I cannot afford to give."

Responsibility to yourself means that you don't fall for shallow and easy solutions—predigested books and ideas, weekend encounters guaranteed to change your life, taking "gut" courses instead of ones you know will challenge you, bluffing at school and life instead of doing solid work, marrying early as an escape from real decisions, getting pregnant as an evasion of already existing problems. It means that you refuse to sell your talents and aspirations short, simply to avoid conflict and confrontation. And this, in turn, means resisting the forces in society which say that women should be nice, play safe, have low professional expectations, drown in love and forget about work, live through others, and stay in the places assigned to us. It means that we insist on a life of meaningful work, insist that work be as meaningful as love and friendship in our lives. It means, therefore, the courage to be "different"; not to be continuously available to others when we need time for ourselves and our work; to be able to demand of others—parents, friends, roommates, teachers, lovers, husbands, children—that they respect our sense of purpose and our integrity as persons. Women everywhere are finding the courage to do this, more and more, and we are finding that courage both in our study of women in the past who possessed it, and in each other as we look to other

women for comradeship, community, and challenge. The difference between a life lived actively, and a life of passive drifting and
dispersal of energies, is an immense difference. Once we begin to
feel committed to our lives, responsible to ourselves, we can never
again be satisfied with the old, passive way.

Now comes the second part of the contract. I believe that in a
women's college you have the right to expect your faculty to take
you seriously. The education of women has been a matter of
debate for centuries, and old, negative attitudes about women's
role, women's ability to think and take leadership, are still rife
both in and outside the university. Many male professors (and I
don't mean only at Douglass) still feel that teaching in a women's
college is a second-rate career. Many tend to eroticize their
women students—to treat them as sexual objects—instead of
demanding the best of their minds. (At Yale a legal suit [*Alexander* v. *Yale*] has been brought against the university by a group of
women students demanding a stated policy against sexual
advances toward female students by male professors.) Many
teachers, both men and women, trained in the male-centered tradition, are still handling the ideas and texts of that tradition on to
students without teaching them to criticize its antiwoman attitudes,
its omission of women as part of the species. Too often, all of us
fail to teach the most important thing, which is that clear thinking,
active discussion, and excellent writing are all necessary for intellectual freedom, and that these require *hard work*. Sometimes,
perhaps in discouragement with a culture which is both antiintel-
lectual and antiwoman, we may resign ourselves to low expectations for our students before we have given them half a chance to
become more thoughtful, expressive human beings. We need to
take to heart the words of Elizabeth Barrett Browning, a poet, a
thinking woman, and a feminist, who wrote in 1845 of her impa-
tience with studies which cultivate a "passive recipiency" in the
mind, and asserted that "women want to be made to *think
actively:* their apprehension is quicker than that of men, but their
defect lies for the most part in the logical faculty and in the higher
mental activities." Note that she implies a defect which can be
remedied by intellectual training, *not* an inborn lack of ability.

I have said that the contract on the student's part involves that
you demand to be taken seriously so that you can also go on taking yourself seriously. This means seeking out criticism, recognizing
that the most affirming thing anyone can do for you is demand that
you push yourself further, show you the range of what you *can* do.
It means rejecting attitudes of "take-it-easy," "why-be-so-serious,"
"why-worry-you'll-probably-get-married-anyway." It means assum-

ing your share of responsibility for what happens in the classroom, because that affects the quality of your daily life here. It means that the student sees herself engaged *with* her teachers in an active, ongoing struggle for a real education. But for her to do this, her teachers must be committed to the belief that women's minds and experience are intrinsically valuable and indispensable to any civilization worthy the name; that there is no more exhilarating and intellectually fertile place in the academic world today than a women's college—*if* both students and teachers in large enough numbers are trying to fulfill this contract. The contract is really a pledge of mutual seriousness about women, about language, ideas, methods, and values. It is our shared commitment toward a world in which the inborn potentialities of so many women's minds will no longer be wasted, raveled-away, paralyzed, or denied.

THE ESSAY OPTIONS: GETTING STARTED

Start by interrogating your reading.

❖ *Solo Activity 2.21* Use TRIAC to help you generate at least two pages of reading notes on the material you're summarizing. In addition, identify and write down two questions you still have about what this essay says. Variation: Instead of using TRIAC, use QEC:CS. ❖

Consider the Logic of Connection

The standard transitional words we use in writing (and in normal conversation) fall into categories, according to the logical connections we want readers (or listeners) to understand. Here's a partial list of what transitions indicate:

- repetition and restatement: *in other words, that is*
- the move to particulars or supporting evidence: *for example, for instance*
- another instance or addition: *and, or*
- difference, contrast, or opposition: *but, on the other hand, however, in contrast, in spite of*
- sequence: *first, second, the last, initially, later*
- logical consequence and inference: *thus, therefore, it follows that, as a consequence, clearly then*
- conclusion: *finally, thus, in conclusion, at last*

All these phrases suggest the explicit or implicit moves that writers make as they work from thesis to restatement to illustration to analysis to conclusion (TRIAC). Writers sometimes use these transitional words and phrases to make the logical movement absolutely clear. Such transitions are often only implied—though, in a paragraph or essay that is well organized, the transitions can always be inserted. The logical moves are there whether the phrases are present or not.

❖   *Solo Activity 2.22*   Using TRIAC, QEC:CS, or another method you know compose an outline that represents the organizational pattern of the source(s) you're summarizing. At each new entry in the outline, use a transitional word or phrase that shows how the new thinking connects with the old. You may or may not follow the same organizational pattern in your summary. At this point, your purpose is simply to be certain you understand the logic of what you plan to summarize. ❖

❖   *Group Activity 2.23*   The sentences in the following paragraph have been scrambled. Reassemble them. Then explain your reasons for putting the sentences in this order by underlining the explicit transitions and inserting—in brackets—the implicit transitions you think are at work. To help you in this task, consider labeling the sentences using the TRIAC scheme. ❖

CAROL BLY
Letters from the Country

Those dreadful soirees he describes, with the eighth-rate singer and the maundering violinist doing a Russian equivalent to "O sweet amaryllis" badly in one corner while people hunch over the samovar, counting on tea as a mood-changing drug to carry them until the piggery of a midnight supper later—this is *particular* information.

It is the secret agenda of the liberal arts conversation: that studying whatever is *other*, in a non-judgemental but simply curious, ready-to-be-amused sort of way, makes people happy.

Chekhov, for example, is not particularly universal.

For some mysterious reason, being informed of how the others do things, how quietly other kinds of life are lived, how other molecules behave in quite other circumstances from the ordinary, raises the ego's joy!

The principle of literature is devotion to the particulars of life.

He is particularly particular.

Start Drafting

No task ever looks more difficult than when you first start it, but once you begin, you're making progress. Drafting a summary can seem harder than it is. Here are some of the common reasons we've heard:

- *I don't know enough yet.* Since a summary asks you to be an expert on whatever you're summarizing, you may find it difficult to actually begin writing your summary; you may not think you're ready. Two solutions can be used at this point: (1) Reread and take more notes, or (2) See if you can outline the original reading. Either of these actions could give you the familiarity you need to start writing.

- *I need to make an outline first.* It makes good sense to consider the overall organization of the summary you're writing. Will your summary simply follow the organization of the original reading? Or will you need to adopt an entirely different organization for your summary? If you're summarizing a chapter in a biology or economics textbook, for example, then the original organization may also work for your summary. Textbooks tend to use straightforward organizational patterns—a concept is named and defined, then it is discussed and explained, and then it is linked to some other concept or placed in some larger context.

  But some material you summarize will not follow this obviously clear pattern. For example, some might start with extensive personal stories meant to provoke readers' attention and sympathy before moving to the generality that the stories illustrate. Other essays may painstakingly use several stories or a series of facts that slowly build a case. You can easily decide that this is not the best form for your own summary.

  It pays to ask yourself how your own summary should go. In general, organize your summary as straightforwardly as possible. Readers refer to summaries to find out what the original, longer essay says, so start by telling them this. Suppose that the essay you're summarizing makes three important points. Mention these at the start by stating each point in the first paragraph before going on to explanations. By doing this, you'd clearly be writing a summary that does not follow the organization plan of the material it summarizes.

- *I don't know how to write a summary without using "I."* We agree that a summary filled with "I think" or "It seems to me that" risk directing readers' attention to you rather than to the material you're summarizing. So here is a suggestion for the first sentence: *In [insert title of what you're summarizing here], [insert author's full name here] [insert action verb such as—but not limited to—asserts/argues/explains/examines/describes . . .].* If we apply this "formula" to the Gettysburg Address, we get this first sentence: *In his "Gettysburg Address," Abraham Lincoln confronts the horror of a Civil War battlefield.*

This may not be the most elegant opening, but it offers a clear beginning that focuses on Lincoln as an author and on his speech as the source.

Consider the Organization of Your Summary

Suppose you're trying to summarize a lengthy and complicated argument that has numerous exceptions, many examples, and is ten or fifteen (or more) pages. Clearly you'll have to decide what is major and what is minor. These content decisions are often difficult—though always necessary. Perhaps equally difficult is the question, "Will your summary mimic the organization of the original source?" Or "Will your summary adopt a more straightforward, direct organization?" In a way, the wording we've adopted here already indicates our suggestion—mimic the original organization whenever it is direct, simple, and clear. And whenever the original's organization is more convoluted or difficult, adopt a different, but simpler and more obvious organization for your summary.

Suppose the original starts with a long personal story about a burglary of the writer's home, and then it goes into statistics about theft and home break-ins, and then it tells another story about a break-in that's even worse than the first story, discusses the people—their backgrounds, their reasons, and so on—convicted of the crime, and then it ends with a passionate plea for more drug treatment centers. Should your summary follow the same organization? It could, but your summary also could focus on the claims and supports the original essay makes by mentioning the other parts only as they clarify the claim or show its truth.

❖ *Group/Solo Activity 2.24* Create a preliminary outline for your summary. Make sure it represents all the major pieces of information your summary needs. Then write a short paragraph that explains why you think the organizational plan in your outline will work effectively for this particular summary. ❖

Get Responses to Drafts of Your Summary

Two kinds of responses can be useful at this point: a response from people who are *unfamiliar* with the original reading or a response from people who are *familiar* with it. People who are strangers to the original will have only your words to inform them. So test your draft to see whether or not it clearly communicates. Ask your reader—a friend or a staff member in the writing center—to let you know what seems clear in your draft and what seems fuzzy or hard to understand. Pay attention to the questions you hear—they're likely to be the same questions other readers would raise. If you can answer those questions now, you'll do a better job of summarizing.

It also pays to ask someone who is familiar with the original to tell you how successfully your summary compares. Does your summary misrepresent or misunderstand anything? Does it leave out something important? Overall, do the points in the summary emphasize those in the original, or is there some imbalance between what seems important in the original and what gets stressed in the summary?

❖ *Group/Solo Activity 2.25* Following the directions just given, obtain responses from at least two readers—classmates, writing center staff, or friends who will give you honest and detailed responses. ❖

Use Quotations

In a 750 word summary, you may have room for the equivalent of about two sentences of directly quoted material from the original. Using even that small amount can help readers actually hear the original material. But what should you quote? Here are some guidelines:

- Do not insert a section of quoted material before the first sentence of your summary.
- Look for quotable phrases or parts of sentences. Such phrases will likely capture the essence of some part of the original, signifying a main point or showing a use of language that seems unique to the writer.
- Work these quotable phrases or parts of sentences into your own sentences, and make sure you identify the quoted material with quotation marks. For example, As Lincoln's speech draws to a close, it focuses on Civil War casualties, the "honored dead," urging all of us to find in their sacrifice "a new birth of freedom."

As you reread your source essay, look for such quotable parts.

Consider Length—Adding Detail or Explanations, Combining Points

If your summary is too short—two pages when you have a three-page maximum, for example—then you probably summarized too drastically. The difference may be in the amount of detail you include: *I had breakfast.* vs. *I had a bagel, half a grapefruit, and a cup of coffee while I read* The New York Times. Adding detail clarifies meaning and adds length.

Or perhaps your summary is too short because it names but doesn't sufficiently explain the key terms or concepts of the original. A summary that's too short may only say, "Rich uses the phrase 'responsibility to yourself' as she urges women to become independent thinkers." A fuller summary, on the other hand, would go on to explain what Rich means by "responsibility to yourself."

Since most summaries have a maximum length, you may find that yours runs over the limit. Shortening some sentences can give you more room for content. See the following examples:

- *Identify and eliminate all "It is true that . . ." sentences.* If you think about it, virtually anything can follow the opening phrase "It is true that." Thus, these sentences unnecessarily postpone what they really have to say. They get written in rough drafts because they give writers a question to answer—What *do* I think is true? Other sentence openers such as "In my opinion" (What *is* my opinion?) or "I think" (What *do* I think?) work the same way, so they serve useful purposes in rough drafts. In final drafts, however, they usually can be revised easily. Here are some examples:

   It is true that some sentences need to be revised.
   becomes
   Some sentences need to be revised.
   I think that Aldo Leopold's essay "The Land Ethic" challenges readers.
   becomes
   Aldo Leopold's essay "The Land Ethic" challenges readers.

Summaries ask for a kind of patience from you that other writing may not—they ask you to withhold your own opinions. And they force readers (us) to think through and thoroughly understand someone else's views before we get to state our own. Ultimately though, this works to our benefit. We do understand someone else more completely. And when it is time for us to declare ourselves, we can use that fuller understanding to our advantage.

Essay Option 2C

Summarize a chapter or a portion of a textbook reading required for another course. Assume that you're writing this summary to a student who has been ill and unable to keep up with the readings. Your summary should be clear enough, detailed enough, and short enough to help this student catch up.

Essay Option 2D

Identify a current movie, and summarize three different movie reviews about it. Do not insert your own opinion; instead, try to report accurately on what the reviewers say. Make sure you quote at least once from each review. In your last paragraph, compare the reviews and explain why they do or don't add up to a clear conclusion about the movie's quality.

SAMPLE STUDENT ESSAY, OPTION 2C

As you work on your own essay for this chapter, consider the strengths and weaknesses of the following student essay. Does it follow the directions? Does it communicate clearly? Use the checklist in Chapter 1 as a guide while you read and evaluate. The professional essay that the student is summarizing follows the summary itself.

SHELLEY FICKES

Where Have All the 'Best Friends' Gone?

"In Praise of 'Best Friends': The Revival of a Fine Old Institution", by Barbara Ehrenreich, describes the institution of best friendship as being on "shaky ground". Ehrenreich contends the best friendships, specifically those among women, are both undervalued and unrecognized in our society. In fact, upon examination of her relationship with her own best friend, Ehrenreich observes: ". . . our relationship has no earthly weight or status. I can't even say the name for it without sounding profoundly silly" (Ehrenreich 304). As she demonstrates in her article, this is because female best friendships have, throughout history, been eclipsed by other types of relationships. Interestingly, women still create and maintain best friendships despite this lack of recognition.

Historically, the great friendships have tended to occur between men. Or at least those are the great friendships we are made aware of: ". . . the only friendships that have survived in history and legend are man-on-man: Alexander and Hephaestion, Orestes and Pylades, Heracles and Iolas" (Ehrenreich 304). Christianity itself, according to the author, did nothing to increase the status of female friendship. Male friendships were seen as a "breeding ground" for traits such as honor, courage, and loyalty. On the other hand, women were to feel shame for being women. And, when two women were together, it could lead to nothing but trouble.

Although women have been involved in passionate, loving friendships for years, the larger society has yet to recognize these relationships. Consequently, in the 20th century, the "companionate marriage" become the ideal, particularly in the middle-class. Rather than acknowledge women's best friendships, it was suggested that women did not need to have female best friends at all. Their husbands would be not only their providers, lovers, coparents, etc., but also their best friends. Unfortunately, as the author notes, "No man can be all things to even one woman" (Ehrenreich 305), and the idea that he could may have done more damage to marriage than anything else in this century.

The great women's movement of the 19th century relied heavily upon the friendship between Elizabeth Cady Stanton and Susan B. Anthony. Even so, when the movement returned in the seventies in the form of feminism, lesbian relationships became the first priority. As Ehrenreich argues, ". . . in our zeal to bring lesbian relationships safely out of the closet, we sometimes ended up shoving best friendships further out of sight" (Ehrenreich 305). In turn, the term "lovers" became the norm. The term "best friends" on the other hand, was taboo.

And currently, in the day and age of working women, best friendship is being brought back in the form of "networking". As the author explains, even though networking is not best friendship, it is an important step in the right direction. At least we are taking note of the fact that women's friendships are valuable. Within the world of networking, however, the value of friendship is predominantly monetary. Thus, when competition in the workplace comes into play networking friendships are bound to hit rough waters.

All of these things have led the author to believe that there is a need "to give a little more space, and a little more respect, to the best friendships in our lives" (Ehrenreich 305). She maintains that best friendships need time, nurturance, and social visibility. Even if that means spending the day with your best friend instead of your spouse or partner. Just like marriage, friendships require effort:

". . . the beauty of best friendship, as opposed to, say, marriage, is that it's a totally grass-roots creative effort that requires no help at all from the powers-that-be" (Ehrenreich 306). It would be nice, however, if they could be recognized as valuable, important parts of women's lives.

BARBARA EHRENREICH

In Praise of 'Best Friends': The Revival of a Fine Old Institution

All the politicians, these days, are "profamily," but I've never heard of one who was "profriendship." This is too bad and possibly short-sighted. After all, most of us would never survive our families if we didn't have our friends.

I'm especially concerned about the fine old institution of "best friends." I realized that it was on shaky ground a few months ago, when the occasion arose to introduce my own best friend (we'll call her Joan) at a somewhat intimidating gathering. I got as far as say-ing, "I am very proud to introduce my best friend, Joan . . ." when suddenly I wasn't proud at all. I was blushing. "Best friend," I real-ized as soon as I heard the words out loud, sounds like something left over from sixth-grade cliques: the kind of thing where if Sandy saw you talking to Stephanie at recess, she might tell you after school that she wasn't going to be your best friend anymore, and so forth. Why couldn't I have just said "my good friend Joan" or something *grown-up* like that?

But Joan is not just any friend, or even a "good friend"; she is my best friend. We have celebrated each other's triumphs together, nursed each other through savage breakups with the various men in our lives, discussed the Great Issues of Our Time, and cackled insanely over things that were, objectively speaking, not even funny. We have quarreled and made up; we've lived in the same house and we've lived thousands of miles apart. We've learned to say hard things, like "You really upset me when . . ." and even "I love you." Yet, for all this, our relationship has no earthly weight or sta-tus. I can't even say the name for it without sounding profoundly silly.

Why is best friendship, particularly between women, so undervalued and unrecognized? Partly, no doubt, because women themselves have always been so undervalued and unrec-ognized. In the Western tradition, male best friendships are the stuff of history and high drama. Reread Homer, for example, and you'll realize that Troy did not fail because Paris, that spoiled Trojan prince, loved Helen, but because Achilles so loved Patroclus. It was Patroclus death, at the hands of the Trojans, that made Achilles snap out of his sulk long enough to slay the Trojans' greatest warrior and guarantee victory to the Greeks. Did Helen have a best friend, or any friend at all? We'll never know, because the only best friendships that have survived in history and legend are man-on-man: Alexander and Hephaestion, Orestes and Pylades, Heracles and Iolas.

Christianity did not improve the status of female friendship. "Every woman ought to be filled with shame at the thought that she is a woman," declaimed one of the early church fathers, Clement of Alexandria, and when two women got together, the shame presumably doubled. Male friendship was still supposed to be a breeding ground for all kinds of upstanding traits—honor, altruism, courage, faith, loyalty. Consider Arthur's friendship with Lancelot, which easily survived the latter's dalliance with Queen Guinevere. But when two women got together, the best you could hope for, apparently, was bitchiness, and the worst was witchcraft.

Yet, without the slightest encouragement from history, women have persisted in finding best friends. According to recent feminist scholarship, the 19th century seems to have been a heyday of female best friendship. In fact, feminism might never have gotten off the ground at all if it hadn't been for the enduring bond between Elizabeth Cady Stanton, the theoretician of the movement, and Susan B. Anthony, the movement's first great pragmatist.

And they are only the most famous best friends. According to Lillian Faderman's book *Surpassing the Love of Men*, there were thousands of anonymous female couples who wrote passionate letters to each other, exchanged promises and tokens of love, and suffered through the separations occasioned by marriage and migration. Feminist scholars have debated whether these great best friendships were actually lesbian, sexual relationships—a question that I find both deeply fascinating (if these were lesbian relationships, were the women involved conscious of what a bold and subversive step they had taken?) and somewhat beside the point. What matters is that these women honored their friendships, and sought ways to give them the kind of coherence and meaning that the larger society reserved only for marriage.

In the 20th century, female best friendship was largely eclipsed by the new ideal of the "companionate marriage." At least in the middle-class culture that celebrated "togetherness," your *husband* was now supposed to be your best friend, as well, of course, as being your lover, provider, coparent, housemate, and principal heir. My own theory (profamily politicians please take note) is that these expectations have done more damage to the institution of marriage than no-fault divorce and the sexual revolution combined. No man can be all things to even one woman. And the foolish idea that one could has left untold thousands of women not only divorced, but what is in the long run far worse—friendless.

Yet even feminism, when it came back to life in the early seventies, did not rehabilitate the institution of female best friendship. Lesbian relationships took priority, for the good and obvious reason that they had been not only neglected, but driven underground. But in our zeal to bring lesbian relationships safely out of the closet, we sometimes ended up shoving best friendships further out of sight. "Best friends?" a politically ever-so-correct friend once snapped at me, in reference to Joan, "why aren't you lovers?" In the same vein, the radical feminist theoretician Shulamith Firestone wrote that after the gender revolution, there would be no asexual friendships. The coming feminist Utopia, I realized sadly, was going to be a pretty lonely place for some of us.

Then, almost before we could get out of our jeans and into our corporate clone clothes, female friendship came back into fashion—but in the vastly attenuated form of "networking" Suddenly we were supposed to have dozens of women friends, hundreds if time and the phone bill allow, but each with a defined function: mentors, contacts, connections, allies, even pretty ones who might be able to introduce us, now and then, to their leftover boyfriends. The voluminous literature on corporate success for women is full of advice on friends: whom to avoid ("turkeys" and whiners), whom to cultivate (winners and potential clients), and how to tell when a friend is moving from the latter category into the former. This is an advance, because it means we are finally realizing that women are important enough to be valued friends and that friendship among women is valuable enough to write and talk about. But in the pushy new dress-for-success world, there's less room than ever for best friendships that last through thick and thin, through skidding as well as climbing.

Hence may campaign to save the institution of female best friendship. I am not asking you to vote for anyone, to pray to anyone, or even to send me money. I'm just suggesting that we all begin to give a little more space, and a little more respect, to the best friendships in our lives. To this end, I propose three rules:

1. Best friendships should be given social visibility. If you are inviting Pat over for dinner you would naturally think of inviting her husband, Ed. Why not Pat's best friend, Jill? Well,

you may be thinking, how childish! They don't have to go everywhere together, Of course they don't, but neither do Pat and Ed. In many settings, including your next dinner party or potluck, Pat and Jill maybe the combination that makes the most sense and has the most fun.

2. Best friendships take time and nurturance, even when that means taking time and nurturance away from other major relationships. Everyone knows that marriages require "work." (A ghastly concept, that. "Working on a marriage" has always sounded to me like something on the order of lawn maintenance.) Friendships require effort, too, and best friendships require our very best efforts. It should be possible to say to husband Ed or whomever, "I'm sorry I can't spend the evening with you because I need to put in some quality time with Jill." He will only be offended if he is a slave to heterosexual couple-ism—in which case you shouldn't have married him in the first place.

3. Best friendship is more important than any work-related benefit that may accrue from it, and should be treated accordingly. Maybe your best friend will help you get that promotion, transfer, or new contract. That's all well and good, but the real question is: will that promotion, transfer, or whatever help your best friendship? If it's a transfer to San Diego, and your best friend's in Cincinnati, it may not be worth it. For example, as a writer who has collaborated with many friends, including "Joan," I am often accosted by strangers exclaiming. "It's a just amazing that you got through that book [article, or other project] together and you're still friends!" The truth is in nine cases out of 10, that the friendship was always far more important than the book. If a project isn't going to strengthen my friendship—and might even threaten it—I'd rather not start.

When I was thinking through this column—out loud of course, with a very good friend on the phone—she sniffed "So what exactly do you want—formal legalized friendships, with best-friend licenses and showers and property settlements in case you get in a fight over the sweaters you've been borrowing from each other for the past ten years?" No, of course not, because the beauty of best friendship, as opposed to, say, marriage, is that it's totally grass-roots, creative effort that requires no help at all from the powers-that-be. Besides, it would be too complicated. In contrast to marriage—and even to sixth-grade cliques—there's no rule that says you can have only one "best" friend.

Chapter 3:
Reading between the Lines

Understanding a piece of writing requires more than just careful attention to what is on the page. To understand, we need to interpret—to ask ourselves some additional questions:

- What do the details mean?
- Are the claims valid?
- Is the writing believable?
- What is the context?
- Who is the intended audience?

Even summarizing requires interpretation. When we summarize we have to consider what *isn't* said—what's implied or assumed. Whether consciously or unconsciously, we are always reading between the lines.

THE EXPERIENCE OF READING LITERATURE

Literature is the best kind of writing for learning how to interpret meaning in this way because in literary texts everything that's true for any reading experience gets intensified, thicker, more obvious. That is, anything you read can be looked at in both these ways: it has a content it wants to convey to you, and in its organization and arrangement it has an experience to make for you. In factual academic prose, the content clearly claims an important place. And the best experience you can have reading academic prose is the experience of understanding it, of seeing its structure and logic. Reading the best academic prose, you're hardly aware of the experience itself at all: you're simply caught up in the expanding clarity of the facts and arguments.

What literature typically has to tell you can often be summarized in cliché: love feels good, love can lead to disappointment, spring is pretty, we wonder how the sky got made, we all get older (unless we die first), grief is hard, betrayal can be destructive to personal relationships, childhood innocence can be vulnerable and touching, and so on. Trouble is, such telling leaves out the truth of emotion and of emotion's important link to thinking and to human motivations.

So literature aims to use language not so much to tell you something flat out as to orchestrate an experience in you. Literature is art. And that's what art does: it makes experience. A movie is a work of art; watching the movie is the experience the movie makes. Often we actually go to a special place for this—a movie theater. A Rolling Stones concert is art too: it doesn't so much want to tell you something as make an experience for you. Same for a Bach Concerto. A Mary Cassatt painting works the same way: it wants to make an experience for you, a very particular experience of looking.

❖ *Solo Activity 3.1* Write a paragraph about an experience with art that you've had in the last six months. Talk about the art—the concert, movie, or the artwork itself. Explain the experience it made for you as you engaged in that art—once the concert or movie started, once you started looking at the painting, once you were "into" the novel, poem, or play. ❖

READING AS A PROCESS

Reading literature, or any challenging book or essay, is just as much a process as the process of composing an essay. It takes time. It involves revision—re-seeing. One reason literature is taught in the university is because this process of re-seeing—this experience of art—is often difficult to manage without the help of others. Few people can pick up Homer or Tolstoy and read them for pleasure. Like writing, reading literature requires community.

❖ *Group Activity 3.2* The following poem was written by the well-known nineteenth-century English poet William Wordsworth. Use the directions that follow it to organize your experience of the poem. ❖

WILLIAM WORDSWORTH

She Dwelt among the Untrodden Ways

She dwelt among the untrodden ways
  Beside the springs of Dove,
A Maid whom there were none to praise
  And very few to love;

A violet by a mossy stone
  Half hidden from the eye!
Fair as a star, when only one
  Is shining in the sky.

She lived unknown and few could know
  When Lucy ceased to be;
But she is in her grave, and, oh,
  The difference to me!

1. *Reading aloud.* "She Dwelt among the Untrodden Ways" is read aloud once, clearly and slowly in class.
2. *First associations.* As you hear the words of the poem read aloud, simply write down whatever goes through your mind—words from the poem that strike you, questions, images, associations, memories, anything that comes to mind. You may have ideas about the meaning of the poem, and this is great; write them down. You may suddenly think of a personal experience, Great. Write that down, too. You may just make a list of random associations. Your goal is to be empirical—not getting the "right" answer but objectively describing exactly what your mind does under the influence of the words.
3. *Listening.* Members of the class share what they wrote, and the ideas are written on the board without comments. As this occurs, each student lists the two or three comments from classmates that resonate the most and make the most sense. This is important; students write down what others in the class have said. They listen.

    Note: The point here is to keep track of responses, rather than to interpret the poem or to fully understand it yet.
4. *Rereading.* The poem is read aloud again. In light of what the class has shared, each student again records associations and free responses.

5. *Tuition*. What we mean by "tuition" is the act of gathering outside information and "expert"—or more experienced—insight. The first four steps draw on and accept your first and second intuitive responses. As William Irmscher said, "Intuition always depends on tuition." Education requires that we draw out what's inside of us, while we also take in what's outside of us.

   This step requires the experience and insight of your instructor, who takes the responses she's heard and—drawing on her own reading of the poem and knowledge of William Wordsworth—makes two or three key points about the theme and style. The instructor gives a mini-lecture, and the class writes down what seems most useful and interesting in what is said.

   To some degree the instructor has a "good" interpretation—one that you need to pay attention to. There are certain things about literature that students can't get on their own—that they need to receive from authority and tradition. On the other hand, the instructor's interpretation is only one good interpretation. Its point is not to cancel your own reading but to inform it. In fact, the instructor's mini-lecture will tie what he or she knows about poetry to the information the class observed about the poem. Much of what students say about a poem on a first reading is pretty good and in tune with the important issues—even if the students don't quite know it yet. A teacher's job in this exercise, as in much of education, is to take what's useful and good in student comments, acknowledge them as useful and good, and then expand, deepen, and connect them with other, larger ideas.

6. *Third reading*. The poem is read aloud a third time. As soon as the last word is spoken, each student should do a five-minute directed freewriting that responds to these two issues:

   • In the course of this freewrite, make quick references to things the class and the instructor said.
   • *My main reaction to this poem is . . . (a working, tentative claim)*. This can be a personal association, such as "this poem made me think of my sister," or an interpretation of it—"This poem seems to be grieving over the loss of a loved one." Since this is a freewrite, don't worry

about making the thesis clear and completely workable
yet. Just get it out there.

- *Where this claim comes from is* . . . (the support). Or, *my
  illustration of this is . . . (the support).* If your focus is a
  personal association, describe the experience and the point
  in the language of the poem when you first started thinking of it. If your focus is an interpretation, draw on the language of the poem to explain it. You may be confused.
  Your thesis may be something like, "The poem really confused me." This is fine, but explain what is confusing in the
  poem.

IMAGES AND IDEAS

As the experience of reading Wordsworth's poem suggests, artists
arrange their materials with considerable care. Since art aims to do more
than merely tell you something—since it wants to both tell you and
make you feel something—artists take the formation of their art seriously. Even if their art seems entirely spontaneous, there's a conscious
decision made to preserve the spontaneity—rather than revise or
rearrange it. As we become more familiar with the many arrangements
the art could take, our experience of the art becomes richer. For example, the more you listen to jazz, the more you know how to listen; and
the more baseball or gymnastics you watch, the more you learn how to
see its many layers and gradations of performance.

In short, art asks us to pay attention to what makes it art. Take
poetry. Even inexperienced readers know that a poem requires them to
read past the obvious. Just the line breaks signal that. In prose, the
sentences break at the edge of the page only because they've hit the
arbitrary margin on the right and the writer simply has run out of
room. But a poem breaks lines on purpose, for reasons of rhythm and
emphasis. The word "verse" actually means "to turn" in Latin, and
that's what our eyes have to do at the end of a line of verse. As a result
of such turns, poems generally have fewer words on the page than
most other prose. Even a quick glance shows that poems are arranged
in some kind of pattern—they stand out more and are surrounded by
white space.

As soon as we see these features of language, we instinctively say to
ourselves—Oh, a poem; we're going to have to slow down. Each word
counts.

❖   *Group Activity 3.3*   Based on this phrase, answer the following questions:

> [Lucy was . . .]
>   A violet by a mossy stone half hidden from the eye!

- Was Lucy bold or shy?
- Was Lucy large and athletic or small and frail?
- What color hair may Lucy have had?
- Was Lucy under pressure or at peace?

Now, how do you *know* any of this? What's in this phrase that suggests these possibilities? How do we know that Lucy wasn't a flower? ❖

This last activity suggests that comparison is one key to the artfulness of poetry. Poems make comparisons. An image is used to imply an idea—a *vehicle* is used to suggest a *tenor*.

- vehicle (a concrete image): *a violet by a mossy stone*
- tenor (Lucy): *the qualities of this person the poet loves*

In some way, the vehicle and the tenor correspond. The qualities of the image suggest the qualities of the idea. To say that Lucy is like an oak tree is to say something entirely different than to say she is like a wood violet. Wood violets are beautiful little yellow flowers that grow briefly in early spring and only in remote and untrodden parts of a forest. They're easily missed. Perhaps Lucy was beautiful but shy. Perhaps she had yellow hair. (We don't know this, of course.) Perhaps in some way she was being pressured by something large and immovable (the rock). Perhaps just this little comparison anticipates the last part of the poem and Lucy's death, since wood violets are so brief.

If Lucy were an oak, she might still be around. She might not be so pretty. Wordsworth might not have loved her.

❖   *Group Activity 3.4*   In light of this, read between the lines of the second comparison.

> [Lucy was . . .]
>   Fair as a star, when only one
>   Is shining in the sky. ❖

❖   *Group/Solo Activity 3.5*   Compare Lucy to five other things.

After each comparison, write a few sentences that spell out what the comparisons might suggest. Be playful. For example, "a computer by a malfunctioning printer" or "an empty beer bottle by a trashy lawn." ❖

❖ *Group/Solo Activity 3.6*   In some ways, the imagery in a poem is the *verbal* equivalent of the *visual* imagery in advertising—imagery that, as we suggested in Chapter 1, can be worth a thousand words. Refer to the ad on page 80, published recently in *Sports Illustrated*. What non-verbal message is conveyed? What elements of the imagery convey that message? Compare the woman pictured in the ad to the girl in Wordsworth's poem. Based on the visual clues, how do we know that the "Jim Beam" woman isn't Lucy? ❖

This kind of comparison is only a part of the reading experience of poems. A good poem manages to combine its elements—every word choice and line break—so the experience seems almost inexhaustible. The poem offers your intelligence and perceptions so much to do that you find yourself doing something slightly different each time. The trick is to pay attention—the words make an experience if you let them and if you participate with them. That participation is reading—without it, the words are just funny black marks on a page in a book.

❖ *Group Activity 3.7*   Choose someone to read the following poem out loud twice. Once you hear the poem twice, read it again to yourself. Then write a paragraph that records what you're seeing, feeling, and thinking about as a result of these words in this order. Once your paragraph is written, discuss how you can or can't really be tested on this poem. ❖

LEX RUNCIMAN
The Boat at Kelly's Lake

It was wooden,
old white plywood,
registered seismographically
every weak breeze, every shift,
the lake peaks widening as they circled,
the underworld set heaving, air
wriggling in brown explosions.
Waterplants waved like sound
pulled by a thick wind.
God was by the pier. Once

I reached my hand down
wrist-deep in it—gooey, slick—

Get in touch with your masculine side.

brought up cupped in a palm
several consistencies of mud
and a salamander
soft under pressure,
spotted yellow, moving
confused in the air, both of us
confused. It fell back
and once in the water
how it fell—clear,
slow, in its own heaven.

THE CONDENSATION OF MEANING

What is true in poems is true for all literature—literature involves the radical condensation of meaning; it always asks for the interpretation of detail. Each word is like a door opening up to a very large room.

What makes reading literature so deeply pleasurable—or so frustrating if we're in a hurry or looking only for the "right" answers—is that we have to make the leap ourselves, in our own minds, from image to idea, vehicle to tenor. In some important way, the words mean more than what they say. Their crucial message is what we make of them—we have to supply it (the message) with our own intelligence, humanity, and imagination.

If an essay can be understood using the TRIAC scheme—topic, restriction, illustration, analysis, closure—a poem can be understood simply as the I in TRIAC without the T,R,A, or C. The T,R,A, and C are our responsibility.

If the process of thinking about writing can be understood using QEC:CS, a poem can be understood as the Q—the question. The experience it makes for us is the E—the exploration—or it's that when we read a poem we are always forced into exploring its meanings, since the meaning is never spelled out.

We can't make this leap or engage in this exploration if we're separated too far in time, geography, or experience from the world of the poem—though with the help of a teacher, a more experienced reader, we can fill in those blanks. In fact, that's one reason to read literature, so our knowledge of flowers, stars, English literature, and England in the nineteenth century—and ultimately of ourselves—can be deepened, stretched, and opened up.

Three specific terms help you understand this dynamic:

- *simile: Lucy is **like** violet*
- *metaphor: Lucy **is** a violet*
  Note: The only difference between a simile and a metaphor is the use of the word "like" or "as."
- *symbol: Lucy*
  Note: A symbol is simply the statement of a vehicle or an image, excluding the idea or tenor. On the other hand, the tenor or idea—the thing represented by the image—in similes and metaphors is actually stated. But note, too, that even when the tenor is stated, the possibilities of the tenor are not exhausted. There are all kinds of additional meanings implied by the image—all the qualities, for example, that we might associate with Lucy.

In this sense, the precision of poetry and the precision of science are quite different. In science, water means one thing and one thing only—the composition of atoms signified by H_2O. In poetry, water can suggest essential life, drowning, floating, loss of self, being in over one's head, or coming out cleansed and ready to start again.

❖ *Group Activity 3.8* In groups, discuss how "The Boat at Kelly's Lake" uses water. Write a paragraph together that expresses your various views. ❖

❖ *Group/Solo Activity 3.9* The literary critic Kenneth Burke once said that words "glow." Each word we use has an atmosphere around it, a set of associations. Some of these are peculiar to our own circumstances—blackberries make us think of our grandmother in Aberdeen. Some of these are cultural and common to everyone within a certain group—snow makes most Northern Europeans think of Christmas.

Quickly write down two or three phrases of whatever comes to mind when you hear each of the following words:

politicians
environmentalists
freedom
church
kitchen
swimming pool
cowboy boots
tatoos

Now meet in groups to discuss two or three of these words. Are your associations similar to others? Why or why not? Where does the "glow" come from? ❖

HOW PROSE CAN BE LIKE POETRY, TOO

The same processes of implication and comparison are also at work in prose narrative. By prose, we mean writing without deliberate line breaks. By narrative, we mean the telling of stories—the concrete description of people, places, and events in time—whether made up (fiction) or based on real events (nonfiction). Narratives often use metaphors and symbols. In a larger sense, prose storytelling is like poetry because it shows rather than tells. Rarely does the author come out and tell us explicitly what the details of the story mean. We have to figure that out ourselves by bringing all our experience and prior thinking to this story that's new to us.

❖ *Group/Solo Activity 3.10* The following nonfiction story also uses the image and idea of flowers—and of gardening as well—to imply a range of emotions and meanings. With pen in hand, read this story carefully, and underline words and phrases that seem significant for whatever reason. Make marginal comments such as questions and first responses. When you finish, write two or three quick sentences that complete this statement: "The moral of this story is _____" We're not suggesting that good stories have morals in this simplistic sense; this is just a useful initial exercise. Fill in the blank even if you're uncertain right now and think you will change your mind later.

Share your responses in groups. As a group, make a list of three things that seem clear to you about this story and three things that are unclear. ❖

MARJORIE SANDOR
The Night Gardener

The house came with a garden. This seemed simple enough, until the woman selling the house looked me dead in the eye and said, "We put a lot of work into that garden; it's going to be hard to leave." The woman was an artist, it turned out, a painter. Her name was Drusilla: she had dark wild hair and the unnaturally steady gaze of a hypnotist at work. Faintly I heard the warning in her voice, the implicit command: you will maintain it, you will not let it die. I nodded, offering what I could to win her favor. We were, after all, newcomers to Oregon, and newly-fled from North Florida's steamy grip. It would be nice to start out on the right foot. Every climate has its unspoken codes, and who knew what dark laws guarded this lush valley with its benign blue summers, where all those people in covered wagons were headed a hundred years ago, suffering hunger and heat-stroke to get to the Promised Land. This was not a legacy I wanted to mess with.

The rest of the morning was my reward. Drusilla invited me to sit at her table as sunlight poured in. She gave our young daughter a bowl of yellow plums and took me around to see her work. Her paintings tended toward the mystical, the feminine: the sacred site at Delphi, the deep insides of orchids. In another age, she would have been secretly consulted for the healing properties of plants, then burned at the stake. There were windchimes and strange coincidences. It turned out we knew people in common halfway around the world. "We want the house," I said, forgetting that my husband, somewhere in the house with her husband, might have an opinion about this too.

All summer, waiting for the loan to close, we took friends to visit the house and its garden. She encouraged us to do this. Come any time, she said, and please, if we're not home, take what you want from the garden. Feel free to come inside, too, she said, showing me where they kept the extra key under a flowerpot. The temptation was too great. Once when they were out of town, the three of us ran through the whole house, right up into their bedroom, running our fingertips along the walls. Back in the garden and only slightly calmer, I cut flowers, while my husband and our daughter gathered plums, nasturtiums, tomatoes, until everybody's arms were full. Just as we were leaving. Drusilla and her husband came home, catching us on the back steps with our stolen bounty. "Hi," I said. "Is this okay?" and though she was nodding, I felt it again, for the quickest slip of a moment, the dark umbilical between herself and her garden, the way I seemed to have come between them like an invader.

"I've never gardened," I confessed.

She smiled—barely—and held me briefly with her eyes. Clearly she already knew this about me: this, and possibly more.

"If you ever need help, don't hesitate to call," she said. "We're only moving a mile out of town. If you want to know where we planted anything, say, the delphiniums, please, please call. I loved this garden." I noticed the past tense. Surely this was sign that she would eventually let go, that I wouldn't be cursed for life. I was spooked, nonetheless.

For the sake of domestic harmony, my husband and I decided to split the gardening responsibilities: he agreed to take on the backyard, with its raised beds for vegetables and perennials, the three-bin composting system, the small lawn. Already he was appraising the beds with a surgeon's cool gaze. "Triage," he said. "We only need about half of it. Our girl's going to need more grass, for cartwheels." Briefly, I admired his fearlessless, his no-nonsense approach, before plunging into my own private sense of inadequacy. For my mission would be to keep from destroying the English-style cottage garden that faced the street, a garden that turned out to be semi-famous in the neighborhood. People from two blocks away dropped by to welcome us, or warn us—which was it? "Oh, you've got Drusilla's garden now," they said. "It's a big favorite around here." Another neighbor was more direct. "I give you a year, two at the outside, before you put in a lawn. Good luck."

But luck was exactly the way it felt, that first season. February: the crocuses came up, small, tentative, easily weighed down, but at last the tulips and daffodils emerged with sturdy authority: even the late winter rains of Western Oregon could not bend them. March, April: a raucous display of azaleas, candytuft, and rhodo-dendrons; a lilac that leaned too close to the driveway, forever wounded by the car. Then it was May, and there were impossible floods of light, and with them yellow coreopsis with blood-red centers, blueberries, daylilies, and a purple butterfly bush just begin-ning to rise above the front window—there was no telling how high it might go. In July, spires of white phlox shone madly in moonlight, shasta daisies leaned heavily against the delicate gold crowns of Coronation yarrow. I spent hours poring over my *Western Garden Book*. It was exhausting just learning the names, and my eyes hurt from the violence of all that light.

I cultivated new friends, two of whom turned out to be veteran gardeners. They humored me, escorted me through maze-like nurs-eries and stood in the front garden with me for hours, discussing ways to "fill in the holes."

For this was the great mystery: there were holes. Big ones. Places where, I guessed, Drusilla had dug up certain beloved perennials and taken them with her, knowing what would befall them if she left them behind.

At last I telephoned her, trembling. "What should be there?" I asked.

"I'll be right over," she said, and quicker than an ambulance, she was with me, standing with tragic calm on the front walk, her dark hair wild as Medusa's. She looked down at the barren space, and in that small eternity, it dawned on me what I'd done: in my spring weeding fervor, I must have yanked out the tender first shoots, in some cases the whole root ball, of several plants.

"Pacific Giant Delphinium," she said.

"How many?"

"Quite a few," she said, not looking at me. "Don't worry, you'll do better next year," she added, in the bitten-off way of someone holding back grief. And she was gone as quickly as she'd come.

All that summer, I collected plants and studied, or pretended to, for I was discovering, in the course of this new life, that it was not really in my nature to study. Rather, I followed whims, pursued a plant purely because I liked its name or its reputation for eccentric behavior. There was the New Dawn rose, *a rampant climber,* also the white bleeding heart with its fringed foliage and delicate white hanging lockets, and cardoon, a cousin of the artichoke favored by Marcel Proust's family cook. My husband, in the backyard, fell in love with mammoth Russian sunflowers: *tough, tolerant, not for tidy gardens.* Our daughter, who steadfastly refused green vegetables at dinner, wandered about plucking chives and breathing a delicate child-version of onion breath onto our dinner guests. Mugwort: *the mother of all herbs,* I read, *cures most ills, gives good dreams.* I imagined myself sewing herb pillows for Christmas, though in fact, I couldn't even do hems. Nevertheless, I called five nurseries trying to track down the seeds, and when I finally found them, the information on the packet frightened me. *Beware: extremely hardy; tends to take over in naturalized areas.* Thereafter, I kept the packet on my work-desk, hoping that the proximity of seeds alone would improve my dreams.

As a substitute for actual effort, I admired the idiosyncracies of my two serious gardening friends: the sophisticated architect from New York who favored plants with exotically shaped leaves and unlikely textures, furry or rubbery, whichever you least expected. She grew magnificent deserty things on a steep hillside: sculpture gardens came to mind, Zen masters meditating among bonsais and raked sand. From all this I gleaned that she was a cool, smart aesthete with strict standards: information that might come in handy later in our friendship. The other one, tall and big-boned and Scandinavian, a painter herself, was mad for daylilies and tall dahlias. In her garden, huge terracotta planters spilled over with deep lapis and azure, hot and lemony Provencal yellows. There was something of the warrior-queen here, a breathtaking aggression of color and height that made me hope I would never find myself in her enemies' camp.

With the summer, too, our immediate neighbors emerged. To our right lived a pair of oceanographers with a nicely sardonic attitude toward their garden. They were the ones who'd given me a year, two at the outside, to succumb to a lawn. Around their own they had planted only the hardiest, most drought-resistant perennials, those that could survive the length of an average research cruise: blueberry bushes and sage, santolina with its silvery foliage and bright yellow pom-poms, its stout constitution. They hinted, barely, that they didn't altogether approve of the painter's gardening habits. "She never weeded," they said. Then, leaning closer: "A lawn is not a crime."

But it was the neighbor on the other side who intrigued me most. Carla, a scientist, had just moved to town. A quiet woman in her mid-forties, she had a pale amazed face that would have looked good under a poineer's cotton bonnet. As we talked over the fence, she told me breathlessly that she and her husband were "experimenting" with a trial separation, confining themselves to the occasional weekend visit. As we looked together at the front yard, with its ruin of sad old grass and spindly shrubberies, she began, hesistantly, to talk about her plans for a garden. A slight tremor entered her voice, a mysterious urgency that drew me, worried me, and which, over the course of the summer, I began to associate with her husband's sporadic visits; the way, on those weekend nights, their two voices floated across the fence as I was trying to put my daughter to bed. It was his voice at first, in long low phrases, a steady monotone that drilled quietly through the air. Once in a while Carla replied, her voice higher than I remembered it. It evaporated quickly, as if she couldn't get enough air. They seemed to be right outside my daughter's window, a drift of unhappy rhythms floating toward her childhood dreams.

One Saturday in late summer when Carla's husband arrived, the bed of his pick-up was piled high with dark soil. "You're lucky, your soil's still in good shape," Carla said to me over the front-yard fence. "We're pretty much starting from scratch." Then her husband cleared his throat, and when she looked at me, I saw that her eyes were bright with tears. "Excuse me," she said. "I'd better get back to it. We only have the weekend."

By day they worked the garden. He dug up the lawn and shoveled in good soil; she planted young perennials: sunroses and pinks, lavender and yarrow, heirloom roses in pale shades, poppies of all kinds. By night, they argued, or rather, she received his low reasonable voice for what seemed a lifetime, then murmured a small reply, after which silence fell, a silence that seemed to last through until Monday morning, when I heard their voices quiet and in balance by the pick-up truck. Then the engine revved and the husband was gone.

My architect friend, visiting the next day, shook her head sadly over their garden. She pointed out that the poppies, as exotic and beautiful as they were, had been planted in straight rows, not grouped in clumps.

"Not a good sign," she said. "What do you know about these people?"

It was January: the time of early dark and serious rains. One night we threw a party—a big one—in which the invited and the uninvited mixed in cheerful chaos. Drusilla herself was among the latter, and though she kept to the edges of the crowd, I saw her every once in while pick up a vase or a book and turn it carefully in her hands in a way that made me think dimly of amulets and little dolls impaled with pins. Midway through the evening, I saw her chatting with my friend the architect, and wedged myself into a nearby corner.

"So what do you think of the garden?" said my friend.

"I think it looks like hell," said Drusilla, swift and sure.

My friend cast a glance my way and I flushed to the neck with embarrassment and something new—anger. Months later, it would dawn on me with no small terror that my friend may have gotten Drusilla to say this while I was within earshot, quite deliberately to make me mad, to jolt me out of my garden dilettantism and into real obsession. She is a very smart woman, this friend, and she had pegged me exactly. Standing there in the corner, humiliated and defiant all at once, I privately declared war. I would show this painter—and everyone else—that I could garden as well as the next person.

My rage persisted. It mellowed only slightly with the constant rains of March, mellowed and shaped itself into a youthful determination, oppositional, competitive, deeply immature, but I didn't care. I was going to have my own garden; I was going to fill in the holes. Behind the candytuft and the fading daffodils, I crouched beside a half dozen young delphiniums and a packet of dahlia tubers, which I'd bought because the picture on the cover showed these to be the tallest of all possible dahlias, and of a weird luscious violent color somewhere between chocolate and blood that suited my current mood. This is where I was, deep in April, when Carla called me over to her garden. She was planting tiger lilies, not in rows this time but randomly, in sweet strange groupings. And although it was the middle of the week, her husband was there too, coming and going with a wheelbarrow full of compost. Carla stood up, smiling, and brushed the dirt off her hands. She reached into her back pocket for an envelope.

"Hey, I've been saving these for you," she said. "Five foot tall purple poppies. They used to be in your garden—a neighbor told me. They're what's missing. I've always wondered what she had there between the butterfly bush and the yarrow. The colors just don't quite make sense."

She glanced back toward her husband, who was still shoveling. "Maybe if we both plant them, we'll have some luck," she said.

Suddenly I saw it: the faint flush of exuberance in her face, a tentative happiness. I understood that she was not talking about missing colors, or even poppies, exactly. As I accepted the packet, I felt as if I'd taken on something more: hope, or maybe even a responsibility of some kind—very small, very old, a fragile tendril of hope that has moved between neighboring gardens for longer than anybody knows.

"I'll give it a try," I said. "How do I do it?"

As she explained it, I heard the old mysterious tremor in her voice. Some night in the dark, she said, put the seeds on a wet paper towel, put the paper towel in a ziplock baggie, and store it for two days in the deepest, darkest drawer of the china cabinet. She told me to do it "just so," as she herself had been instructed by her neighbor on the other side. Otherwise they wouldn't germinate. I went home, and that night did exactly as she bade.

It was three nights later, as I lay in bed, that I realized I'd forgotten all about the seeds. It seemed crazy to garden in the dark, but I couldn't sleep. I got dressed, went downstairs, and took the plastic bag out of the drawer. Soon I found myself kneeling in the front garden, the wet paper towels in my hands splattered with dark seed. White phlox towered over me in the moonlight, the bleeding hearts hung their fragile white lockets down, the daisies gave off an acrid, musty smell, almost fetid—how could I not have noticed before? And though the neighborhood was quiet at last, I remembered the voices of Carla and her husband rising and falling in the dark, all those seasons of hope and difficulty pressing up so close to our own.

But the poppy seeds had germinated, and were waiting: they clung wetly to my palms. I had to rub my hands against the soil to get the seeds to leave me. As I knelt there amidst the crazy abundance of that second season in Drusilla's garden, I knew, finally, how to claim it for my own. I kept my hands in the cool evening soil a moment longer. Some people say that plants can talk, can tell you want they want. Can they listen, too?

It's hard to say what I wanted to ask for, exactly. A good growing season, abundance in both our gardens. For a saving magic to bloom between them. "These are for Carla," I whispered.

And I stayed right there, hunkered down in the dirt a little longer than was strictly necessary. It was hard to leave, and why should I? At last, nobody was watching. Everyone was asleep but my garden and me.

❖ *Solo Activity 3.11* Reread the story, and note any moment when the narrator and the characters are engaged in the act of reading between the lines—such as reading the meaning of what others say, reading faces, or reading situations. Then write a paragraph arguing that "The Night Gardener" is really a narrative about the need all of us have to interpret ambiguous situations and complicated people. Support that point with three examples. ❖

❖ *Solo Activity 3.12* Reread the story a second time. This time, note any passage you think points to the meaning of the story. Nowhere does the author actually come out and say, "Now here, my friends, is the point." She observes what Wayne Booth calls an "authorial silence," giving us details and leaving it up to us to figure out what they mean. But in any carefully structured story—such as this one—certain details and patterns of detail point to what that implied meaning is. Look for those details. You may want to consider the following questions:

- What is suggested specifically in the first paragraph of the story? What is suggested by the last paragraph? Do you see any parallels between the first and last paragraphs?
- What is the significance of the narrator's neighbor and her husband planting a new garden?
- What is the significance of the narrator planting the flowers at night? What is the significance of those particular flowers?
- What is the significance of the kinds of flowers the narrator plants throughout the story, the style of planting she does, and her approach to gardening?
- What might gardening represent here? What has it represented in your experience or in other stories you've read or heard?
- What is the significance of the title?

After the second read, stop and do a final freewrite that responds to the following question. You are the author, and you've just given a reading of this story to a group of students. A student asks, "So what does this story finally mean?" which is the Q of QEC: CS. Answer the question, and cite details in the story—the E and C. (We're not suggesting that there's an easy correspondence between what the author intends and what a reader interprets. This is just a useful exercise.) ❖

POINT OF VIEW

Two other issues are important for understanding poetry or prose that uses fictional techniques: tone and point of view. A writer always has choices when it comes to point of view, particularly in fiction. Since a fiction writer invents the characters—since in a sense she's the God of this universe—the writer can choose to tell us as much or as little as she wants about what's going on inside the character's heads. Controlling the flow of information, withholding some or all of what may be said, and forcing us to look at the story from a certain angle or with a certain bias determines what interpretations are possible for us to make.

The conventions of fiction offer fiction writers these basic choices for point of view:

a. *Dramatic or objective point of view.* The writer is like a fly on the wall or a video camera, simply recording everything he or she sees from the outside without giving us access to the consciousness of the characters.

b. *Third-person unlimited omniscient point of view.* The writer tells us what's going inside the head of every character, always using the third person—she thought, he felt, they worried, they resented, Cameron was persuaded but refused to admit it, Olivia longed for his arms. . . Thus, readers always know more than any of the characters do. This is the direct opposite of the previous choice.

c. *Third-person limited omniscient point of view.* The writer tells us what's going on inside of the head of one character, looking at everything that happens from his point of view—"Wayne sauntered into the room, unimpressed by what he saw. . ." Thus, readers understand one character more fully than any character in the story might.

   Note that except in certain unusual cases, no omniscient point of view—neither b. nor c.—is available to the nonfiction writer. The nonfiction storyteller doesn't know for sure what's going on inside the heads of real people. The writer hasn't made them up because they're actual people—so the nonfiction writer can only choose to tell the story from the objective or first-person point of view.

d. *First-person point of view.* The writer tells us a story from the point of view of "I", since the writer is a character in the story—"I sauntered into the room, unimpressed by what I saw." First-person narrators can only tell us what's going on inside their own head—they must make inferences based on detail about the inner state of the other characters.

Note that in a short story, novel, or even a personal essay, the first-person narrator is not necessarily the writer, though there may be many similarities. The storyteller is always one of the characters. In a first-person story, readers often feel as though they become the "I" character.

❖ *Solo Activity 3.13* What is the point of view of "The Night Gardener," and what inferences does that point of view force us to make? In other words, how does it force us to read between the lines? How would the story change if it were written from another point of view? ❖

TONE OF VOICE

A final way to begin understanding the nature of both poetry and storytelling is to think about tone of voice. Is the writer being sarcastic? Serious? Happy? Sad? Joyous?

❖ *Group Activity 3.14* Read the following line aloud in three different tones of voice, trying to change the meaning of it each time—Man, isn't the weather terrific today? Now try the same thing with "I love you." Discuss the elements of your voice that signalled the changes of meaning? Of body language? ❖

How does written language convey these qualities of the spoken voice? Printed language, after all, is silent—the words just sit there on the page entirely without sound. How does something visual like a word or phrase—these funny little black marks on the page—signal something oral like the voice? Punctuation can do some of that work. "Man, isn't the weather terrific today!" suggests something different than the same sentence with a question mark. Typeface also can have some effect— "Man, *isn't* the weather just **TERRIFIC** today?"—though there's more ambiguity here.

❖ *Solo Activity 3.15* Write three versions of "I love you" so you communicate three different ways readers will hear those words. Use punctuation and typeface to communicate the differences. ❖

In general, the issue of tone can only be decided in context, taking into account the rhythm of the sentences—the place of the line in the story, what's come before or after it, what character is saying it, what the larger themes are, and so on.

This is particularly true with the stylistic or tonal device of irony. If it's pouring rain outside, and has been for weeks, and someone walks into the room and says, "Isn't the weather terrific today," this person has obviously said the opposite of what he really means (unless he's crazy). That's irony: when what's said is the opposite of what's meant. Everyday conversation is full of irony—"I **love** my English composition class," "Don't you find calculus really easy?" "I could care less whether I go out with Danny"—though it's often hard to detect the same levels of meaning in written text. One sign of good critical reading skills is the sensitivity of your "irony meter." The capacity to detect irony suggests the larger sense this book is trying to urge—that words always have the potential to mean more than they say.

❖ *Group/Solo Activity 3.16* Describe the tone of the following lines from "The Night Gardener." What makes you think this?

> In another age she would have been discretely consulted for the healing properties of plants, then burned at the stake.
>
> I cultivated new friends. . .
>
> It was hard to leave, and why should I? At last, nobody was watching. Everyone was asleep, except my garden and me. ❖

❖ *Solo Activity 3.17* Mark three passages from the entire story where the narrator interprets or is unsure about the tone of what people are saying to her. ❖

FILLING IN THE GAPS

On all these levels of imagistic language, point of view, and tone, reading poetry and fiction is a matter of "filling in the gaps," as literary critic Wolfgang Iser put it. Things are always left unsaid, and those unsaid things are what draw us deeper into the story, stimulating our imaginations. We have to supply meanings for what's only hinted at, just as the narrator in the "The Night Gardener" has to figure out how to fill the mysterious holes in her garden (left when she pulled up flowers that she thought were weeds!).

❖   *Group Activity 3.18*   The following poem uses gaps in a playful and obvious way to make a larger point. Fill in as many of the gaps as you can. ❖

WILLIAM STAFFORD
Final Exam: American Renaissance

Fill in blanks: Your name is _____ _____Ido Emerson.
Your friend Thor _____ lives at _____Pond; he owes you
rent and an ax. Your neighbor who lives in a house with
_____ gables won't respond to another neighbor, Herman
_____ , who broods about a whale colored _____ .
You think it is time for America to _____ .

In a few words, tell why.

❖   *Group Activity 3.19*   Explain in one sentence what the larger point of the poem is. Make a list of reasons why you think this. What elements of the poem lead you to think that this is its larger meaning? ❖

Essay Option 3A

Using your experience from Activities 18 and 19, write a two- to four-page essay that explains your interpretation of the theme, point, or underlying message of "Final Exam." Your thesis will be a more elegant version of the sentence, "The point of the poem is _____." It can appear anywhere in the essay.

The remainder of your essay should explain the details that led you to this conclusion. For audience, think of both the class and your instructor, with emphasis on the instructor. Think of this as a conventional school assignment. Your essay's underlying purpose will be to demonstrate to your instructor that you understand the central ideas of this chapter. Use its terms and concepts as you explain why you think what you think about the poem. In other words, your interpretation of the poem will serve as a "final exam" on the ideas and methods of "reading between the lines."

Suggestion: Relate the Stafford poem to Adrienne Rich's essay in Chapter 2.
Option: Follow the same general directions, but focus on any poem of your choice.

LITERATURE AND LIFE

We called the first essay option a conventional academic writing assignment, and it is. But reading poetry and fiction in this way is also great training for life. After all, life is more like a poem or a story than like an article where the thesis is clearly stated and all the implications are spelled out in succession. Rarely do the clouds part and some voice speak out loud and clear about the reasons things happen to us. Life seems to *show* rather than *tell*. Like the narrator in "The Night Gardener," we always read between the lines of our friends and our problems, trying to figure out what they mean and what to do.

❖ *Solo Activity 3.20* Think of a recent conversation you had with a friend or family member. List the three major things you said to each other. Make another list of three things you *didn't* say to each other but were somehow communicated. For example, your girlfriend may have said that she didn't want to go to the movies; what you understood from this, maybe, is that she was tired. Finally, make a third list of those elements of facial expression, body language, tone of voice, and so on that communicated the implied message. In other words, what led you to read between the lines of your friend in the ways you did, (always granting that your interpretation may have been wrong)? ❖

❖ *Solo Activity 3.21* Look closely at a student in a class you're taking, someone you don't know well. Write a profile of this person, a description of what this person is like, supporting your inferences with as many details as you can think of: clothing, body language, gender, and so on. ❖

❖ *Solo Activity 3.22* Assume you've been reported missing. Assume you are the detective in charge of investigating this disappearance. You've come to the missing person's dorm room or apartment to see what you can learn about his or her habits and character. Inventory everything you see that may give you clues about the missing person, with a brief phrase or sentence after each item that records what you think that item implies about the person. Consider things such as posters on the walls, pictures, books, CDs, how clean or messy the room is, the kinds of clothes hanging in the closet, and so on. Based on this evidence, speculate about where the person has gone and whether the disappearance is willing or unwilling. ❖

❖ *Solo Activity 3.23* Read one of your classrooms as if it is a poem. Study the details of the physical layout and what they suggest about the attitudes of your university toward students and education. How many students can the room hold? Are the desks bolted to the floor? Are they arranged in an amphitheatre that extends upward from a raised platform where the teacher stands? How are the desks related to each other spatially; for example, can students face each other? What about the age and condition of the building? ❖

Our lives are surrounded by white space with gaps to be filled everywhere. One condition of being human is the constant effort to fill those gaps with whatever intuition and knowledge we have. Life supplies us with detail after detail. Our job is to read past those details to what they might imply; our job is to assemble those details into possible and provisional meanings—and then to revise those interpretations yet again when the details change or our perspective shifts. Every person we encounter is a narrator with an individual point of view, and we are narrators, too. At least in this life, omniscience isn't possible. So we watch, listen, negotiate, ask questions, try again—the mystery of selves always eluding us. As literary critic Robert Scholes said, the world is full of texts. We're always reading them. It's as natural as breathing.

Essay Option 3B

Choose one of the "texts" in Activities 3.20–3.23, or choose one of your own. Then read between its lines—that is, write an essay that reflects on the values, assumptions, points of view, ideas, and issues that are implied but not actually stated by that text. Unpack what's packed in. Make explicit what's implicit. Bring in the foreground what's in the background. In short, read the text as if it is a poem.

Ground your essay in a more eloquently stated version of this thesis statement: "The main message hidden in this text is _____." Support your speculations by linking them directly to details that *are* stated or explicit in the text or object you are studying. Conclude by reflecting on why this kind of "reading" may be important to you or anyone else. What's gained from reading between the lines in this way?

For audience, consider one of these two options: (1) the academic audience of classmates and the instructor or (2) a "real world" audience that consists of some person or group who really needs to be informed of what you think. For example, if you expand on Activity 3.20, you could write the essay as a letter as an explanation or apology to a friend or loved one. If you expand on Activity 3.23, you could write the essay as a letter to the dean of your college or president of the university that describes the nature of the education you've been receiving—either to praise or blame.

READING LITERATURE AS TRAINING FOR READING OTHER KINDS OF WRITING

If literature can teach us how to read life, it certainly can teach us how to read other kinds of writing—even the supposedly "non-literary kind." In fact, there is no language completely devoid of the style and thickness that characterizes literature. As Richard Lanham pointed out, there's a spectrum. The "transparent" language, such as phone books, encyclopedias, and so on, aspires to be completely neutral and objective. It's on one side. On the other side is poetry and fiction, language that's obviously stylized, tends to be opaque, and attracts our attention as much as the meaning behind it. Between the two is language we might think of as "translucent"—it admits some light of meaning, while it somewhat distorts the style and bias of the author. An article in a news magazine may qualify here.

Language on the transparent side, however, isn't totally transparent; every window is a little distorted. No language is entirely objective. Think briefly about phone books. They could be organized differently from the way they are—by occupation, income, or race; or with all the names and phone numbers listed under categories like "Professors," or "Those Making $50,000 or more," or "Asian." The alphabetical order of phone books suggests democracy—everyone is equal, though until recent times, women were often listed as part of a pairing, and usually as the second person in that pair, such as "Mr. and Mrs. Fred Jackson." In some phone books, those who pay an extra fee can have their name printed in bold. We always can choose to withhold our address, which may suggest a person who is more introspective or private than others.

The white pages with people's names come first and then the yellow pages follow with advertisements. People come first. Or do they? What does it mean for the yellow pages to be so loud, bold, and attention-grabbing? What dominates a phone book visually, and what does that suggest about our values?

❖ *Group/Solo Activity 3.24* Read between the lines of the following sentences taken from a sign posted at the entrance of a research forest. Consider these elements:

- the level of formality of the words
- the tone of the words
- the "glow" or connotations of the words
- their physical arrangement and sequence on the sign
- the apparent reason for such a sign
- the assumptions the sign seems to be making

In addition, think metaphorically about the words. For example, imagine what the person behind the words looks like—how he or she may be dressed, age, and the expression on his or her face. Think, too, about the sort of person this sign assumes you to be—its implied attitudes about you. What is the implied understanding of what a forest really is? ❖

Public Access Rules

- In order to protect research forest resources, stay on roads and authorized trails designated for your mode of travel.
- Do not block gates or roadways to emergency vehicle access.
- While recreating, yield to Forest vehicles and be courteous to other recreationists at all times.

❖ *Solo Activity 3.25*   Rewrite these three sentences and change the style to imply an entirely different message about forests and people. ❖

Though the sign in the research forest presents itself as entirely "unpoetic," as severe and bureaucratic, this style of writing conveys a meaning that is just as powerful as writing that uses metaphors and symbols. For that matter, the sign *does* use a metaphor, though it is less obvious here than in poetry (e.g., *mode* of travel, *blocking* gates). Metaphors are unavoidable and intrinsic to all language.

Even selection implies meaning. Early editions of *The Worldbook Encyclopedia* featured few entries about women or people of color. In recent editions, you'll see many. Length signals meaning, too. If the encyclopedia devotes five pages to "electricity" and one paragraph to "existentialism," something is implied about what this encyclopedia values.

❖ *Group/Solo Activity 3.26*   Locate a full-page magazine advertisement for either a vehicle (car or truck), a cologne or perfume, or a service (for example, an insurance company). Bring this advertisement (or a photocopy of it) to class. In your group, choose one of these ads and read it as you would a piece of literature. Assume that every aspect of the ad has been considered and chosen in order to communicate meaning. Write a paragraph that identifies and discusses four messages essential to the meaning and success of this ad. ❖

INTERPRETING THESIS-DRIVEN PROSE

Most of the writing you read in college textbooks consists of top-down, thesis-driven language. The writer's effort is to be as clear as possible about the major point, to support that point with details, to identify how those details fit the claims, and to link each sentence with obvious transitional words and phrases. The effort is toward explicitness.

This is the kind of writing we focus on in this book—the kind that we've described as Claim/Support and used TRIAC to help you understand. But even in this book, we've left a lot out. We can't say everything there is to say or everything we know about a subject. Writing is a process of deciding what to include and what to leave out, simply in the interest of economy and coherence. Sometimes, these are conscious decisions. Other times, writers unconsciously leave out huge areas of concern. In the same way, writers unconsciously project their attitudes—about politics, their sense of authority, and their regard for the reader. We can't help doing this in our writing, just as we can't help it in real life. Everything is attitude.

❖ *Group/Solo Activity 3.27*   Read between the lines of the following paragraph from *Lincoln at Gettysburg: The Words That Remade America*, a scholarly book for a general readership by social critic and intellectual historian Garry Wills. Answer the questions that follow.

GARRY WILLS

from Lincoln at Gettysburg: The Words That Remade America

The Gettysburg Address looks less mysterious than it should to those who believe there is such a thing as "natural speech." All speech is unnatural. It is artificial. Believers in "artless" or "plain" speech think that rhetoric is added to some prior natural thing, like cosmetics added to the unadorned face. But human faces are *born*, like kitten faces. Words are not born in that way. Human babies, unlike kittens, produce a later artifact called language, and they largely speak in jingles, symbols, tales, and myths during the early stages of their talk. Plain speech is a later development, in whole cultures as in individuals. Simple prose depends on a complex epistemology—it depends on concepts like "objective fact." Language reverses the logic of horticulture: here the blossoms come first, and *they* produce the branches.

- What sort of reader does Wills seem to imagine? What level of knowledge does the author seem to assume in readers? What level of interest and intelligence does the author seem to imagine?
- What arguments are brought up by the author? Can you sense what the scholarly debate is about, and who the author may be disagreeing with—(in general terms)?
- What is Wills's tone of voice? What is the author's style? What image of the writer do the words project—What is he wearing? How old is he?
- What metaphors does Wills use? What jargon is used? ❖

❖ *Group/Solo Activity 3.28* Choose a scholarly journal in your major or some area of interest. Pick an article from the latest issue, and compare the first paragraph of that article with Wills's paragraph above. Read between their lines. What different assumptions about audience, purpose, and the nature of language do the two authors make? Both are doing "academic discourse"—that is, they write about ideas and make arguments about those ideas. What differing notions of that enterprise are implied? ❖

What's obvious is that all specialized discourse assumes an audience of other specialists who share a knowledge of certain jargons and histories of ideas within that field. If certain things couldn't be taken for granted or assumed as general knowledge by the reader, every piece of writing would be a thousand pages long. The problem for beginners who read scholarly articles is that they're not inside that community yet. They can't read between the lines without years of study. They don't know what's taken for granted or what's assumed. In a sense, that's the whole purpose of education—to help outsiders become insiders and to enable students, over time, to take for granted what certain communities already take for granted.

❖ *Group/Solo Activity 3.29* Make a list of important jargon words from your latest job. If you worked in a grocery store, you may include such phrases as "night stocker," "checker," and "bar codes." List at least five terms, and briefly define them. Then share your terms with others. How are these jargon terms alike and different from the jargon terms you are encountering at the university? ❖

All scholarly discourse assumes that details are worth dwelling on, taking apart, and looking past. This type of writing always assumes complexity. Gary Wills, after all, writes a 317-page book about the Gettysburg Address—a speech that's only 272 words long! His book claims that those 272 words capture the essence of American life in the middle of the nineteenth century, that the words of the speech are stylistically powerful, that much, much is contained inside them, much that is worthy of unpacking and considering. That's the nature of intellectual work. What we should read between the lines of every piece of academic writing is a belief in the value of reading between the lines.

With this in mind, literature is the best training of all for critical thinking and reading. It's like all language, only more obvious and intense. If we can comprehend a metaphor that is obvious and intentional and thick, we become more skilled at critical thinking and the implicit meaning in all kinds of writing.

Essay Option 3C

Follow the same directions here as you did for Essay Option 3B, but apply them to these texts:

- A section of your College Catalogue or Schedule of Classes—for example, the description of a department and its offerings and the general table of contents
- The Web page of your university or department
- Any of the classrooms on your campus; look at the age of the building, the arrangement and number of chairs, the color of the walls, the number of windows, the presence or absence of certain kinds of equipment, the distance between teacher and students, and so on
- The description of a course that is offered during a particular term
- The table of contents of any textbook you're using in a class; a chapter or several pages of a textbook; look at the size of the pages, the typeface, the use of illustrations, the style of the language, its arrangement on the page, the sequence of material, and so on
- Any poster or notice on a bulletin board, kiosk, or wall on campus, whether it's an official university notice or a hand-made notice about a party on the weekend. Look at one particular text of this kind and unpack its meaning, or read and interpret one particular bulletin board or kiosk—what does the collection and combination of material at that site imply about the nature of your campus?
- A map of your university—where the buildings are located in relation to each other, the amount of parking, the size of the buildings, the relation of the campus to the town, the amount of green space, and so on

For audience, again choose among two options: (1) an academic audience or (2) a "real world" audience.

THE ESSAY OPTIONS: GETTING STARTED

One way to understand the question (Q) for this chapter is to simply ask, What do I think about this poem or text? Or what do I think is the most important meaning or theme in this poem or text?

The Exploration (E) can take several paths. Literature invites comparisons. On one hand, when we read a poem or story, we naturally say, "I had an experience just like that." And because we've had a similar experience, we understand the poem better. We can relate to it or identify with it.

Just as your experience can help you understand the poem, the poem can help you understand your experience. It's not that you're always "reducing" the poem to what you already know, but in a sense you "raise" what you know to the level of the poem's complexity and insight, which allows its depth and structure to enlarge and improve your own understanding. The poem becomes a device for helping you see things you didn't see before.

❖ *Solo Activity 3.30* Draw a line down the center of a sheet a paper. Title the left side, "What My Experience Teaches Me About the Poem." Title the right side, "What the Poem Teaches Me About My Experience." Make lists under both heads, and fill up the page. If you choose a nonpoetic "text," substitute that text for the word "poem." ❖

At the same time, as we suggested in Group Activity 3.2, it's also necessary to move beyond your own responses and beyond the text itself in search for the thesis. However valuable your own experience can be as a point of departure, certain ideas can be discovered only outside yourself—ideas that may become very important to you as a person. That's what libraries are for. And classes. As we have stressed before, reading requires community.

❖ *Group/Solo Activity 3.31* Refer to the following poem by William Stafford, as well as several quotes from his interviews and speeches about poetry. As you read them, underline the things that give you more insight into "The American Renaissance." On a sheet of paper, list these words and phrases. Skip a space at the bottom, and jot down two or three summary phrases that capture the main points and the main ways this supplemental material "adds up." In addition, reread the two Stafford quotations we used in the "Preface to Students" at the beginning of this book. ❖

WILLIAM STAFFORD
Learning How to Lose

All your years learning how to live to win,
how others judge you, who counts—you know
it's wrong: but those habits cling that brought you
this freedom. You know how to earn it but
you don't know what it is—a friend that you
make is conquered, like an enemy.

Somewhere you'll rest, have faith, even
lose sometimes, accept the way you are, say
easily to the world: "Leave me alone, Hours.
I'm just living here. Let Now win."

Don't have any standards outside the feeling you have as you write. Just follow your impulse, enjoy what happens. Permit yourself to like what you are doing (if you feel any qualms, then veer toward what feels good—why oppose the only compass you have?)

The first thing you think of is really worth writing down. And the second. And the third . . .

If a student learns to seek praise and avoid blame, the actual feel and excitement of learning and accomplishing will be slighted in favor of someone else's reaction. The student's own, inner, self-realizing relation to the materials is displaced. Anyone who customarily seeks outside rewards rather than inner satisfactions will be disabled, it seems to me, for all higher and original accomplishment. And that kind of teaching and "learning" will corrupt both student and teacher. For teachers will begin to feel themselves arbiters and guardians rather than participants in the excitement of skill and discovery.

I assume that there is no ceiling on one's education, that . . . out there in the realm of our mutual seeking we all—students, teachers, and yes, even our bosses—can continue to learn, without the distraction of pats on the head or raps on the knuckles. Education is too important and exciting to be dominated by thoughts of the hovering red pencil or the happy smiling face pasted in the margin.

When I write a poem it's like I glimpse something far off—just a little strip of something actual. It's like seeing a strip of the universe between the slats of a picket fence. You are passing, and between the pickets you glimpse a little of what's beyond. And then I write another poem, and I get another glimpse, another strip of light through the fence. And then another, another. But I never know if the successive glimpses are connected. Behind the fence, I never know if all those strips of the universe have continuity, a connected substance.

Discovering and Sharpening a Thesis Statement

When you're getting started on a paper you're searching for a thesis—a point of view, or that specific thing to write about. All the notetaking and prewriting is a means to that end. At some point, an idea emerges.

❖ *Solo Activity 3.32* Make a list of all the words and phrases from the poem, from the chapter, and from any of the prewriting you've done that seem interesting or important to you. Jot them down in any order. Reread the list, and rank the ideas that you like the best or seem the most workable by numbering them 1, 2, 3, and so on in the margin. Now make an X next to the items that seem related in any way to the idea you've marked (1), or draw arrows from those details back to the idea. Do you have enough specifics to make up the essay (you still haven't come up with a thesis)? If not, quickly read the poem or text again, and see what other relevant details you can find.

On a separate sheet of paper, take the top two to four ideas on your list and somehow sketch out their relationship. Are any of these ideas somehow related? (You may try to informally apply the idea of rhetorical diagramming from the first chapter here.) Is one idea, for example, a subset of another? Does one idea oppose another? Which of your favorite ideas just don't fit with the rest? It's not possible or necessary to spell out this process in a linear and mechanical way. You just doodle and sketch. You draw a lot of arrows, and at some point a kind of thesis grows out of all the details you've listed. ❖

In Chapter 1, we suggested that good thesis statements are never merely restatements of commonplaces and that they should always try to answer the question of significance: Who cares about this idea? Why does this matter? Here are two more tips to sharpen your thesis statements:

1. As John Ramage and John Bean suggest, think about both the audience and how you want that audience to be changed by your essay:

   Before reading my essay, my readers think this way about my topic _____

   After reading my essay, my readers will think this different way about my topic _____

2. Return to the formula we suggested for Essay Option 2 in Chapter 1, and apply it to this topic: "Everyone says _____, but I think _____." Ramage and Bean have the same pattern in mind when they recommend that you begin your thesis statement with "although" or "whereas"—a strategy they say can give your thesis a persuasive tension and interest: "Though most people believe X, this essay asserts Y."

   Not: The Clinton White House scandal has had both positive and negative effects on the discussion of sexual morality in this country.

   But: While many people think the Clinton White House scandal has undermined moral values in this country, it has actually forced us all to reaffirm our basic standards of decency and honesty.

❖ *Group/Solo Activity 3.33* Apply tip 1 to the topic of your essay, and then restate the second sentence (After reading my essay, my readers will think _____) in the form of a sentence that begins with "Although." Write all your sentences on the board, find the one or two that seem the best, and critique the rest using these as models. ❖

A Suggestion for Writing a Rough Draft and Revising It

Although Stafford doesn't use the term "freewriting," that's basically what he means when he talks about following your "impulse" and permitting yourself to "like what you're doing" in the material we included in activity 3.31. It makes sense if you're writing *about* Stafford to write in the way he recommends. Do what he advises in the quote about not "having any standards" and getting out a draft as quickly and straightforwardly as possible.

As you revise your rough draft, however, follow this pattern: claim (T), illustration (I), analysis of how the illustration fits the claim (A). This is an adaptation of the TRIAC scheme, with a special emphasis on what follows the illustration. Students often make a claim and support it with detail from the text. This is fine, but then they move on. The quote just sits there as if its relevance is self-evident as if it's obvious how it supports the claim. But if it was were obvious, there would be no need to make the claim in the first place. The point is that we're all involved in the act of interpretation. So to show that act, it's necessary to follow up the quoted line or passage with analysis of how that passage—the words, rhythms, images, themes—actually matches up with the inference you've made. This is how you do the equivalent in literary analysis of "showing your work" in math.

You can follow this pattern within a paragraph or across paragraph boundaries—the T and I are one paragraph and the A is another, for example. Then you repeat this pattern with each of the other major points you make.

❖ *Solo Activity 3.34* Add one to three sentences of analysis to complete the following brief statements of illustration and thesis:

> Wordsworth compares Lucy to a "violet by a mossy stone" [I], which implies that she's a fragile and isolated creature [T] . . .

> Throughout "The Night Gardener," Sandor implies that taking care of flowers is parallel to the living of life [T]. As she puts it, for example, "I cultivated new friends" [I] . . . ❖

Jargon and Style

Throughout this chapter, we've drawn on the basic terminology of literary analysis by introducing terms such as point of view, metaphor, symbol, and so on. We also allude to such literary theorists as Wayne Booth, Kenneth Burke, and Wolfgang Iser. The point of this terminology is to sharpen your sense of how literature works and to give you a precise way of talking about that experience of words.

Maybe it's obvious that the writing topic for this chapter aims at drawing you into such an experience. Everything in this chapter should have some application to your understanding of Stafford's poem or whatever "text" you're discussing.

❖ *Solo Activity 3.35* Reread this chapter, and underline at least three terms or passages that help you in responding to the topic. ❖

At the same time, we want to celebrate the directness of the writers we've highlighted. Both Wills and Stafford, for example, do the careful, hard thinking that characterizes intellectual work; yet they do it in a language free of unnecessary abstraction and jargon. Some jargon is necessary. Abstraction, in a sense, is the goal of intellectual work—arriving at some language to understand the overall operation of an idea, process, or form. And yet too often, academic discourse is paralyzed by obscurity, indirectness, and even deliberate, arrogant wordiness—language that's designed not to inform but to exclude. Well-intentioned students often think they have to write in that unnatural and affected register to be taken seriously as "college writers." So they find themselves at sea, floundering in language they don't really understand.

The key to academic writing, especially for students, is to take the big words and difficult concepts and translate them into direct, straightforward language. If you can do this, you've shown your genuine understanding.

❖ *Group Activity 3.36* Translate the following three sentences into simpler prose that says the same thing. If you're not sure what the original means, come as close as you can. Note: There are hints in this exercise of possible thesis statements for the paper on Stafford.

Example: Stafford's repeated deployment of lacuna within the general linguistic fabric of the textual event privileges not the objective meaning of the poetic referent but implicitly argues for the intersubjectivity of all analytical acts and for the reader's inherent obligation to remedy such lacunae.

Translation: Stafford leaves gaps in the poem that the readers have to fill for themselves.

1. The metaphorical exploitation of the genre of academic examination implicitly problematizes and indeed ironically calls into question the very notion of quantitative evaluation of so-called literary "knowledge."

2. The figurative evocation of Emerson, Hawthorne, and Thoreau are not as thematically relevant to Stafford's implicit

conceptualization of the goals of education as the negative figuration of the blank space itself—an anti-symbol, as it were, of ideological frames of reference beyond explicit formulation.

3. Ironic implication is the dominant rhetorical strategy in the poem, creating a highly charged metaphorical frisson between the ostensive declaration of the surface features and the deep intentionality of the statement, which in fact subverts those surface features. ❖

Essay Option 3D

Write a two- to four-page essay in the form of a letter to a friend or family member. Argue that your reader should read Marjorie Sandor's essay, "The Night Gardener." Informal letters don't need thesis statements, but this is a mixed form—adopt the informality of a letter, address the letter to this specific person, but organize what you say around a single, clear thesis that you illustrate with detail. What's the main reason this person should read the essay, and what details help support this claim? Somewhere in your essay, include an analysis of a specific passage from the story.

Essay Option 3E

Write a two- to four-page essay in the form of a letter to a friend or family member—with the provisos listed in Essay Option 3D about letter writing. But this time, assume that your audience is struggling with some sort of a personal problem. The thesis in your letter is that one of the main ideas in this chapter, "reading between the lines," can be helpful in solving the problem. Explain the idea, and support your claim that says it is useful by analyzing a particular text—literary or nonliterary. In other words, somehow argue to a specific person that the skills of reading literature can be applied to the reading of life.

Essay Option 3F

Write a formal memo to the Dean of the School of Engineering, Business, or Science at your college or university that argues, on the basis of this chapter, that all majors in these areas should be required to take at least two literature courses. Illustrate by talking about a particular text.

SAMPLE STUDENT ESSAY, OPTION 3B

As you work on your own essay for this chapter, consider the strengths and weaknesses of the following student essay. Does it follow the directions? Does it communicate clearly? Use the checklist in Chapter 1 as a guide while you read and evaluate.

KATE LAMONT

Reading Koi

The fish have not been fed for weeks but they don't seem to mind. After all, it's nearly November, so their metabolism must be gradually slowing down with the coolness that approaches as we progress to the near-dead stop of the winter chill. Their motionlessness, now hanging, suspended in the depths of the pond, is quite a reversal of their activity of months gone by.

My initial encounter with the pond was last May when I was hired and the General Manager informed me that among other duties, one of my responsibilities would be to make sure that the koi were fed (but not overfed). It is a concern highlighted by a small laminated paper sign propped upon a stick amongst the starry-flowered reeds that reads *Please Do Not Feed The Koi*.

Unsympathetic as it may sound to certain passers by who compassionately acknowledge the greedy slurping of the fish upon approach, after just a few hours observing koi it becomes apparent that they are gluttonous creatures. An evidently distant relative to the common goldfish, they would probably eat themselves into a watery grave if granted the opportunity by a careless caretaker, as goldfish are known to do. Yet such an exquisite example among an array of fishes in the world must be taken care of and provided the proper nutrition in order to survive and sustain its luster. The koi would likely lose some glory if sustained solely on the breadcrumbs scattered from pudgy five-year-old hands whose owners' mothers disregard the sign.

The food I do feed them comes in a bright green bag slashed with curious black characters that might as well be hieroglyphics to me. I assume it is Japanese, since they are Japanese koi, and I marvel at a language so unfamiliar, curious at a product marketed in the United States without one word of English on its packaging (especially as an accessory for a pet that has become so popular in this country). The koi pellets within are bb-sized and brown, reeking of a salty, fish-like scent. I doubt the koi can smell it despite the strongly offensive odor.

However, from the behaviors of the koi in the active summer months, I can read and understand which senses they have that are highly developed. As I scattered handfuls of food across the surface of the pond, the fish readily bundled up in swarms near where I stood startled and darted into the depths of safety once the shadow of my arm extended over them. This indicates a keen sensitivity to light and the darkness of shadows by sight, which results in a quick reactive response.

The same thing happened when a glossy blue dragonfly flitted across the surface of the pond on a blazing summer afternoon. All of the fish within the immediate vicinity of the shadows quickly swarm away. Though the dragonfly is a fraction of the size of even the smallest koi, such a shadow above the water would indicate the potential danger of a predator, such as a bird that might similarly fly across a pond in search of prey. In a man-made pond such as this, the Great Blue Heron and nocturnal hunters such as raccoons are the main enemies of koi. However, none have been killed in this pond, which I determine must be because of its depth in which the fish can hide, out of the reach of their predators.

A different curious behavior I noticed about the koi directs my attention to another of their keen senses. One day as I was upstairs in the building adjacent to the pond, I heard the UPS truck driving up the gravel road, and as I looked out the window, I saw that the swarm of bright fish followed the truck around the curve from one side of the pond to the other as the truck passed by. Fascinated, I walked from one side of the pond to another, observing as they, likewise, followed me. This behavior implies that the koi must have a heightened sense of sound and sensitivity to vibration. Their tendency to follow people make the koi seem tame, somewhat like a dog, though they seem to me to be much more a part of nature even in captivity that any domesticated animal or pet.

So why the fascination with koi as an animal that people pay hundreds of dollars for to keep in ponds and aquariums? I think it partially has to do with the power to hold part of the beauty and wonder of nature in a semi-controlled environment that people can enjoy and learn from. I heard or read once that any amount of time spent watching fish swimming is a mentally and physically therapeutic as an equal amount of time spent in meditation. It is supposed to have an actual, physical calming effect on the body to watch this graceful underwater motion, which must be why so many doctors' offices have fish tanks in the waiting rooms.

Whether this theory is scientifically proven to be true or not is irrelevant. I ascribe to the idea based on the calming experience in my own life and what I have gained by simply watching the koi in their fluid underwater dance each day at my job. Not merely the fish in the pond, but the whole surrounding experience of the rustling red maple nearby and the warming sun pressing upon my bare shoulders on a summer afternoon all contribute to the pleasant feeling I associate with feeding and gazing at the koi.

I notice the variation in their sizes with probably five very old and very large ones who were the starting breeders in the pond. There is a full range down to the smallest ones, who are the newest editions native to the pond and span little more than six inches. Likewise, in their coloration there is a diverse array from vibrant crimson red, bright yellow and orange, scattered with black spots to the youngest gray ones who only began to show a shimmer of yellow on the dorsal side in the last weeks of August. One of the largest ones, One-Eyed Jack, has only one eye and I wonder how he lost it or if he just came way from the beginning. I think he seems wise, which may be ridiculous for a fish, but there is something heavy about the solemnity of the creature, as if he has a story to tell.

Their colors sparkle in the sun and shimmer on the tops of their heads around the black spots that remind me of embers dying down but just glittering in a fireplace. Sometimes I scatter their food in several areas of the pond to watch them overlap and weave their various colors among themselves as if creating a brilliant fabric. The colors remind me of the yarn, orange and bronze and tipped with white that my grandmother used to knit an afghan when I was child. Likewise, the sun on my back when I stand by the pond makes me think of its warmth.

Does it seem strange to read fish? To read a pond as if it were a poem? An initial reaction might be yes, but I argue that it is not. All aspects of the world around us are texts just waiting to be read, as a closed book on the shelf. Yet unlike the book, which we have to actually open and spend time to read, we effortlessly read the world everyday, interpreting things that are not explicit and unconsciously encompassing them to incorporate into our individual perspectives. With attention to what we are reading and how we read it, the everyday world can become fascinating and more fully appreciated, as what we experience takes on the associations and the weight of images used in poems to illustrate the intricacies in life that are reflected in the literature that we write to read.

Chapter 4:
Linking Causes and Effects

PREDICTING THE FUTURE

Let's begin this chapter with an activity:

❖ *Group/Solo Activity 4.1*   Get out a sheet of paper. (Scratch paper will do fine). Assume that you are standing in the doorway of a kitchen. You intend to go to the refrigerator so you can pour yourself a glass of milk. Draw the floor plan of this kitchen (any kitchen you know) on your paper by pretending you're a camera looking straight down from the ceiling—draw the kitchen walls, show where the doorway is, and sketch the countertops and other kitchen features. Use an R to show where the refrigerator is; an S to show the sink; an ST for the stove; and an X for your position in the doorway. Draw this before going to the next paragraph.

To get from the doorway to the refrigerator—or from X to R— you must first cross half that distance, right? Draw a solid line halfway from X to R. To get halfway to the refrigerator, you must first cross half the distance to halfway, right? Draw a line like this (- - - - -) to indicate half the distance to halfway. And to get half the distance to halfway, you must cross half that distance, right? Draw a dotted line (......) to show this distance.

By now, you should see a pattern of decreasing distances. Clearly, since in each case you must cross half a distance before you can cross the other half, and since mathematics tells us that any distance between two

points can be halved, clearly you will never be able to reach the refrigerator: there will always be another distance to be halved before you can
go on. Right? ❖

If you just finished Group/Solo Activity 4.1, then you were
exposed to one of Zeno's paradoxes. Also known as Zeno of Elea, this
philosopher and mathematician lived in southern Italy about 450 B.C.
His argument urges one set of causes leading to a particular effect: since
each distance must be crossed halfway before it can be crossed all the
way, and since we know that every distance—no matter how small—can
be halved (all of these are causes), the effect is that we can never get anywhere. If you believe Zeno is wrong, why?

This paradox also illustrates one of the principal aims of an effort
to link causes and effects—the hope that people can accurately predict
an outcome or effect based on certain causes. We make such efforts all
the time. Consider a monthly budget—it's our effort to anticipate
expenses so we make sure our money lasts. The assumption is if we stick
to the budgeted expenses (causes), then at the end of the month we'll
still have enough funds to cover the last of the bills (effect). Another
example illustrates that if we dress warm, sleep right, eat right, and get
a flu shot (causes), then maybe we won't get sick this winter (effect).
Each example uses cause and effect linkages in the effort to predict what
may happen in the future.

❖ *Group/Solo Activity 4.2* The following problem, first published by
Bean, Drenk, and Lee, asks you to consider causes and effects. If you
don't know anything about flotation, ask others in the class for help. The
point here is not so much to test your knowledge of physics, as to give you
experience discussing how a series of causes and effects leads to a process
with a predictable result.

Problem: Imagine you just put a big block of ice in a bucket and then
filled the bucket to the brim with water. The ice is now floating in the
bucket, and the water level is exactly level with the top rim. Draw a cross
section of a bucket with the ice and water in it. Draw your ice block so
that part of it shows above the rim of the bucket with a small portion
above the water line—remember that ice floats on water—and the larger
proportion below the water line.

Now assume that you wait several hours for the ice to melt. Ignor-
ing any evaporation, what will happen? Will the water level in the bucket

remain exactly the same? Will the water level drop? Or will water over-flow the rim of the bucket?

Decide your answer, and then write a paragraph of a page or less that explains what happens. Assume you're writing to a classmate who doesn't have the right answer yet. ❖

EXPLAINING THE PAST

We use cause and effect thinking to try to explain the past, too. For example, why do some people spell more accurately than others? That question can take us to the old truism: the larger a person's shoe size, the greater that person's spelling accuracy. Cause and effect, right? And what about information from the National Opinion Research Center at the University of Chicago? Or statistics from the Associated Press that indicate, "jazz fans, gun owners and those who lack confidence in the president are among the most sexually active Americans" (*Corvallis Gazette-Times,* Jan. 15, 1998 p. A8). Cause and effect again, right? Or consider this example from *Eve Spoke,* a book that addresses human intelligence and language evolution:

> The speed at which people travel is one measure of technology. For millions of years 2 or 3 miles in an hour was the limit set by humans' walking pace. About six thousand years ago horses were domesti-cated, and the maximum sustained rate jumped to about 15 miles per hour. That speed held constant until the early decades of the nineteenth century, when steam-powered locomotives were invented. Fifteen miles per hour was about the pace of the first steam-powered railroad trains, but within 70 years the maximum speed exceeded 100 miles an hour. By the 1940s military fighter jets flew at 200 miles an hour. Twenty-five years later commercial air-lines routinely cruised at 540 miles an hour. Military aircraft now exceed 2,500 miles per hour and space shuttles and satellites circle the earth at 14,000 miles an hour (83, 84).

With all these examples, we can conclude that human beings—having progressed from the ability to move at two miles an hour to 14,000 miles an hour—must now be 7,000 times smarter than human beings 6,000 years ago. Yes?

❖ *Group/Solo Activity 4.3* Consider a recent decision you made—either the decision to attend college or the decision to attend this partic-ular college. Write that at the top of a piece of paper (e.g., My Decision to Attend This School). Consider this decision an effect. Underneath this head, list all the causes—all the *why's*—that contributed to your decision.

Once you've listed all the causes you can think of, circle those that seem most important. What causes, if they'd not happened or you thought differently, would have changed your decision? Then write several sentences explaining how, in your view, you really did make this original decision. To what extent (or not) did you actually consider all these causes? ❖

If you just worked Activity 4.3, then you've just engaged in the effort to link causes to a particular effect in your own life. And you tried to do so using one of the most common methods we have for understanding our own lives—to work backwards from a present fact in the effort to explain how it came to be.

Medicine offers many examples of the effort to link causes and effects. A person arrives in a doctor's office with a set of symptoms and complaints. The doctor's effort is first diagnostic—an effort to recognize a pattern already observed in other people and detailed by other doctors. Once a diagnosis is identified, then the doctor prescribes treatment.

Medical researchers carry this a step further—they seek to understand how the patient's condition originated. They want to discover the step-by-step nature of the problem so they can interrupt or modify the sequence. Thus, they often work backwards from effects in order to understand how to change the causes, and therefore the effects, in the future. Thus AIDS researchers work backwards from symptoms to the *causes* of those symptoms to the causes of the causes of those systems. Effective treatment will mean identifying a way to interrupt the step-by-step chain of causes that ultimately lead to the ill health that HIV-positive individuals risk.

In fact, the effort to link causes and effects can work in either direction—*backwards,* to try and figure out how some present condition came to be, or *forwards,* to try and predict how something will go. We're often interested in one direction more than the other. Say you break your arm. In a sense, the cause doesn't matter—your arm is still broken. The question becomes, what treatment is best? In other words, what series of causes will yield the best effect? Does the bone need to be stabilized with pins or screws? What size cast is necessary? In short, what series of causes will result in a healed bone?

Once your arm has been treated, then you may go back and determine the cause of the break. If you broke your arm in a fall while skiing, then perhaps the fall was due to your own misjudgment of snow conditions, or perhaps to a split second when your ski tips crossed. Beyond a resolution to ski more conservatively, perhaps nothing more can be learned from this accident.

However, if you broke your arm on the job when a rack of paint cans fell on you, then you may need to investigate many causes. Were the paint cans stacked carefully? Were they stacked too high? Were the racks strong enough to hold the weight of the paint cans? Who stacked them? Should the cans have been stacked in that particular place at all?

❖ *Group/Solo Activity 4.4* Consider some medical or other relatively minor mishap in your own life (e.g., a broken bone, a flat tire). Construct the best step-by-step chain of causes that led to the effect—what contributed to the broken bone? What led it to happen? Or why did the tire blow? What conditions caused it? List these conditions in the order in which they occurred. If you can't identify all the causes, explain why you can't.

Once you have your list of causes, think of each cause as an effect. Then try to identify at least one cause for that effect. For example, one cause for the flat tire was because the tire was worn. The tire was worn, because I didn't have enough money to buy a new one. Do this analysis for all the causes you originally identify.

As you look at this analysis, does it support a simple and straightforward explanation for the original event? Or does your analysis support a more complicated, less simple explanation for it? ❖

Once you start looking for the play of causes and effects, you'll find them everywhere. Weather forecasters get paid to assess causes and effects. You talk with a good friend who seems suddenly distant or sullen (the effect), and you wonder what you could have said (the cause). You work on a paper in a class (the cause) and wonder what kind of grade it will get (the effect). You consider your own education and wonder where it will lead. Sometimes you may even wonder why you were born to one set of parents and not another, or why you're living where you are and not on the other side of the globe.

CAUSE AND EFFECT AS PROCESS ANALYSIS

In many cases, it makes sense to think of cause and effect as a process—as a series of causes and effects. What happens? Then what happens next? How does it happen? Why does it happen this way and not some other way? You get into a car and turn the key, and that action closes an electrical circuit to the starter motor. Thus, a series of causes and effects leads to a smoothly running engine—if the car is in good repair. If you turn the key and nothing happens, then some part of the cause-effect chain is broken. To fix the problem, some knowledgeable person will need to know how to consider all of this as a process and how to examine each of its steps.

❖ *Group Activity 4.5* Consider a jury trial in which the driver of a car hits a pedestrian in a crosswalk. The cause—the car hitting the pedestrian—and the effects—the pedestrian's injuries and the driver's charge of vehicular assault—are clear and not in dispute. The car did, indeed, hit the pedestrian; the district attorney's office did decide to press charges.

As a juror, do you now have enough information to convict the driver? If not, what else would you want to know in order to determine the driver's innocence or guilt? What evidence could you imagine that may lead you to a finding of "not guilty"?

Finally, what does your response say about the ways causes and effects are linked and judged? ❖

CO-RELATION AND CAUSATION

Early in this chapter, we said, "Consider this old truism: the larger a person's shoe size, the greater that person's spelling accuracy. Cause and effect, right?" In fact, you can be pretty sure, even without extensive proof, that what we did (on purpose) was confuse co-relation with causation. Co-relation says two things, large feet and superior spelling ability, are true—they're related but merely because they're true at the *same time*. Causation says that one thing, large feet, causes the other—more accurate spelling. This particular co-relation—larger feet and better spelling existing at the same time—is actually accurate, though only in a limited sense: when it's applied to grade school-age children. But we would find it pretty difficult to show that larger feet actually cause people to be more accurate spellers. To summarize—just because two things happen to be true at the same time does not necessarily mean that one has caused the other. It may mean that, and it may not. More study is needed to know for sure.

❖ *Group/Solo Activity 4.6* Identify three different examples of co-relation—two things true at the same time. Make one of your examples outlandish (e.g., the sun is out, your wallet is empty, there-fore the sunshine emptied your wallet.). Make a second one less out-landish and make the third example ambiguous enough that it actually could be part of a cause-effect relationship. ❖

AN EXAMPLE OF CO-RELATION AND CAUSATION: "DO WOMEN BENEFIT FROM STUDY AT ALL-FEMALE SCHOOLS?"

Take, for example, this question: Do women get a better education at all-female schools? We can translate this question to highlight its cause-effect character this way: If women go to all-female schools (the cause), do they get a better education (the effect)?

An article by Wendy Kaminer in *The Atlantic Monthly** examines this question. The article traces the history of same-sex education and the legal rulings on the question, but the analysis ultimately rests on a discussion of causes and effects:

> . . . proponents of all-girls schools rely on social science to support the claim that segregation by sex fosters achievement in girls. "Stud-ies show . . ." is the usual lead-in to any defense of single-sex schools. In fact studies do not show that girls fare better in single-sex schools. "There does not seem to be research support for this per-spective," the sociologist Cynthia Epstein politely observes. Epstein, the author of *Deceptive Distinctions: Sex, Gender, and the Social Order* (1988), adds that there is no consensus among psychologists as to the existence of psychological or cognitive differences between the sexes, and that the evidence for the need for single-sex education and the justice of single-sex schools is highly equivocal.

Notice what Kaminer does as a thinker and writer—she affirms the need for an accurate, reliable link of causes and effects. She finds that supporters of same-sex schooling reach conclusions based on an assump-tion that women and men learn differently. That assumption, if true, could easily be seen as part of a chain of causes and effects—*because* men and women learn differently, women studying at all-female schools would be able to learn as females learn and without the distraction of a competing male style (the effect); and *because* these women would learn under more favorable conditions, women from all-female schools would gain some advantage over women studying at co-educational schools

---

* "The Trouble with Single-Sex Schools" by Wendy Kaminer, *The Atlantic Monthly*, April, 1998.

(the effect). But is this chain of causes and effects, in fact, accurate? It is accurate only if the chain stays unbroken.

By quoting Cynthia Epstein—a presumably reliable expert whose work suggests that the chain in this example is inaccurate because there is little evidence that supports a claim for single-sex schooling—Kaminer then turns to look at the sources that suggested otherwise. These sources asserted a cause and effect relationship that show an advantage to same-sex education. Kaminer's effort now will be to show that these studies are based on a flawed grasp of the way causes and effects are linked:

> Perhaps the most frequently cited studies (claiming advantages to all-female schools) were conducted by M. Elizabeth Tidball, who reviewed the educational backgrounds of female achievers. In her first widely cited study, published in 1973, Tidball examined a random sample of women included in *Who's Who* and found that disproportionate numbers were graduates of women's colleges.

Kaminer goes on to question whether or not the effect—getting included in *Who's Who*—can be explained by the single cause of going to a women's college.

> What do these studies (that is, Tidball's study above and other similar studies by her) tell us about the relationship between single-sex education and achievement? Virtually nothing. Tidball made the common mistake of confusing correlation with causation.

In short, Kaminer indicates that while Tidball may have observed a relationship between single-sex education and women's achievement, she did not show that one led to the other.

Of course, Kaminer is making an argument. And so it makes good sense for her to now turn to some other explanation—some other chain of causes and effects—for the relationship Tidball observed. Here's part of Kaminer's analysis:

> Tidball's 1973 study focuses on women who graduated from women's colleges in the years before elite men's colleges were integrated; until the mid-1970s ambitious, high-achieving females gravitated to the Seven Sisters (elite women's colleges) because they were among the most selective and prestigious institutions open to women. Students at these schools were self-selected for success, like their male counterparts in the Ivy League. They also tended to be well connected; many may have owed their success to the males present in their families more than to the absence of males from their classes.

❖ *Group/Solo Activity 4.7* Analyze the quoted portion of Kaminer's discussion as just presented above. What cause-effect relationships does it affirm as truthful—or likely to be truthful—and what relationships does it assert are untruthful or merely examples of co-relation? List these on paper.

Once you finish your list, write your opinion of Kaminer's analysis. In your opinion, what has Kaminer effectively shown? What do you think still needs proof? Be ready to explain your opinion as to the causes (what Kaminer says) and effects (what you now see to be accurate or true).

Note: In fairness to Kaminer and her article, we must emphasize that only a small portion of her discussion has been reproduced here. ❖

USING QEC:CS IN LINKING CAUSES AND EFFECTS

QEC:CS can easily be adapted to the effort of linking causes and effects. The question (the Q in QEC) in such situations is always a variation of one or more of the following:

- Does A cause B?
- Is A by itself enough to cause B?
- Do A and B merely exist at the same time?

Any effort to examine or explore these questions (the E in QEC) will lead to various conclusions (the C in QEC). And any claims (yes, A does cause B, or . . .) will end up being supported by whatever evidence has been gathered. So any effort to identify and explain the links between causes and effects is always an effort to make a series of claims (e.g., this causes that) to show why and how such claims are true.

❖ *Group/Solo Activity 4.8* Read the following article "Good News For Poor Spellers." Identify the major questions the article raises, and list them under the letter Q. Indicate the methods of examination that were used to answer those questions, and list them under E. Finally, indicate the conclusions, and list them under C.

Once you have your QEC analysis on paper, what claims do you think it would support? Would these be claims of causation or just co-relation? Be ready to explain your reasoning. ❖

MARILYN VOS SAVANT
Good News for Poor Spellers

A reader asked if you believe that spelling ability is a measure of education, intelligence or desire. I was fascinated by the survey you published in response. The implication of the questions is that you believe spelling ability may be related to personality. What were the results? I'm dying to know.
—Judith Alexander, Chicago, Ill.

The biggest (and best) news is this: The result of our spelling experiment, in which 42,603 readers took part (20,188 by postal mail and 22,415 by e-mail), indicates that poor spelling ability has *no* relationship to general intelligence.

On the other hand, education, intelligence and desire *must* have a relationship to *excellent* spelling ability: If one has little education, intelligence and desire, one surely will not be able to spell. But my theory is that even if one has the basics, personality traits may still stand in the way. Or perhaps one's traits may boost one into the ranks of excellent spellers—in particular, the trait for being meticulous.

Readers first were asked to rank their spelling ability on a scale of 1 to 100. Choosing an answer established a personal assessment range for each individual. Readers then were asked to rank other traits on that same range. In my analysis, I first noted an individual's spelling rank and then noted which other quality he or she ranked closest to his or her spelling rank.

I considered that quality (or more than one) to be the most closely related to that individual's spelling ability. This greatly reduced the effect of subjectivity in self-assessment. In other words, I may not know what an individual means by ranking his spelling ability as, say, 75—but *he* does. So, no matter what his actual ability is, and no matter how accurately he managed to assess it, I could still determine the quality that related to it closer than anything else for that individual. By ranking other qualities on the same scale, the individual pointed it out himself. I call this technique "self-normalization."

The answer to "Where would you rank your ability to follow instructions?" (which is a personality trait interacting with general intelligence) related most often to spelling ability. It was followed by "Where would you rank your ability to solve problems?" (which is general intelligence alone). And this was followed by "Where would you rank as an organized person?" (which is a personality trait alone).

Here's where the good news appeared: The first two relation-ships were top-heavy, meaning they related strongly for top spellers but hardly at all for bottom spellers. In fact, of the worst spellers, only 6% ranked their ability to follow instructions closest to their spelling ability, and only 5% ranked their ability to solve problems closest to their spelling ability!

But one of the three significant relationships was consistent from the top spellers down to the bottom spellers: organizational ability. The top spellers were the most organized, the average spellers were in the middle, and the bottom spellers were the least organized. In other words, organization paralleled spelling ability closest of all.

In short, here's what this means: Our experiment indicates that if you're a top speller, you're more likely to be more intelligent than average, better able to follow instructions than average and more organized than average. On the other hand, if you're a bottom speller, your general intelligence and ability to follow instructions are *not likely* to be lower than average, but you are *more likely* to be less organized. This suggests it is possible that a lack of orga-nization drags a speller down.

I included the question "Where would you rank your leader-ship ability?" only to validate my methods, because I was confident that leadership ability had nothing to do with spelling ability. This was borne out by the data: It related least often. I also included the question "Where would you rank as a creative person?" because I doubted that creativity had anything to do with spelling ability (or the lack of it), but I still was curious about it: It related virtually the same.

Because they are not categorized by spelling ability, here are some results just for fun: When they have trouble balancing their checkbooks, 59% of all the respondents said they give up and change their balance to match the bank's. About housekeeping habits, 65% said, "At my place, everything is all over the place." As for time management, 52% have no time to think about it. Even if they're not in a hurry to get to work, 81% don't make their beds every day. And in most matters of the mind, 89% call themselves "decisive."

In the best spellers, however, noticeable differences are found everywhere except in the area of decisiveness. When they have trouble balancing their checkbooks, only 36% (instead of 59%) give up. The others keep at it until they account for every penny. Only 49% (instead of 65%) admit to being a bit messy. The rest maintain, "A place for everything, and everything in its place." With regard to time management, only 34% (instead of 52%) have no time to think about it. The others prioritize as best they can. And when they are not in a hurry, only 57% (instead of 81%) don't make their beds. The rest do.

In sum, it appears that spelling ability may be more related to personality than has been assumed. What to do about it? Keep in mind that the difference between a good speller and a bad speller is not huge—just a few letters here and there! Yes, I'm serious. Remember that even bad spellers can spell most words perfectly. I suggest being more meticulous about spelling: That is, try harder. If you work on a computer, go ahead and use your spell-checker; but whenever it finds a misspelled word, stop and hand-write the correct spelling a dozen times. Otherwise, keep a dictionary handy. Whenever you're not sure how to spell a word, don't guess! Look it up. Then write it down a dozen times. If you do this without fail for the next six months, your spelling willing improve dramatically.

Maybe the best news of all is that so many readers took part in a *spelling* survey! This says that we're interested in far more than movie stars and fashion. Speaking for myself, I think it says that Americans are being underestimated! Thanks a million for your help.

About our methods in this poll . . .

Our experiment was not a scientific poll. First, only readers who wished to participate did so, so the data were reported selectively. Second, the participants' assessments of themselves were subjective, so one good speller might be different from another good speller. Here's how I handled these concerns:

First, because readers reported selectively, numbers were not reported. That is, it was not reported that "*n percent* of Americans are good spellers." Second, because readers assessed themselves, labels were not reported. That is, it was not reported that "n percent of Americans are *good* spellers." Instead, relationships were noted.

CAUSES, EFFECTS, RESEARCH, AND THE SCIENTIFIC METHOD

Though we've not said much about it directly, research often becomes crucial when you link causes and effects. For example, after a traffic accident, authorities investigate what happened. They study evidence, interview participants and witnesses, take measurements, note weather conditions and time of day—all in an effort to assemble the various factors that played a part in the accident.

Similarly, scientific researchers have determined an investigative process—the scientific method—in order to scrupulously examine cause-effect linkages. They sometimes work this way to understand the present (How did this come to be?) and other times to predict the future (How can we prevent an effect from occurring?) Insurance investigators and fabric manufacturers might work together testing various materials to see which ones burn readily, which ones produce toxic smoke, and which ones burn less readily and with less injurious smoke. Or ecologists and foresters work together to see how logging practices change watersheds. Eye specialists study the results of ultraviolet radiation on the health of the eye.

The scientific method itself is designed to offer researchers a consistent method for such inquiry. It begins with a question and hypothesis, then identifies an experiment—a way to test the question and then a way to proceed to a collection of data yielded by the test. Finally, it analyzes the data for whatever conclusions or claims that data might support. Here's a crude example: remember, we're not marine biologists):

- *Question:* A marine biologist notices signs that an ocean reef is suffering. This observation leads to the question, "Why is the reef suffering?"
- *Hypothesis:* The reef is suffering because of the volume of industrial wastes pumped out of a drainage pipe a quarter of a mile away.
- *Experiment:* A healthy reef is recreated in a lab setting—a large tank. The laboratory reef is exposed to increasing levels of the same industrial wastes pumped out of the drainage pipe. The levels are increased at intervals of three weeks.
- *Data:* Measures of the reef's health are collected every other day for the duration of the experiment.
- *Analysis and Conclusion:* The data is discussed in terms of the original hypothesis. The data could confirm the original hypothesis, or it could show some weak relationship or no clear relationship at all.

❖ *Solo Activity 4.9*   Make a list of at least four questions that draw your intellectual interest and that scientific study could begin to answer only by looking at causes and effects. Example: geologists look at current land forms in order to try to understand the question, "What forces made those land forms?"

Of these four questions, which one would you actually like to investigate if given the chance? Write a paragraph explaining your interest and the ways you think the question could be or ought to be investigated. ❖

❖ *Group Activity 4.10* Based on your individual work for Solo Activity 4.9, compile a group list of all the questions you arrived at individually. Once you complete this list, decide which department or unit in your school may actually investigate that question. If you cannot identify any department or unit, then note that. ❖

MULTIPLE CAUSES, MULTIPLE EFFECTS

The scientific method tries to ensure the accurate linking of causes and effects. But the success of the method gets challenged whenever causes and effects become particularly complicated. For example, consider the issue of urban growth—or its opposite, loss of urban population. Cities are complicated places. How does a person accurately construct a scientific inquiry that can predict the addition of, say, ten percent of the current population over the next three years? Or how can city managers or urban planners predict what will happen if three local manufacturers close, and the local economy thus loses those payroll dollars?

Or consider the example of global warming: How can scientists confidently predict the effects of reductions in the use of Freon gas—the gas used in air conditioners and other processes? Computer models now try to simulate the complex dynamics of city population changes or atmospheric changes. But the linking of causes and effects is made more difficult by the sheer number of factors that come into play.

Essay Option 4A

Identify some medical condition that interests you. For example, you may know someone with diabetes or an older relative who had polio. Maybe you suffer from seasonal allergies or suffered knee damage from sports or arthritis.

With this medical condition in mind, construct a question or series of related questions that you'd actually like to have answered (e.g., Exactly what happened to my knee when I fell on it? What was the medical and structural result? How are such injuries treated now? Or what exactly caused polio? Why don't we hear much about it now? Is it still a problem?).

Then go to experts who can contribute to the answers you seek. Go to whatever books or live people or Web sites convince you they are reliable and authoritative. Make sure you consult at least four outside sources, and keep track of them to present at the end of your report in the format your teacher specifies.

With sources consulted and research results clear in your mind, write a five- to seven-page report, including your source page, that explains the medical condition in terms of causes and effects (e.g., If you're talking about seasonal allergies, what chain of causes and effects leads to the symptoms?). Aim your report at people with the same questions you had when you started—so if you're writing about your knee injury, assume that your readers have just suffered the same injury and have the same questions you had.

Using cause and effect linkages, explain what you learned. Use drawings or charts that might help readers understand. End by drawing whatever conclusions seem both clear and helpful to your readers (e.g., what can people do to reduce the effects of seasonal allergies?). Make sure your essay itself supports these conclusions.

MULTIPLE EFFECTS, MULTIPLE RESPONSES, MULTIPLE VIEWS

With complex questions, controversy often arises. Why? One reason has already been indicated—the complexity of the question makes the investigation itself difficult. But controversy can also result whenever the same causes produce multiple effects—some good, depending on your perspective, and some bad. Many economic controversies revolve around multiple effects. For example, a wish to keep shirt or dress prices low may produce at least these two effects: (1) jobs once performed in America, where labor costs are high, are now performed overseas, where labor costs are lower; and (2) those shirts and dresses carry price tags that are considerably lower than they would otherwise. Most of us would agree that lower prices (the effect) are a good thing. Most of us who don't own clothing companies would also agree that losing your job (another effect) is not a good thing.

❖ *Group/Solo Activity 4.11*   Consider a controversy local to your school, town, or state, and see if you can understand its multiple effects—some viewed as positive, with others as negative or unimportant. Identify all the possible effects, and be ready to explain how they create conflict. ❖

THE CASE STUDY: CONSTRUCTING A WHOLE NARRATIVE

It is precisely the seeming randomness and complexity of life that makes the effort to link causes and effects so important. And case studies—literally, the study of individual cases—seek to capture this complexity and nuance, with the assumption that if we can understand individual cases first, then we can begin to generalize accurately about causes and effects.

In *Reviving Ophelia,* a book that discusses the difficulties and pitfalls that girls in our culture face as they reach adolescence, psychologist Mary Pipher presents a number of composite stories from her clinical practice. In her attempt to treat people, Pipher's task is to help her patients figure out causes. As in any medical practice, Pipher's patients are suffering—they have already reached a situation in which the effects they live with are no longer tolerable.

❖ *Solo Activity 4.12* Closely read the following discussion of "Amy," age 12, from *Reviving Ophelia.* Copy three sentences you think show important *causes* and three sentences you think show important *effects.* Once you've copied these six sentences, write a paragraph about how easy or hard it was to choose which sentences to copy. ❖

MARY PIPHER
Amy (12)

Joan brought Amy in for counseling because she and Chuck were divorcing. Last year Amy had been lively, lighthearted and fun-loving. This year she was quiet, withdrawn and serious.

Joan was an articulate schoolteacher who was venomous on the subject of her husband, Chuck. He was evil incarnate, the Adolf Hitler of husbands and without a good motive to his credit. She poured out her anger while Amy shrank deeper into my couch. Amy looked like she was evaporating as her mother talked, her serious little face grew smaller, her body more childlike.

Joan explained how she and Chuck had tried counseling, but that Chuck, even though he was a therapist himself, wouldn't cooperate. She had done her best, but he sabotaged her efforts to save the family. And now that she had filed, he was doing everything he could to destroy her life and turn Amy against her.

Joan listed her concerns about Amy. She had lost five pounds since May. She wasn't communicating and was avoiding friends and activities. Joan finished by saying, "I think she's depressed by her dad's behavior."

I asked for examples of Chuck's behavior. "Do you have all day?" Joan asked. "We're fighting for custody and he keeps pressuring and bribing Amy to choose him. He puts me down constantly and he sets me up to be angry. Last week he called to change visitation three times. He disappoints Amy by not coming when he says he will."

Weakly Amy protested, "He comes when he says."

Joan continued as if she hadn't heard. "We have psychologists evaluating Amy for the custody decision, but I wanted someone to help her with the stress of the divorce."

With some reservations I asked to talk to Amy alone. In the last few months she'd talked to attorneys, judges and psychologists and her trust for adults was at an all-time low. From her point of view, I was just one more adult who was supposed to be helping but wasn't.

I asked how her summer was going and she answered so softly I had to ask her to repeat herself. She said, "It's rained a lot and I haven't been able to swim as much as I like to."

I thought she was giving careful answers to me and probably to everyone else as well. She'd learned that what she didn't say didn't get her in trouble. I talked to her about divorce, how it stresses out kids and makes them feel alone and weird. I said that I'd seen lots of kids who were sad and mad about their parents' divorce. I told her about other kids in her predicament and I put happy endings on the stories. Amy relaxed as I talked and asked me questions about the kids in the stories. But when I asked about her, she resumed her frozen face.

I said, "Most kids hate to choose which parent to live with."

"Both of them want me and I hate to hurt their feelings." Amy shook her head miserably. "Besides, some days I hate Dad and some days I hate Mom. Some days I hate them both."

I asked about living arrangements. "Mom and I still live at home for now. Dad has an apartment in the town where he works. I don't know anyone there and I can't stand his place. Mom says that she'll have to move though, especially if Dad gets me."

She sat up straight and said, "I don't want to live with either of them right now. They're both screwed up. I want to run away from home."

We talked about running away—its dangers and appeals. Amy, like most twelve-year-olds, wanted to run to family. Older kids want to go to the coast or to move in with friends. Amy dreamed of going to her grandmother's house in Minnesota. She asked for her parent's permission, but both had wanted her with them this summer.

Once she started, Amy loved to talk. She told me about starting her period at her dad's house. She had supplies at her mother's, but nothing at her dad's, and she had to ask him to go buy her pads. Later her mom got in a fight with him because he hadn't brought her home. She'd wanted to share Amy's first period. As Amy said, "She thought it should be a mother-daughter thing."

She told me that both parents tried to buy her love with presents. "If I wanted to, I could ask for a racing bike or television right now." Worst of all was how her parents talked about each other. "They both pretend they don't rag on each other, but they drop hints all the time that the other one is the craziest, meanest person they know."

Her biggest worry was starting junior high next year. If she lived with Dad, it would be a new school where she had no friends. If she lived with Mom, all the kids would know her parents got divorced. She said, "I don't know how I'll get my homework done. Mom helps me with math and Dad knows French."

She told me how ashamed she was of the divorce. She had tried unsuccessfully to keep it secret and had been embarrassed when kindly adults offered her sympathy. She avoided her friends because they might bring it up. She was sure she had the strangest parents in America.

I said, "They have lots of competition for strange, believe me." She smiled for the first time that day, and I caught a glimmer of what the pre-divorce Amy must have been like.

I ended the session by calling Joan in and suggesting that Amy go spend a few weeks with her grandmother while the adults worked things out. After she returned, we'd talk again and maybe Amy could be in a divorce group for young teens.

Joan said, "Chuck will never agree with this." I offered to call him.

Chuck was immediately angry when he heard I'd seen Amy. I talked to him about releases, consent to treatment and confidentiality. Then, after he calmed down, I asked him how Amy was doing. He said, "Since the separation, she's a different kid." Of course, he had his own theory about Amy, "Confidentially," he said, "Joan is the biggest bitch on the planet."

I listened patiently while he bad-mouthed Joan. As he talked, I thought how miserable these two people had made each other and how right it was that they divorce. But unfortunately, because they had Amy, they couldn't really separate. In fact, in some ways they would need to negotiate and coordinate efforts even more now that they lived in separate households. And the same things that destroyed the marriage could keep them from adequately parenting Amy over the next few years.

I reminded myself that underneath the parents' anger was pain. No doubt they both needed guidance sorting through this failed marriage. But my job was to help Amy. I feared that unless these parents settled down, Amy was at high risk for depression and, perhaps later, delinquency. I wasn't sure these parents were capable of putting Amy's needs first and working as a team, but I had nothing to lose in trying to help them do this.

I suggested Chuck and Joan come in for some divorce counseling. I told Chuck that it's better to talk about Amy in therapy than in an attorney's office. It's cheaper and non-adversarial. Perhaps because he himself was a psychologist, he had to agree.

Chuck said he was willing, but he doubted Joan would do it. I offered to talk to her. I could see Amy's drawn face as I hung up the phone. Maybe while she was at her grandmother's I could have Chuck and Joan in for some sessions. Maybe by the time she came home and started junior high, they would have started to do what adults need to do in situations like this, which is to put their own pain aside and help their child.

Case studies offer clear advantages: they can capture and hold in accurate relation a very large number of influences. Therefore, they can present a complicated truth. For example, watching a student for twenty-four hours, recording everything the student does, and then interviewing the student afterwards so as to further understand that twenty-four hours might yield a fairly accurate picture of the many decisions students make in a twenty-four hour period. We might infer from this case study some useful truths about college students and college life.

In fact, we learn quite a bit both informally and formally from the observation of individual case studies. We watch television and see the fate of a particular pride of lions in Africa, and thus we begin to understand how all lions live. We watch a documentary on an accident victim recovering from brain surgery, and we begin to learn more about how all human brains work. We watch the members of our families—our parents, aunts, sisters, or brothers—and draw conclusions about what we, ourselves, should or should not do. We may even apply what we get from reading a novel or short story in much the same way.

But case studies can be misleading, too. They can encourage confusion by suggesting that one example is the same as all examples. Or they can suggest that one example observed now can also be extended to apply to future examples not yet in existence.

❖   *Solo Activity 4.13*   Imagine this bit of personal history: a documentary film/sound crew started following you around yesterday, exactly 24 hours before the meeting time for this class. And they left you just as you walked into class today.

Would they have recorded a "typical" day in your college life? Based on all of what they saw, what conclusions might they come to about you? About your college experience? About college students on your campus? About all college students? How comfortable or uncomfortable would you feel being selected for a case study?

If you actually volunteered as a case-study subject, what about you would the researchers be interested in? Why would you be a good case-study research subject? ❖

Essay Option 4B

Interview someone in your family about an event that was particularly important to the course of his or her life. Consider "family" as widely as you wish—include friends who are close enough to you that they feel like family. Make sure you understand the event itself. Then direct your questions to the *causes* and the *effects* of the event. Make sure you fully understand as much as your interviewee is willing to tell you.

It's important for you to recognize that, for some events such as disasters like floods or house fires the causes might have little to do with your interviewee. Some things cannot be foreseen or prevented. In such cases, the event becomes a cause that leads to many effects. Other events, such as a marriage, a divorce, a decision to change jobs, etc., may have a long history of causes. Focus your interview—and develop your essay—so that you do justice to the particular event your interviewee discusses.

Following the interview, bring two authoritative sources into your discussion. Use these authorities to help you draw conclusions about whether or not the causes and effects your interviewee discusses are at all typical. If your interviewee discusses divorce, your authoritative sources should be experts on divorce. If your interviewee has spoken at length about the causes of the divorce, you should use your sources to show either how these particular causes are common or how they are unusual.

Assume that you're writing this essay for all the other members of your family or circle of close friends—those currently present and those who might join later. Your main effort here is to present some personal history and to interpret or contextualize it in light of what experts say. Secondarily, you're creating a record that may prove interesting and valuable to your family or personal history.

THE ESSAY OPTIONS: GETTING STARTED

Two essay options have been offered so far in this chapter; others can be found at the end. All the options have these things in common—they require research, they ask you to analyze and often summarize what you learn, they ask you to pay particular attention to the linkages between causes and effects, and they ask you to present your findings to an audience that has little or no prior knowledge of your essay's content.

Generate Research Questions

It's easy to assume that when we research, we research topics. But more accurately, we research questions—we want to find answers. If you're registering for classes and your schedule allows you to take only classes that start after 4 p.m., then you'll turn to the schedule of classes with one obvious question in mind—what courses meet after 4 P.M.? That's a small example of doing research.

❖ *Group/Solo Activity 4.14* Assume you have a budget of $5,000 to buy a used car. What questions should you ask in order to get a car that will last and will fit your needs? List as many of these questions as possible. Once you finish your list, decide which four questions really would make a significant difference in your decision. Of these four questions, which ones would call for some kind of research? For each of these questions, discuss what you may actually do in order to learn the answers to those questions. ❖

Researching: Interviewing Live Sources by Using the Journalist's Questions

Essay Option 4B relies heavily on a personal interview. You've been doing personal interviews virtually all of your life. Say you've heard good things about two movies, *Chinatown* and *Sophie's Choice*. You don't know much more than people say these movies were "good." You could go to a movie guide or other print source, or you could ask around. "Have you ever seen *Chinatown?*" "Yeah, it's a great film." "Who stars in it?" "Jack Nicholson." "What about *Sophie's Choice?*" "Another great movie; Meryl Streep is the main character."

The effort to ask around is exactly the same effort as an interview. The major differences are that an interview is more carefully planned and more carefully recorded. The journalist's questions can be very useful here:

- *Who?* Which people were involved? Which people have played major roles? How would you describe them?
- *What?* What happened? What was the order of events?
- *Where?* Where did this happen? How would you describe this place?
- *When?* What time of year did this happen? How old were you? What time of day did this happen?
- *Why?* What made it happen as it did? Or, how did it happen? What made or allowed it to happen this way?

Of these questions, *why* will lead you most directly to discussion of causes and effects, and *what* will lead most directly to a discussion of sequence, which allows a sense of how causes led to effects that became causes, and so on.

❖ *Solo Activity 4.15*   If you plan to interview live sources as part of your research effort, gather your questions now. Stay away from yes/no questions unless you plan to follow up with questions that ask for further explanation. ❖

Researching: Investigating On-Line and Print Sources

Though you may also be able to use interview sources, the first Essay Option will require you to consult on-line and print sources, too. On-line and print sources generally offer more in the way of information, simply because they're often easier to access than live human beings who have busy schedules. Most libraries stay open late, and the Internet never closes or sleeps. But the sheer quantity of information in a library or on the Web can be overwhelming. Two considerations will make life easier: (1) an awareness of the questions you want your sources to answer, and (2) an understanding of how information is typically stored in the library and on the Internet. Actually, some brainstorming and writing down your questions can help you find information.

❖ *Group/Solo Activity 4.16* Make a list of the questions you need or want to answer in your essay. To do this, start by completing each of the following prompts. Make your responses full and specific to your specific paper:

- I want to understand what _____
- I want to understand when _____
- I want to understand how _____
- I want to understand why _____
- I want to understand who _____

Working in pairs or larger groups, read your responses to each other. As you listen to what others want to find out, see if you can help them sharpen their research goals (e.g., Do you mean you want to find out about ligament damage in general, or do you mean you want to find out more about that particular knee ligament you just mentioned?). ❖

If you've used live sources for your research, then you may have gotten the names of particular researchers or the titles of some useful sources. With those names and titles, your search in a library catalog or on the Web becomes much easier. Virtually all computer-driven library catalogs and all search engines on the Web will require you to type some words to direct your search for information. If you have an author's name or know the specific title of an article or book, you will be able to quickly discover whether your library has that work by that person.

If you just completed Group/Solo Activity 4.16, then you should have some specifically worded sentences about your research interests. The wording you used to complete those prompts may help you search for information in a library catalog or on the Web. Computer programs search by comparing words you type to the many records stored in their databases. It is likely that some of the words you're using in your research also will be the words that lead you to useful information. Try them when you're prompted for words in titles or subject areas. Some of them may work, while others may not. If you type "lord," the computer will locate many matches; at least half of them will relate to things like the Lord's Prayer, though what you may be looking for has more to do with English royalty.

Research librarians work at almost every college library. They help people locate information in their own libraries and in other libraries via interlibrary loan and similar agreements to share resources. They probably use the World Wide Web daily. These professionals can save you considerable time and frustration, if you ask.

Anticipate Your Need to Quote Accurately and to Document Sources

If you plan to interview, how will you remember, recall, or make record of what you hear? Do you plan to record the interview if the interviewee agrees? Or will you simply take notes? One way to help with notetaking is to list your major questions on paper—with one question per page at the top so you can use the rest of the page to make notes about that particular question.

When you go to print or on-line sources, make notes about the information you typically need for documentation. For on-line sources, you'll need to copy down the Web address (http://. . .) so readers can check the site themselves if they wish. If your on-line information can be printed to your computer, the printout will often contain the Web address. For print sources, you should copy the author's name, the title of the article or book, the publisher, the publisher's location by state or city and country if outside the United States, and the copyright date. If this seems time-consuming, and you're standing at a copy machine anyhow, you may want to simply photocopy the title and copyright pages, and then staple them to any other information you copied from the same source.

Whatever you do, keep track of your source information as you go. Few things are more frustrating than tracking down source information after you've written the paper and already quoted from those sources.

Consider What You're Learning in Terms of Causes and Effects

Essay Option 4D at the end of this chapter asks you to report on the design and findings of the Framingham Heart Study. In this study, as in most research efforts, some causes and effects might be relatively clear and direct, while others are fuzzy or puzzling. In some cases, links might be shown though the actual cause-effect mechanism may still be unclear. As you report on this research, it's important for you to clearly explain what experts know for sure, what they believe could or might be true, and what they frankly aren't sure of yet.

Other Essay Options in this chapter may show the same range— from certainty, in terms of causes and effects, to reasonable conviction to puzzlement or uncertainty. You can look hard at print sources and press your interview subjects to explain, but you still may find instances where the cause and effect relationships remain unclear.

❖ *Group Activity 4.17*   Once you've done considerable research and have begun to get what seems like a firm grasp on your material, test it by trying to explain it to others. Take turns in your group. As you listen, ask the questions that naturally come to you in your effort to understand what you're hearing.

For each person who explains, designate another group member to record these questions and then pass them to the writer/researcher. Once everyone has had a turn, each of you should have a list of the questions the group asked. Use these questions to help you flesh out and make clearer your own understanding and make your own essay more concise. ❖

Consider Your Claims and Supports

In a sense, all the information you gather and choose to report serves as either a claim ("here's what is true") or a support ("these authoritative sources tell me so"). But this isn't exactly what we mean here.

Suppose you're working on the Essay Option that asks you to interview a family member about some significant event in his or her life, and then to place that interview information in some larger context. In essence, that Essay Option asks three large questions: What happened? In what ways is this case study typical or not? What can or should we learn from this example and from the experts consulted? Of these three questions, the last two focus directly on claims and supports.

Understanding the claims that your paper makes will directly affect your focus and level of detail. You'll want to focus readers on information that makes the claim clear and supports it effectively. If you can see that the case study is typical—as experts define "typical"—then it will be one of your claims. Readers will expect to see the evidence.

Each of the other Essay Options asks you to draw conclusions of some sort—to show why the evidence you gathered supports those conclusions. You may not discover those conclusions until you're well into the research and writing process. But it's important to recognize that (1) as with virtually all academic papers, this one finally rests on a series of claims and supports, and (2) once you know those claims, you can organize or reorganize your presentation so the supports stand out and answer readers' questions.

❖ *Solo Activity 4.18*   Consider your essay in terms of the claims it makes and the supports it offers to explain and validate those claims. Write down at least two major claims that arise out of your investigations.

Under each claim, list the parts of your paper that help illustrate and support that claim.

Once you've done this, make a revision plan. What do you need to add or cut? What needs to be longer or clearer? What needs to be reordered in this paper so that readers can see the cause and effect relationships?

Here's an example of a claim: "My interview with Malik _____ , a well-respected marine biologist, tells me that even now scientists who are women or minorities face difficulties not shared by their male colleagues." With this claim in mind, it should now be possible to test the rest of the paper—does it support this claim or not?

Assuming the previous claim can be supported, the research on this topic must show that at one time, women faced considerable hurdles in order to maintain careers. But the wording of the claim also suggests that this situation, while not yet fully remedied, is also not as bad as it once was. ❖

❖ *Group Activity 4.19* Take turns discussing your essay's claims and supports. Be ready to explain the claims your essay makes and the supports it uses. And be ready to listen to and ask questions about the claims and supports of the other essays by members of your group. ❖

Summarize Carefully, Quote Accurately, and Account for Your Sources

Chapter 2 discussed the use of quotations, and we refer you to that material. In addition, we want to add that a research report—whether it uses live, print, or on-line sources—often asks for summarizing skills. You cannot reproduce your sources completely, nor should you summarize them so severely that the complexities they discuss are entirely lost. In other words, it's likely that you'll want to use some quoted material— text reproduced word-for-word—as a way for readers to "hear" the source. And it means that you will sometimes shorten and paraphrase what you hear or read.

Whenever you directly quote or paraphrase material based on a specific source or a small set of sources, then you are obligated to signal those origins to readers. Various disciplines employ different systems to accomplish this. Three common systems are the Modern Language Association (MLA), the American Psychological Association (APA), and the University of Chicago graduate school—usually referred to as Chicago style). Handbooks usually give the specific instructions for these styles.

You must understand what style is required, and then follow it scrupulously. If you don't follow it, then all your research can look suspicious. Without proper documentation, your work will look sloppy— and this raises questions about accuracy in readers' minds.

Essay Option 4C

Collect your area newspaper for a week. From them, locate five stories that clearly hinge on some kind of cause-effect analysis. From these five stories, select two and use them in an essay to show how common cause-effect questions are. Using these same two examples, explain how the cause-effect relationships would typically be proven, and show why it matters that cause-effect relationships be established rigorously and accurately. Assume you're writing to anyone who may read the newspaper.

Essay Option 4D

Research the design, scope, procedures, and findings of the Framingham Heart Study. Summarize what you discover. Discuss the ways that the study's results indicate cause-effect linkages and the ways they indicate co-relations. End your discussion by explaining whether or not any of the findings of this study have caused anything in your own habits or in the way that you were raised. Write this for other classmates, and assume that they've never heard of this study.

SAMPLE STUDENT ESSAY, OPTION 4C

As you work on your own essay for this chapter, consider the strengths and weaknesses of the following student essay. Does it follow the directions? Does it communicate clearly? Use the checklist in Chapter 1 as a guide while you read and evaluate.

TANYA WILLIAMS

Joe Camel and HIV Testing

The process of understanding or explaining cause-effect relationships in our daily lives is so natural that we often do not recognize it as a process at all. If the dishwasher in the kitchen is leaking, I attempt to discover why. Similarly, if a letter is returned to me unopened, I consider possible explanations. Is the address wrong? Was the postage insufficient? Or even, what have I done to offend this person? Indeed, cause-effect questions are such a frequent method of understanding the present and predicting the future that the complicated nature of cause-effect relationships is often overlooked. In order to better understand and appreciate the frequency and complexity of cause-effect relationships, I located a number of articles from *The Oregonian* that exemplified some kind of cause-effect analysis. The two articles discussed below reflect a variety of methods for proving cause-effect relationships as well as the importance of establishing such relationships accurately and thoroughly.

In an article titled "Teen Smoking increased 73% in Joe Camel years, study says" (*The Oregonian*, Oct. 9, 1998), Russ Bynum reports the results of a study conducted by the national Centers for Disease Control and Prevention. This study seems to indicate a link between an increase in teenage smoking between 1988 and 1996 and the introduction of Joe Camel to R. J. Reynolds' advertising campaign. The agency's research was based on surveys of nearly 80,000 Americans between the ages of 12 and 66. Researchers then extrapolated nationwide estimates from that sample. The participants were asked whether they ever had a daily smoking habit, and if so, when they started smoking.

The article is particularly interesting in terms of cause-effect relationships because although the report clearly states: "tobacco ads that rely heavily on giveaways and youth-friendly cartoons are partly to blame," the study itself proves only that the number of Americans under age 18 who smoke daily has increased 73% during those years. It is also interesting to note that in an attempt to explain these statistics, the government looked first and only (as far as we know) at ` targeted' advertising by tobacco companies. The evidence they offer in support of such claims is based, not on extensive research on the impacts of Joe Camel on teenage smoking, but on co-relational data regarding the concurrence of the introduction of Joe Camel in 1988 and the steady increase of daily smoking rates that same year. Juxtaposed so, the national Centers for Disease Control and Prevention are suggesting a cause-effect relationship, although the facts do not thoroughly and conclusively prove that to be the case. In failing to accurately establish a cause-effect relationship between tobacco ads and the increase in teen smoking, this article exemplifies the tendency to mistake co-relation for causation, as well as the importance of thorough and relevant research in establishing cause-effect relationships.

The second article I reviewed, "All pregnant women should be tested for HIV, panel advises," appeared in *The Oregonian,* October 15, 1998. This article is centered on a cause-effect relationship that looks both forward and backward in its efforts to prevent mother-infant HIV transmission. Reporter Lauran Neergaard outlines the conclusions reached by The Institute of Medicine in its study of the role of HIV testing of pregnant women in both early detection efforts and in the prevention of mother-child transmission. In addition, the article also explores other possible effects of mandated HIV testing for pregnant women, including the potential problems of such a policy.

The article exemplifies the importance of cause-effect relationships both in explaining the present by looking to the past, and in predicting the possible effects of a particular cause, thus anticipating the future. In this example, the Institute's study was motivated by an awareness that "too many pregnant women who should be tested are not, meaning they miss taking the drug AZT, which can significantly cut their chances of spreading HIV to their babies." The success of AZT in mother-child transmission prevention has already been established and the Institute's conclusions rely heavily on the past performance of AZT in the treatment and prevention of HIV transmission. The study itself relies on the cause-effect relationship between mothers taking AZT and the decrease of HIV in newborns.

The Institute's resulting recommendation that HIV testing be among the battery of tests all pregnant women take was met with mixed reactions and poses some interesting implications for individual state's laws regarding HIV testing and counseling, doctor/patient relations, as well as society's perception of HIV testing in general. In short, the effects of this recommendation are more complicated and less obvious than the main objective of early HIV detection and prevention of transmission between mothers and their babies. These *other* effects must also be considered by the Centers for Disease Control and Prevention in their review of the policy. In this case it is particularly important that the cause-effect relationships be established and sufficiently supported with research because the implementation of this recommendation is not only costly, but emotionally weighty as well. Inarguably, a policy as far-reaching and widely impacting as this one would have some unforeseen effects, effects that cannot be accurately measured or accounted for presently. These too, must also be considered. Clearly, the main objective of this study and its subsequent recommendation are in the best interests of mothers and their children and society as a whole, but as is the nature of cause-effect relationships, there is more to the picture than that.

These two newpaper articles reflect not only how common cause-effect questions are, but also, just how complicated and ambiguous these relationships can be. Proving such relationships requires thorough research, the ability to ask the right questions, and the desire to seek out the less than obvious in determining both possible causes and possible effects. The importance of accurately establishing cause-effect relationships is also evident in these two articles. If these relationships are insufficiently researched, mistake co-relation for causation, or display other evidence of faulty reasoning the message and information they relay will be misleading. As exemplified in the Joe Camel article, statistics and research conducted independently of one another but simultaneously do not conclusively prove a cause-effect relationship. For the tobacco industry, this flawed reasoning amounts to bad press. For the careful reader, the assertion of a cause-effect relationship without adequate support raises questions both about the author's reasoning and the political agenda of the national Centers for Disease Control and Prevention. The process of determining cause-effect relationships can be quite complicated, particularly when the effects have yet to occur. This process, and the scope of possibilities that must be considered in implementing a policy such as mandatory HIV testing for pregnant women, requires careful consideration of all parties and points of view involved. Cause-effect relationships are not always as straightforward as "if A then B." If all possibilities are not considered, the tendency to oversimplify can result in misleading information and flawed thinking.

Bynum, Russ. "Teen smoking increased 73% in Joe Camel years, study says." *The Oregonian*, 9 Oct 1998, early ed.: 1.
Neergaard, Lauran. "All pregnant women should be tested for HIV, panel advises." *The Oregonian*, 15 Oct 1998, early ed.: 1.

Chapter 5:
Analyzing and Making Arguments

The latest research on Neanderthal speech suggests that, while those near-relatives of ours probably sounded different than modern human beings—their vocal tracts indicate a less precise, more nasal pronunciation—they probably did use a kind of proto-language. And chances are, they often disagreed with each other. Still, human beings have survived and dominated other animals—not because we're larger (think of horses), stronger (think of bears), or better adapted to a particular environment (think of snakes). We're here because of culture—because we can talk with each other and forge agreements about how to act. But such agreements are rarely unanimous, and they often prove complicated to achieve.

❖ *Solo Activity 5.1* Write a paragraph about how your family manages to agree or disagree about your end-of-the-year holiday plans, your July 4th celebration, or any other regular but important family gathering. Consider these kinds of questions as you write: Who makes the plans? How many people are expected to agree with these plans? Do you all agree or not? Do you agree to disagree? Is everyone happy with the plans each year? Do some family members privately complain but publicly go along? Are there factions or alliances between family members? Has it always been this easy (or hard) to orchestrate family gatherings?

If your own family seems dull or unsuitable for this exercise, consider another family you know. How well (or poorly) do they manage to agree about the celebration of Thanksgiving or the New Year? As you consider these questions, try to isolate the deciding factors. ❖

Efforts at persuasion are hardly the exclusive province of families. Sociologists and observers of American culture routinely note the presence of commercial messages almost everywhere, including logos or brand names on our own clothing. Our bodies become billboards and commercials for some company or cause. Look at your own clothing and that of your classmates. How many company advertisements do you see, even in a room supposedly given over to education rather than sales? Can you spot any anti-commercials—messages meant to offer contrast to straightforward corporate or organizational affiliation? The number however, is not as important as any possible effect—which takes us to the next activity.

❖ *Group Activity 5.2* Appoint someone to list on the board all the company slogans and trademarks you see in your classroom. Start with what you and your classmates are wearing, but also include any other advertisements or efforts at persuasion that are visible in the room.

Once you agree that the list on the board is complete, individually write at least six sentences on paper that discuss the degree to which these efforts at persuasion affect you (or not) in any way. Include any reasons you or others might have for wearing the clothes that advertise a company, brand, cause, or organization. Explain why you think what you think. Then come up with a counter-argument for at least one reason someone could offer to disagree with what you say.

Once you finish this paragraph, form groups of five and read your paragraphs out loud. Then, work as a group to write a paragraph that reflects *all* the views you just heard. ❖

MEDIA PERSUASION

Now consider all the television ads you've ever seen and heard, all the billboards you've passed on roads and highways, all the product banners you've seen at sporting events, all the magazine and newspaper ads you've read, all the radio spots you've heard, all the political ads you've seen and heard, and all the editorial comments you've been exposed to. The ancient Greek philosopher Aristotle had something to say about such efforts of persuasion. He would classify them according to their method—those appealing to our logic and intellect (appeals to *logos*), those using a personal endorsement from someone we trust (appeals to *ethos*), and those that try to convince us emotionally (appeals to *pathos*). Thus, most—but not all—newspaper editorials appeal to our sense of intellect and thoughtfulness, or logos. Michael Jordan's effort to sell underwear capitalizes on his widespread recognition as a basketball player, or ethos. And a car advertisement that tells us driving *this* car model is relaxing makes an emotional appeal presumably based on our stressful lives, or pathos.

❖ *Solo Activity 5.3*   As homework, look through one or more mass market magazines (*Time* or *People* are examples) and identify an ad that uses appeals to logic (logos), another that appeals to the trustworthy character of someone (ethos), and a third that is designed to appeal to your emotions (pathos). Bring these ads—or copies of them—to class. For each ad also write and bring to class a paragraph that explains why you have interpreted that ad as an appeal to logos, ethos, or pathos. (Save the ads; you may need them again for Activity 5.5.) ❖

An advertisement's tactics—the way someone or something tries to persuade us—can always be questioned. Should we really trust a sports star who tells us which shampoo to use? Does the sports star really use the product? Is this person's use similar to our own? Is that, by itself, enough to convince us?

Should we buy a particular brand of margarine solely because its ads tell us it's lower in fat than most other margarines? That may be logical, but suppose we find out this margarine tastes horrible? And should we really choose a car because the ad tells us we'll be lucky in romance? What about mileage, warranty, safety record, or frequency of repairs? Do these things matter?

Here's the bottom line: one way or another, every advertisement wants to direct your attention in very particular ways. Therefore, it makes good sense to ask yourself these two questions—What factors am I being directed to look at or consider? And what factors am I being encouraged *not* to consider?

❖ *Group Activity 5.4*   Overnight, page through a recent general interest magazine and look at the advertisements. Find at least two ads that seem "suspicious" to you. In other words, as you pay fuller attention to the ad, you see little or no good reason to agree with its attempt at persuasion. Maybe the logic simply doesn't hold up. Maybe you see little or no reason to be convinced by a celebrity or other spokesperson. Maybe an emotional appeal seems to overlook other important considerations.

Bring these two ads to class. In groups, discuss the ads all of you collected, and identify three that seem particularly bad to you—their tactics questionable. For each one, write a paragraph that explains the ad's primary appeal—to logical intellect, to trustworthy character, or to emotional action?—and the reasons you think it fails. ❖

PERSUASION AND BELIEVABILITY

Even if the tactics that a persuasive message adopts seem appropriate, that does not necessarily mean those tactics will always persuade. We still need to examine the tactics—or arguments—themselves. An ad could convincingly tell us that product A lasts fifteen percent longer than its competitor, product B. It may also leave out the fact that product A costs fifty percent more than product B. In short, its logic may be accurate but so incomplete that we can't trust it.

If it appeals to us based on the trustworthiness and character of a spokesperson, then we need to ask whether that person's character is actually trustworthy, given the persuasive message we're meant to agree with. Do we want to believe every spokesperson who is lucky and well-known enough to land an advertising contract? Does it affect their credibility that they're getting a sizable sum of money for their endorsement? And if we claim that we know all this—that we're cynical and immune to such influence—then why do advertisers keep paying celebrities so much money?

Finally, is an emotional response a reliable barometer of something's worth? Should we smoke a particular brand of cigarette because we like the image associated with the brand? Should we smoke at all? Is a decision to smoke a logical decision? An emotional one? What about a decision to stop smoking?

❖ *Group Activity 5.5* Meet in groups and exchange the ads you used for Activity 5.3. Looking at each new ad you have just received, analyze it and decide whether it appeals primarily to logos, ethos, or pathos. Once you have made this analysis, decide as a group which of the ads makes the most persuasively successful appeal to logos, the most successful appeal to ethos, and the most successful appeal to pathos. Be ready to explain your reasons. ❖

It may seem like we've spent a considerable amount of time on advertisements. We've done this for three reasons: (1) since living in American culture means you're swimming in advertisements, knowing how they work—or want to work—can help you keep your head above water, (2) seeing how advertisements work can help you analyze prose arguments you read, and (3) your own advocacy efforts might lead you to use some or all of these same persuasive tactics. But it's time to move from advertisements to prose arguments.

READING PROSE ARGUMENTS: RECOGNIZING INDUCTIVE ARGUMENTS

Besides Aristotle's appeals to logic, character, and emotion, you should be aware of two other persuasive strategies—induction and deduction. An *inductive* argument builds its case on the basis of specific examples; these examples often get presented as stories about specific people. An inductive argument about the need for national health care may feature several individuals whose stories each indicate a need for such a program.

For example, we might hear about a single mother who is trying to raise two young children, one of whom has chronic kidney disease. As we read in detail about her difficulties, her child's illness and medical expenses, and her horrible choices and frustrations, we might come to the conclusion that a national health care program should be instituted.

If we came to that conclusion, we might do so partly on the basis of emotions—in this case, on our sympathy for that family. But we also might believe that the single story we heard is actually a representative one. For this sort of inductive reasoning to hold true, then the sample—the story of this family—should, in fact, be typical. It should actually represent the needs of such a large number of people that government has the responsibility to act and help meet those needs—just as government acts to protect our need for safety by organizing law-enforcement agencies.

This kind of inductive reasoning works from representative examples to assertions about a larger generality—because this family needs health care, and this family is typical, and a measurably large number of families also need this care, the government should act to provide it. While inductive reasoning often plays on emotions, it also can be logically questioned. Is the example given in its completeness? Is the example really typical? How many instances does the example really represent? And will the proposed solution really meet the need? If you can provide positive answers to these questions, then the inductive argument gains power.

Notice that we're looking from a new perspective, at the issues raised in Chapter 1. That chapter argued that "Everyone says _____ , but in my experience I have found _____ ." Your task in Chapter 1 was to claim your own experience—not to claim that your experience holds for everyone else.

Your task now is to move toward making larger claims—claims that might apply to someone other than yourself, but carefully, reasonably.

❖ *Solo Activity 5.6*   Consider your own direct experience—either as a participant or a firsthand observer—of some controversial issue. For example, should states impose stiffer penalties for under-age drinking? Should a divorce be harder to obtain than it is now? Should states allow a "training wage" lower than the minimum wage for employees who are less that 18 years old? Should tobacco advertising be banned? Should tobacco companies be held liable for illnesses due to tobacco smoking? Should academic cheating be grounds for an "F" in a course? Should your campus abolish fraternities and sororities? Are athletics too highly valued or too slighted by your campus administration? Should condoms be available in high school restrooms?

Write a paragraph of at least six sentences that identifies the issue (as your first sentence) and then sketches your experience with it. Once you finish your paragraph, ask yourself whether your experience seems sufficient for a valid inductive argument. Write a second paragraph that gives at least two reasons why you believe it is or isn't sufficient. ❖

Essay Option 5A

Extend Solo Activity 5.6 to essay length—roughly five pages. In this longer format, give more attention to your experience itself. Explain it with care and detail so readers can understand not merely what happened but also how it felt and what it made you think about. In the second half of your essay, make a claim about your story and its relation to the controversy you know about firsthand. Then show how your experience supports your claim.

ARGUING FROM STATISTICAL DATA

Another kind of inductive argument works not merely from a single example, as a case study, nor from a handful of similar examples, but rather from many examples. When researchers compile the evidence of such examples—the data—the result is a set of numerical representations of those examples, or what we call statistics. We hear statistics cited all the time: a politician quotes statistics to show a rising or falling crime rate; polls literally *are* statistical representations of opinions. Are all statistics valid? Should we be persuaded by them?

INDUCTION: VALIDITY AND PERSUASIVENESS

We've seen two major kinds of inductive argument: arguing from a single or small group of examples, and arguing from the statistical representation of a large group of examples. Each method has its potential drawbacks.

Let's go back to the earlier example of the single parent struggling with the illness of her child—is this really typical, and does it represent many millions of people? And let's also assume that a national health care program would meet the needs of those many millions of people. Thus, we assume that the inductive reasoning is true or—to use another word—valid. Does this necessarily mean that the inductive reasoning is also persuasive? Are you persuaded enough to divert some of your tax dollars to such a program?

❖ *Group/Solo Activity 5.7* Assume that you just heard a wrenching, painfully detailed explanation from each of four different families about their need for national health care. Each of the families is different in its own way, but they share the following facts in common: a family member is seriously ill; the adults in the family either work full time or provide full-time care to the family member who is ill; the family's income cannot pay for medical bills and yet it is too high to qualify for current low-income government health care programs; and because of the family health care debts, other family members are penalized—for example, the family has lost its house or siblings aren't able to attend college. Assume further that a national health care program would address the health care needs and the financial concerns of not just these four families but of many families like them. Also assume that the inductive argument has validity. Why might some people grant the validity of the argument and yet still not be persuaded to endorse a national health care program? ❖

As you may have discovered if you thought through Group/Solo Activity 5.7, it is entirely possible to grant the accuracy of inductive reasoning and still not be persuaded by it. Why not? Because complicated problems—and health care is one of them—bring a large number of values into play. When it comes to advocacy and persuasion, values and beliefs are at least as important as accurate reasoning. An inductive argument for national health care eventually comes around to a discussion about the role of government and the collection and spending of tax dollars. People who believe government should keep out of the private lives of its citizens might grant the validity of an inductive argument for national health care, and then vehemently disagree with any effort to establish such a program.

What about the validity and persuasiveness of statistical arguments? All we can say about them is to be wary and investigate the realities that the statistics purport to portray. For example, a commuter airline suffers double the number of crashes from the previous year. How many crashes are we talking about? It may be as simple as one incident one year and two the next. Were other factors at work, too? And maybe this commuter airline also tripled the size of its schedule. So one statistic—the number of crashes this year versus last year—shows an alarming rise. But the number of crashes per flights may actually have gone down. One statistic makes the airline's safety record look bad, while the other shows an airline making significant improvements in safety.

❖ *Group Activity 5.8* Overnight locate at least one news article that quotes statistics in order to make some point. Do your own analysis of this use of statistics. See if you can figure out some other and unmentioned factors that could make the newspaper's use of these statistics either wrong or incomplete.

In groups in class, bring your example and your analysis. Look at each example in turns and then decide on two that illustrate what you believe could be the particularly shaky use of statistics. Be ready to explain your reasoning. ❖

INDUCTIVE FALLACIES

The primary inductive fallacy—a hasty or overly broad generalization—has been suggested already. An inductive argument lacks validity whenever its example can't be generalized—what's true for one case isn't necessarily true for all others. For example, one person in a class bought a term paper, therefore all others papers are in question. This is simply a false generalization. In addition to the false generalization fallacy, watch out for these others:

- *The pattern-is-proof fallacy.* Because it happened this way once, it always happens this way. Example: The fact that you ate lunch yesterday, and the day before, and the day before that all proves that you ate lunch today.
- *The slippery-slope fallacy.* Because we do a little bit of X, we'll then inevitably proceed to do a lot of X. Example: Because you ate brussels sprouts as part of your dinner yesterday, you now will have brussels sprouts at every meal.
- *The truth-is-personal fallacy.* Merely because person so-and-so says it, it must be false. Or because person so-and-so says it, it must be true. Example: Since my parents believe it, it must be true for everyone.
- *The everyone-says-so fallacy.* Because a poll shows that seventy-two percent of those asked believe in the truth of X, X must be true. Example: Aliens must exist, because so many people say they do.

❖ *Group/Solo Activity 5.9* Write at least one additional example for each of the inductive fallacies previously discussed. ❖

❖ *Group/Solo Activity 5.10* Consider the everyone-says-so fallacy regarding television polls. These polls invite people in the station's viewing area to call in and voice their opinions on some controversial issue or to vote yes or no on some controversial question. How do you view such polls? To what extent do they persuade you?

What about polls conducted by the random and scientific sampling of a small percentage of individuals in order to determine public sentiment? Do the results of these polls persuade you? Write a paragraph that explains to what extent either of these methods gives you trustworthy information.

Finally, is there a difference between trustworthy information and persuasive, rationally compelling information? ❖

RECOGNIZING DEDUCTIVE ARGUMENTS

Simply put, inductive arguments work from specifics to assert a generalization. In contrast, *deductive* arguments start with one or more generalizations or premises in order to assert an accurate specific conclusion. Here's an example of a deductive argument:

Generalization: All convicted murderers deserve the death penalty.
Specific observation: You are a murderer.
Specific conclusion: You deserve the death penalty.

In this deductive argument, if you agree with both the truth of the generalization and the truth of the specific observation, then the conclusion cannot be denied.

Now consider this deductive argument:

Generalization: Fish swim.
Specific observation: You swim.
Specific conclusion: You must be a fish.

Again, if we grant the truth of the premises—the generalization and specific observation—then the conclusion must be true. Note: is it true that *only* fish swim?

❖ *Group/Solo Activity 5.11* Reread the previous two short deductive arguments. Write a paragraph of at least six sentences that explains why you would or would not accept the arguments as persuasive. ❖

Deductive logic is a large, complicated field of study. We can give you only a little taste of it here. Needless to say, deductive arguments can fall prey to a number of fallacies. One of the most common is the either-or fallacy, as in "you're either a saint or a sinner" or "either we can trust our neighbors or we shouldn't let our kids trick-or-treat on Halloween." Either-or statements work well for matters of simple fact, such as "either you're a registered voter or you're not". But whenever complexity enters the picture, then either-or statements lose their accuracy. Even a seemingly simple "either-or" statement such as "either your tire is flat or it's not" ignores the many gradations between an accurately inflated tire and one that will not support the weight of a car.

Another common form of argument is the tactic of unwanted or absurd conclusions. It works like this: Take any argument that you disagree with, and then agree with it. Then show how it will result in horrible consequences. For example, suppose that many people in your town or city oppose the use of public monies to fund public transportation, such as buses, subways, or light rail systems. You could argue with them at first by accepting their position of "OK, let's assume that we shouldn't spend public dollars on public transportation" and then by showing the resulting negative consequences:

> A decision to not fund public transportation will limit people's transportation choices. So in a time of steady population growth, more and more commuters will need to use cars. This will put added strain on an already overburdened freeway system. We'll find ourselves more often stuck behind large accidents. Or we'll have to leave for work at 5:30 a.m., which means we won't see our children before they go to school. Our insurance rates will rise. Our stress level will increase. Who really wants these outcomes? The real questions here should be how much will effective public transportation cost? What government and public partnerships can help meet that cost? And how quickly can we get good efficient systems up and running?

Notice that this persuasive tactic depends on identifying outcomes that most people will agree are undesirable. This form of persuasion can be attacked in two ways—by showing how the identified outcomes are actually unlikely or incorrect, or by showing that another, better option or solution, other than the one proposed, also will prevent these unwanted outcomes.

❖ *Group/Solo Activity 5.12*   Choose two of the following advocacy statements. For each one, write a paragraph that grants the assertion and then shows how it will lead to all sorts of unwanted consequences. This is an exercise, so you don't necessarily need to agree with your own argument.

- Young children should not be taught the myth of Santa Claus.
- We do not need more gun control.
- Free speech means free speech—we should let people say whatever they want to say.
- Students should think of themselves as consumers, with their teachers being the merchants, or the sellers, of education. ❖

❖ *Group/Solo Activity 5.13*   Read through the statements for Group/Solo Activity 5.12. Compose an advocacy statement about some issue that concerns you. Then write a paragraph using the tactic of unwanted conclusions as a way to advance an argument that you genuinely do hold. ❖

CONSIDERING AND QUESTIONING ASSUMPTIONS

Suppose that perceived increases in crime convince voters to pressure their state legislature to do something about this problem. As a result of such pressure, the legislature decides to enact tough mandatory sentences for convicted criminals and to spend an additional ten percent of the state budget on new prisons. This set of decisions rests on a variety of assumptions:

- It's better for judges not to have much discretion in sentencing—the circumstances of a particular case don't matter really, so do the crime, and serve the time.
- Locking up criminals protects society by keeping these people off the streets. This is a better use for state dollars than other things that are not funded.
- Mandatory prison sentences serve as a deterrent. Would-be criminals consider these consequences, and some of them decide not to commit crimes.
- Prison terms work. When prisoners are released, their experience in prison will be an effective deterrent against committing new crimes.
- The public sees these new laws and feels safer and well-served by their legislators.

But are these assumptions really accurate? Do longer mandatory prison sentences present the best response to increased crime? Would diverting some of those tax dollars to job training programs or drug treatment programs be any more effective?

Our point here is this—until the assumptions are identified and examined, we cannot really be sure whether the new prisons and the new, stiffer penalties are really a good idea or not. If the assumed truths turn out false, then the argument for stiffer penalties and more prisons might not be as attractive as the legislature first believed.

❖ *Group/Solo Activity 5.14* See what assumptions you can detect behind these two persuasive statements. You should be able to identify at least three for each case:

1. Tobacco advertising ought to be banned.
2. Minors ought to be required to tell their parents before obtaining an abortion.

Now write two more statements similar to the previous two, but focus on different issues. If you do this alone, identify at least three assumptions that underpin each of your statements. If you do this in a group, exchange statements and work to identify the assumptions that support the statements written by someone else. If you have trouble, ask others in the group for help. ❖

Let's turn now to another example—the following newspaper column. You'll see that it's eleven paragraphs long and each paragraph is numbered. Read the writer's effort at advocacy, and then turn to Group/Solo Activity 5.15.

Mona Charen

Majoring in Sex

Colleges let students waste valuable time on these courses

Imagine a youngster home from college circa 1976. Her father asks amiably, "How are your studies going?" The young lady responds, "Well, I'm majoring in sex." Depending upon the father's view of premarital sex, his response might range from horror to mild amusement. But never, never would a father in mid-'70s America have imagined that his daughter was speaking the literal truth. (1)

Those were halcyon, innocent days compared to today's academy. Today, leading universities will take tens of thousands of your dollars to offer courses (and sometimes even majors) in such subjects as "Lesbian, Gay and Bisexual Studies," "Queer Lives" and "Sexuality Today." (2)

According to *The New York Times*, at the University of Virginia, co-educational pairs of students use Play-Doh to mold genitals. "If we can discuss the heart, stomach and elbow without embarrassment," explains Susan Tate, who teaches the Play-Doh course, "we should be able to talk about the penis, clitoris and vagina without laughing." (3)

This is an academic subject? How are the students graded? One shudders to ask. Those who show the least embarrassment get A's? (4)

At Brown University, an Ivy League-school, students can major in something called "Sexuality and Society." Now, even if one could imagine a serious scientific study of sexuality within the context of psychology or physiology, it's difficult to imagine that there would be sufficient material to comprise a major. But the inclusion of the word "society" gives the game away. This is not an academic discipline. This is propaganda. (5)

The New York Times reports that among the required courses in this field of study are the biology of gender (whatever that means), an introduction to gay and lesbian literary and cultural studies; the history of sexuality, and a course called Queers and Culture (which appears on the student's transcript as "Identities/Communities," the better to bamboozle future employers). (6)

One former student who majored in Sexuality and Society, and who now works for a gay health center in Boston, was lavish in his praise of his undergraduate training. "What I really like about queer theory is that rather than looking at minority or dissident sexuality vs. the mainstream, we question a lot of basic assumptions we have about sexuality," Marshall Miller told the Times. (7)

Ordinary Americans, hearing about this perversion of higher education, must think that universities are off in some peculiar world of their own. But consider the case of the State University of New York. The New Paltz campus hosted a conference on women's sexuality titled "Revolting Behavior: The Challenge of Women's Sexual Freedom." Topics covered included sex toys and sadomasochism—both of which were enthusiastically endorsed by the "scholars" involved. The title of the sadomasochism lecture was "Safe, Sane and Consensual S&M: An Alternative Way of Loving." (8)

One of the members of the board of trustees of the State University of New York, Dr. Candace de Russy, appointed by Republican Gov. George Pataki (elections do matter), attended the conference and immediately called for the resignation of the president of the university, Roger Bowen, who gave opening remarks at the conference. De Russy called the conference "a travesty of academic standards" that had "absolutely nothing to do with the college's undergraduate mission." (9)

Obvious, one would have thought. But de Russy was slapped down by the other trustees and by the ever-reliable New York Times editorial page. The conference on "women's sexuality" may have made some people uneasy, sniffed the Times, but it deserves protection "on grounds of free speech and academic freedom." De Russy, the voice of the establishment admonished, should halt her "destructive assaults on the institution she is supposed to be safeguarding." (10)

Something queer is going on here, and it isn't just queer theory. America's elites have completely lost their judgment and common sense. College is a unique opportunity for students to revel in the riches of learning passed down through three millennia. There is more beauty, mystery and wonder in the world than any student can hope to taste even in four full years. To waste any of that precious (and expensive) time on nonsense is almost criminal. (11)

❖ *Group/Solo Activity 5.15*

    a. Look carefully at paragraphs one, three, five, and six. For each paragraph, decide what kind of argument the author presents. Is that paragraph an appeal to logos, ethos, or pathos? Is it an effort at either inductive or deductive reasoning? Try to recognize the tactics the author uses. For each of these four paragraphs, write two sentences that identify the tactics you see.

    b. Once you've identified the persuasive strategies the writer uses in those paragraphs, decide whether or not the strategies seem to be used intelligently. Again, don't yet consider whether or not you agree with the reasoning. Rather, consider whether the reasoning seems careful and accurate, or whether it appears to fall prey to one or more of the fallacies discussed earlier in this chapter.

    c. Look now at the author's overall presentation, and try to characterize it accurately. What strategies are employed in paragraphs one through ten that presumably lead to the conclusions given in paragraph eleven? Write your own paragraph that analyzes the paragraphs one through ten overall.

    d. Setting aside your opinions on women's studies or gender studies, how would you critique the author's effort at advocacy? In other words, given the strategies she's chosen to use, do you find that they have been used intelligently and rationally? Remember, you may agree with the author's conclusions for your own reasons, yet still find her persuasive effort incomplete or fallacious. The question here pertains to how the argument is made, not whether you tend to agree with it.

    e. Do your best to find something in this piece that you agree with and find persuasive. Then make the same effort to find something you disagree with or find poorly argued. Now, based on all your attention to the author's piece as an example of advocacy, come to at least two conclusions about advocacy that are either new to you or have been emphasized again in this activity. ❖

Essay Option 5B

Copy a relatively short editorial or advocacy essay, such as the one you just read, from a newspaper or general interest magazine. Analyze all the methods the writer uses in the effort to persuade. Does the piece fall prey to any of the fallacies described earlier in this chapter, or does it consistently avoid them? Make a preliminary claim about the quality of the reasoning as you find it in this piece, and make sure your analysis clearly supports it.

Then, in the second half of your essay, explain the reasons that you are inclined to agree or disagree with the position as advocated—your second major claim. If your opinion comes from knowledge that's not given in the original piece, explain its sources (e.g., your own experiences, other books or articles you've read, etc.). If your opinion results from the persuasive quality of the piece you copied, then explain why you find it so persuasive.

CONSIDERING ADVOCACY AND AUDIENCE

If you've watched any television at all, then you've seen commercials. And you probably recognized a long time ago that, while anyone could be watching any commercial, some of them seem to be addressed to you and others clearly are not. Recall two commercials—one that included you and seemed pitched to you, and another one that seemed aimed at an audience that doesn't include you. How did you recognize these distinctions? What was it about the commercials that told you whether or not you were a part of their intended audience?

Prose arguments certainly consider who might read them. After all, the first task of any advocacy effort must be to hold the attention of the target audience. A piece of prose advocacy that insults its readers or fails to consider their likely responses will probably not be read, just as you are sometimes inclined to hit the mute button when a commercial comes on the television. A prose argument that goes unread is one that has failed.

❖ *Group/Solo Activity 5.16* Return to Charen's newspaper column. Write a paragraph that answers each of these questions:

a. Assuming that Charen wants to sell newspapers, how successful is her column?

b. Assuming that Charen wants to convince readers that "America's elites have completely lost their judgment and common sense," how successful is her column?

    c. Assuming that Charen wants to polarize her readers—those who already agree with her feel more agreement, while those who already disagree feel more disagreement—how successful is her column?

    d. Based on what Charen actually says, what audience do you think she wants to reach? Why do you think so? ❖

Aristotle analyzed the strength of any argument in terms of its appeal to a particular audience. An argument that may succeed when addressed to MTV viewers might fall flat when addressed to those who routinely identify with the American Movie Classics channel. What we say and decide *not* to say has everything to do with audience, with the people we imagine sitting in front of us and weighing what we say—grimacing, nodding, looking quizzical, laughing, agreeing, or disagreeing. You already know this intuitively. For example, you wouldn't wear a bathing suit to job interview, except maybe as a lifeguard.

❖ *Group/Solo Activity 5.17* This is a classic exercise to demonstrate the importance of audience. Assume that you're writing four letters to four different audiences. The subject of each is the same—your immediate and urgent need for some additional cash. Break into four groups. Group 1 conveys this fact or request to your mother or father. Group 2's letter is to a close friend, which may or may not include a request—it may simply be telling the story. Group 3's letter is to the student loan officer at your college or university or to some other official who is capable of issuing a check. Group 4's letter is to the student government loan fund, which is administered by your elected student representatives.

Read the representative letters aloud to the class as a whole, leaving off the salutation. How can you tell which audience has been addressed? In your discussion, consider both the content and word choice of the letter. Hint: Even punctuation can indicate audience, as in "Dear Sir:" versus "Hi Mom,". ❖

ARGUING FROM ANALOGY

Chapter 6 will address comparisons in more detail. But a discussion of advocacy would be incomplete if it didn't mention the use of comparisons—or analogies—as another tactic used primarily to undercut or diminish the arguments you oppose. Such an argument uses this structure: A is like B, where A refers to something you want to call into suspicion, and B is something either unlikely or impossible. Thus, someone who wanted to convince you that you should study without music blaring may say, "Studying with music blaring is like trying to sing underwater." Here are two more examples: "A prose summary of a poem holds all the grandeur of a 3" × 5" photo of the Grand Canyon," or "Arguing against drug treatment programs is like arguing that the world is flat."

Note that this kind of argument is often meant to be dismissive or at least distracting. It works to undercut rational, careful thought by attempting to refocus the debate.

❖ *Group/Solo Activity 5.18* Complete the following analogies:

- Sharing a room with a brother or sister is like _____
- Cramming for a test all night before an 8 a.m. test is like _____
- Working three jobs is like _____
- Sleeping late on Saturday is like _____
- Watching _____ (insert a sports team) is like _____

Now create four more analogies using the same pattern. Try to make two of them outlandish and obviously funny or wrong, and make the other two more serious and pointed. ❖

Arguing from comparisons can be useful if the comparison itself is then discussed. For example, suppose you want to argue against a curfew for people under eighteen years of age. You may say that, "Imposing a curfew on people younger than eighteen is like requiring everyone shorter than 60 inches to wear only black shoes. In both cases, a group of people are classified according to arbitrary criteria, and their choices are then restricted." Thus, the analogy is both presented and interpreted.

Such an argument can be challenged by asking what aspects of the comparison are either not valid or not included. The comparison used in the curfew argument leaves out the question of whether or not those under 18 are mature or responsible enough to have the same freedoms as those who are 19 years old or 49 years old. The analogy simply avoids that aspect of the question. So the analogy may be useful, but it also may not be sufficient by itself. An argument against a curfew may need additional appeals, such as those discussed earlier in this chapter.

❖ *Group/Solo Activity 5.19* Identify and write down two issues or arguments. Then challenge each by using an analogy. Finally, for each issue and its accompanying analogy, write a paragraph that explains a strength and a weakness of the analogy. ❖

ARGUING FROM AUTHORITY

Many academic arguments find their persuasive power by appealing to authorities that most readers will find credible. A journal on cardiac disease will publish articles almost exclusively from physicians who specialize in cardiac diseases. And an editorial board of such recognized experts will decide which articles to publish. In academic settings, such a journal is called a "peer-reviewed journal" or a "juried publication." You can tell if a journal is peer-reviewed by looking at its editorial composition.

On-line Web sites have complicated our ability to determine what information proceeds from careful and expert inquiry and what proceeds from the imagination and half-understandings of someone who knows enough to construct a Web site. Some information on the Web is entirely trustworthy and authoritative; some is accurate but also influenced by a wish to promote a cause or a particular viewpoint; and some is simply fanciful. When in doubt about the authority of an on-line source, consult a professor or a research librarian.

Many discussions outside academics also rely on authoritative sources. When a young child swallows some cleaning fluid from under the sink, a parent will call the poison control hot line. In effect, the parent seeks the input of an expert in order to know how to react to a potentially dangerous situation. Or when bad weather looms, all of us look to weather forecasters and especially to the U.S. Weather Bureau. They may not be perfect, but we know they have training, experience, and access to technology that we simply cannot match ourselves.

Much of the advocacy writing done in college refers to experts in order to explain and justify claims that we could not make based on our own personal experience. Not only is this strategy well-recognized, but it can be one of the most successful and persuasive advocacy strategies—particularly when readers agree that the authorities cited are indeed believable.

❖ *Group/Solo Activity 5.20* In a paragraph, recall a time when you found the need to consult an expert or authority—either in person, in print, or on-line. What answers were you looking for? Did you get them? Were they accurate? If you do this activity in a group, listen to each other's paragraphs. Then write a group paragraph that gives advice on how or when to consult experts. ❖

❖ *Solo Activity 5.21* Look through textbooks for other classes, and locate a clear example of an argument based on the use of an authoritative source or sources. Photocopy that page, and write a paragraph that points to the example and explains why you think the argument is either believable or suspect. ❖

Essay Option 5C

In the *US News and World Report* article, "No Books, Please; We're Students," the author makes a variety of claims about college students. Analyze this argument. Consider it first in terms of its appeals to logos, ethos, and pathos. Then analyze its use of induction and deduction. Your analysis should answer these two questions: (1) How well constructed, or not, is this argument?, and (2) To what extent, if any, do you agree with its claims?

Your response cannot be longer than 1,500 words—about six double-spaced pages. Recognize that your response is an effort at advocacy—it should attempt to convince readers that its analysis is sound, and it should offer whatever appeals or inductive or deductive reasoning you deem persuasive in order to either partially or fully agree or partially or fully disagree with the claims the author makes. If it is necessary or useful for you to consult sources other than this article and your own life experience, you are certainly encouraged to do so.

Finally, assume that your response will be published by *US News and World Report* next month when they reprint Leo's original essay. Thus, you and Leo share the same wide audience.

JOHN LEO
No Books, Please; We're Students

Incoming college students "are increasingly disengaged from the academic experience," according to the latest (1995) national survey of college freshmen put out each year by UCLA's Higher Education Research Institute. This is a rather dainty way of saying that compared with freshmen a decade or so ago, current students are more easily bored and considerably less willing to work hard.

Only 35 percent of students said they spent six or more hours a week studying or doing homework during senior year in high school, down from 43.7 percent in 1987. And the 1995 survey shows the highest percentage ever of students reporting being frequently bored in class, 33.9 percent.

As always, this information should come with many asterisks attached: The college population is broader and less elite now, and many students have to juggle jobs and heavy family responsibilities. At the more selective colleges, short attention spans and a reluctance to read and study are less of a problem. But a lot of professors are echoing the negative general findings of the freshman survey.

"During the last decade, college students have changed for the worse," chemistry professor Henry Bauer of Virginia Tech said in a paper prepared for an academic meeting this week in Orlando. "An increasing proportion carry a chip on their shoulder and expect good grades without attending class or studying."

Bauer has kept charts for 10 years, showing that his students have done progressively worse on final exams compared with midsemester quizzes, even though they know that the same questions used on the quizzes will show up on the finals. He thinks this is "indisputable" evidence of student decline, including a simple unwillingness to bone up on the answers known to be coming on final exams.

"Inattentive, inarticulate." His paper is filled with similar comments from professors around the country. "The real problem is students who won't study," wrote a Penn State professor. A retired professor from Southern Connecticut State said: "I found my students progressively more ignorant, inattentive, inarticulate." "Unprecedented numbers of students rarely come to class," said a Virginia Tech teacher. "They have not read the material and have scant interest in learning it." Another professor said that many students only come to class when they have nothing better to do. At one of his classes, no students at all showed up.

So far the best depiction of these attitudes is in the new book, *Generation X Goes to College,* by "Peter Sacks," the pseudonym for a California journalist who taught writing courses to mostly white, mostly middle-class groups at an unnamed suburban community college.

"Sacks" produces a devastating portrait of bored and unmotivated students unwilling to read or study but feeling entitled to high grades, partly because they saw themselves as consumers "buying" an education from teachers, whose job it was to deliver the product whether the students worked for it or not.

"Disengaged rudeness" was the common attitude. Students would sometimes chat loudly, sleep, talk on cell phones and even watch television during class, paying attention only when something amusing or entertaining occurred. The decline of the work ethic was institutionalized in grade inflation, "hand-holding" (the assumption that teachers would help solve students' personal problems) and watering down standards "to accommodate a generation of students who had become increasingly disengaged from anything resembling an intellectual life."

Engulfed by an amusement culture from their first days of watching "Sesame Street," "Sacks" writes, the students wanted primarily to be entertained, and in a poll he took his students said that was the No. 1 quality they wanted in a teacher. The word "fun" turned up often in student evaluations of teachers, which exerted powerful sway over a teacher's career. At one point, a faculty member suggested that "Sacks" take an acting course so he could improve his student evaluations.

The entertainment factor is popping up at many colleges these days—courses on "Star Trek," use of videos and movies, even a music video on the economic theories of John Maynard Keynes. Economics light for nonreaders.

But the book goes well beyond conventional arguments about slackers, entitlement and dumbing down. Students, he says, now have a postmodern sensibility—distrustful of reason, authority, facts, objectivity, all values not generated by the self. "As children of postmodernity, they seem implicitly to distrust anything that purports to be a source of knowledge and authority."

"Sacks" and some fellow teachers concluded they were "in the midst of a profound cultural upheaval that had completely changed students and the collegiate enterprise from just 10 years earlier." Oddly, he presents his boomer generation as the defender of traditional order against generation X, but the heavy campaigns against authority, objectivity and an adult-run university were boomer themes of the Sixties now rattling through the culture. But he's right about the depth of the upheaval. We can expect greater campus conflict and upheaval in the years ahead.

Essay Option 5D

Consider an issue that already interests you and is likely to use statistics in an effort to convince people one way or another. Such issues might include local land-use planning, environmental debates about various regulations, decisions about increasing or decreasing the local public transportation options, economic decisions about the use of tax dollars, arguments about the efficiency of schools in actually teaching students, and so on. If you can draw on experience of more limited, local issues, including some on your campus, then please do so.

Review the issue specifically in terms of how the people involved use statistics to prove or support their claims. Does the use of statistics in this issue work to clarify appeals, or does the use tend to simplify or unrealistically portray aspects of the controversy? Assume you're writing to the people who are investigating the issue for the first time. Explain what you believe they can trust and what you think they should find suspicion with—these will be your claims. Make sure your evidence and examples support your claims.

ESSAY OPTIONS: GETTING STARTED

Consider Your Essay's Methods

This chapter has identified a variety of persuasive methods. Your first task as the writer of an essay should be to consider how you want to construct your own argument or effort at persuasion. Each of the options suggests the methods to use, so your effort should be to use those methods in order to understand what you want to say.

Consult Your Own Experience

Some issues you consider may fall outside your own direct experience, and this may be the case especially for academic arguments. A question such as, "Identify the two most important causes of the civil rights movement of the 1960s" asks you to write advocacy—to answer the question is to make an argument for your analysis. You may or may not have any direct experience to draw upon—instead, you'll draw on your reading experience, which is part of your general experience, too.

Leo's article in Essay Option 5C clearly makes an argument about college students and how they have changed over time. Written in 1996, Leo's argument draws on sources and experience more or less contemporary with the mid-1990s. And you certainly have experience of your own to draw on—experience more current and up-to-date than any Leo could summon. So this Essay Option gives you a perfect opportunity to make decisions about how much or how little you want to trust and use your own experience. In fact, each Essay Option in this chapter asks you to consult your own experience to some extent.

❖ *Solo Activity 5.22* Make whatever kind of notes you want to in order to begin sketching what you know firsthand about your issue. If you freewrite as a way of getting material on the page, then use this method; or if you like to make outlines, do this. Do whatever you often do to get yourself started on the thinking that you need to do. As you brainstorm, think about what parts of your experience seem relevant—which parts either support or contradict the assertions you want to make.

Then create a second set of notes or freewrites aimed at bringing any of your relevant reading knowledge to paper. At this point, write it in any way you recall it. ❖

Consult Sources Outside Your Experience

Leo's article quotes an annual survey done by UCLA's Higher Education Research Institute. Can you find out whether this survey has continued since 1995? Are surveys by other organizations also published? Are there any books or articles about college students and their attitudes? Does anyone survey college professors about their views of their students? Has any author published any kind of response to *Generation X Goes to College?*

With any of the Essay Options, answering these questions will inevitably take you to sources both on and off campus. Advocacy without support and knowledge becomes nothing but browbeating.

❖ *Solo Activity 5.23* Do some on-line searching to discover what information is available relevant to your Essay Option. First check your college's catalog—for both books and articles. If your college library has joined with other institutions to pool library resources, you may be able to search the holdings of several institutions at the same time. In addition, consult at least one index of publications in order to help you locate published sources.

To complete this activity, you should bring printouts of at least three potentially useful sources. If you can't find three, write a paragraph that explains what search efforts you tried, even though you were not successful.

Note: Reference librarians spend their time keeping track of innovations in electronic searching and information gathering. If you are not familiar with your library's capabilities in this area, consult one of these librarians. ❖

Write a First Draft

Working from your notes, start writing your first draft. You may decide to write straight through, beginning with a first paragraph and proceeding from there. On the other hand, you could start by writing a portion of your own thinking that seems clearest to you right now. After all, no rule says that a first draft must be written in the order in which it will be read.

❖ *Solo Activity 5.24* Begin drafting your focus essay. Work from your notes, from the analyses and quotations you've gathered from earlier activities, and/or from any outside sources. Write what seems easiest to write. If that means starting "in the middle," then do that—you can write the front and back later. Be ready to make a photocopy of this draft and turn it in if your teacher asks for it. This draft must be at least three pages in length. ❖

Get Response to Your Draft; Give Your Response to Others

As in all writing situations, it's difficult to be both the person who writes—and therefore knows something about how the thought is supposed to inform the words—and the person who reads—and therefore must make meaning of only the words on the page. This can be particularly difficult if your subject or focus is somewhat new to you. College writing situations will often ask you to write about material that you had little knowledge of three weeks or a month previously. Two actions can help give you a clearer picture: (1) reading what others have said—and the degree to which they've said it clearly, and (2) hearing from other readers what your words on the page communicate to them. Whether you feel you really know the subject or not, this kind of response *getting* and response *giving* can be crucial to developing both your thinking and your words on the page.

❖ *Group Activity 5.25* Working in groups of three, read each other's drafts and offer responses to the writers. Use these questions to help you offer useful feedback to each other:

- As the draft relates a story or example, can you understand the specifics? Are all the necessary who, where, what, and when questions clearly answered? What questions do you want to ask the writer in order to clarify what's on the page?

- Does the draft include quotations from other sources? Do those quotations really serve a strong purpose, or do they seem somehow forced? What suggestions would you make to improve the use of experience and quotations outside the writer's own?
- Can you clearly see the persuasive tactics used in this draft? Comment briefly on one that works particularly well. ❖

Consider Audience

Let's assume at this point that you have a pretty clear idea about your own position—you know (mostly) what you feel, think, and therefore want to say. Consider all of that your content. Now try to look at the content as your readers might. This step is crucial, because all persuasion assumes an audience. So how will your audience react? What counter arguments might they make? What explanations will they need to see in full context? What phrases and vocabulary might they find offensive—would you write to people in the '70s by referring to them as "old people"?

❖ **Solo Activity 5.26** To what extent, or not, is audience a factor in the Essay Option you've chosen? Write three statements about how audience considerations should affect *what* or *how* you say it in your essay. ❖

SPEAKING ADVOCACY: MAKING ORAL ARGUMENTS

Advocacy is always social. Even when you argue with yourself, you're pretending there are two of you. And since advocacy is always social, you may often want to advance your own position orally and in person. This will sometimes mean making a speech—a planned presentation—to a commission or those involved in decision making.

Making Planned Presentations

As you may guess, the key lies in planning, which we can divide into four phases: understanding the issue, understanding your own stance, deciding what you want to say, and deciding how you want to structure it for presentation. Understanding the issue is essentially an exercise in listening and analysis—what are others saying, and how are they coming to their conclusions? Based on what premises? Based on what evidence? Based on what values? After working through previous parts of this chapter and earlier sections of this book, such questions should be familiar to you. Everything you know about summarizing, challenging commonplaces, and linking causes and effects should come into play as you try to understand the complexities of an issue and the wide spectrum of opinions. There are no shortcuts here—either you have familiarized yourself with an issue and what people are saying about it, or you still have that to do yet.

A thorough understanding of an issue does not necessarily lead you to a clear or simple position. Complex issues generate controversy precisely because they are complex. And perhaps the best position, as you see it, seems either very complicated or in some ways contradictory. (See Chapter 6 for more on embracing contraries.) But if you've been assigned a speech, you will need a thesis—a claim. Perhaps your claim is that the issue itself is deceptively complicated. Whatever it is, you need to identify it for yourself; you have to decide.

Recognize that the sort of careful planning we're urging also goes a considerable distance toward combatting shyness or stage fright. Think of it this way: shyness or stage fright comes from a focus on you and on worry about your performance. If you can shift your internal focus to what you genuinely understand about that issue, then that issue becomes more important to you. You focus less on yourself and more on your content and the importance of that content. You think more about the message than about the messenger.

❖ *Solo Activity 5.27* Consider the variety of controversial issues that surround you—some in your family, some in the various communities you're part of, some of them larger societal concerns. Of all these issues, you will know some quite well, either because you have direct experience or because you have already worked to learn about them. You may only be partially aware of others: people talk about them or report them on TV or in newspapers, but you're really too uninformed to take a position.

Identify two issues that you do know, and two others you've only heard about. Presume that in two weeks, you're required to give a five-minute presentation that advocates your position on one of these four issues. Which issue would you pick, and why would you pick it? Write a paragraph that explains your choice. ❖

Assuming that you know your issue and your own position, the next step is to plan your actual presentation. To do this, we offer the following pointers:

1. Consider how much time you have for your presentation. A five-minute presentation is one thing, while a thirty-minute speech is quite another. In five minutes, could you build a careful, step-by-step logic? Or would a well-chosen example be better?

2. Consider who you're speaking to. Will your listeners already know quite a bit about the issue—or at least think they do? Do you want to challenge this knowledge? Do you want to take advantage of it? Or will your audience probably admit to some degree of unfamiliarity, thus looking to you for information and education? What can you present that will give your audience a sense of confident understanding of the issue?

3. Consider what most influenced your own conviction. What experience or facts made the difference for you? Will that same experience or those same facts similarly influence the people to whom you're speaking?

❖ *Solo Activity 5.28*

a. Presume that you've been assigned to make a five-minute presentation that responds to Leo's article printed earlier in this chapter. Write at least three sentences that address each of the three planning considerations just discussed.

b. With the previous considerations clear in your mind, it's now time to outline your actual presentation. You can use any outline form you want—and find easy to refer to—but make sure it shows the main points you plan to address in the order you plan to make them. Make sure this outline does not exceed a single page. ❖

Consider Making Overhead Transparencies or Handouts

If your presentation asks listeners to link of a variety of elements in a particular logical way, you may want to illustrate this logic with a transparency you could project and refer to as you speak. Using transparencies carries some drawbacks, such as our habit of staring at the screen. Your audience will likely do just that—stare at the transparency you're projecting rather than pay attention to you or what you are saying. Hint: When the transparency has done its job, turn off the overhead projector. Your audience will then refocus its attention on you and what you are saying.

Handouts can accomplish the same usefulness, but they also offer similar potential for distraction. If you use a handout, tell your audience when to look at it and explain what they're seeing. When the handout has served its purpose, use a transition phrase such as, "Let's turn to another issue now," that tells listeners to shift attention back to you.

❖ *Solo Activity 5.29* Assume that you plan to make a presentation that will last at least five minutes. Make either an overhead transparency or a handout that could support your content and make it easier for listeners to grasp your points. The best examples will illustrate a structure or a logic without necessarily trying to fill in all the linkages and explanations; the speech itself should do that. ❖

Recognize Important Similarities and Differences between Papers and Speeches

Speeches are papers heard once and not read at all. While speeches need to be at least as organized as papers, speeches should highlight this organizational structure at every opportunity. These tips should help:

- Consider numbering each item in a list, and announce the total number early. For example, "Three reasons lead me to this conclusion. First . . . The second reason . . . And finally . . ." Verbally point this out for listeners since they are not readers—they cannot stop and reread an earlier portion.

- Use transitions to repeat your main points. Listeners do not manage the same uniform level of high concentration as they listen. You know this yourself—you can begin by listening carefully and intently, but sooner or later your mind will take an independent track. As someone making a speech or giving a presentation, you cannot know when your audience will do this, but you can be fairly sure that they will. So repeat your main points. Thus, you may preface a second reason by showing how it logically relates to the first one. And in the process, you may use a phrase or part of a sentence to remind readers of that first reason:

  . . . not only does athletic competition teach the value of practice—the first point your speech made—it also teaches the value of team work . . .

or

. . . as important as the value of practice can be, it is not the only benefit to athletic competition—participants also learn the value of teamwork . . .

or

. . . if the value of practice is the first benefit of athletic competition, what is the second? It's the value of teamwork. . .

In short, tell listeners what you plan to say, say it, then tell them what you said.

- Acknowledge that you're sharing a space with other human beings and not merely consulting a printed set of notes. In other words, look at the people to whom you're speaking. Realize that you have something in mind that they'd like to hear about. Try to make this social situation as comfortable and human as you can.

   In addition, consider using phrases that acknowledge you're making a speech and the audience is listening: "At this point you may be wondering . . ." or "Skeptics might object that . . ." Such phrases might not be appropriate for formal debate, but they can be effective as logical tools—they can signal a turn in the discussion—and as tools that show you want to include your listeners in the thinking that your speech represents.

Practice and Time Yourself

Practice is just another way to become more familiar with your subject and with the voice you want to use to say it. Try to sound like a smart, prepared, composed version of yourself. If you practice, you will actually be those things. And time your presentation. If you have never done this before, you will be surprised at how limited a five-minute presentation can be. And remember one advantage you always have over your audience: you know what you want to say, and they have yet to hear it.

SAMPLE STUDENT ESSAY, OPTION 5C

As you work on your own essay for this chapter, consider the strengths and weaknesses of the following student essay. Does it follow the directions? Does it communicate clearly? Use the checklist in Chapter 1 as a guide while you read and evaluate.

SCOTT GALLAGHER

But, I Have a Question!

"You lazy, good for nothing kids with your loud music and rock-n-roll sensibilities!" shout Peter Sacks and Henry Bauer in John Leo's article, "No Books Please; We're Students." Looking down from their lofty offices in academia, Sacks and Bauer have proclaimed incoming students "inattentive, inarticulate," and, overall, worse than those of a decade before. Their pronouncement is, however, a gross generalization drawn from few facts and a select group of opinions and not representative of all incoming college freshmen.

Leo's article refers to the UCLA's national survey of college freshman (1995) as initial support for his argument. He quotes from the report that students "are increasingly disengaged from the academic experience," and refers to the statistics that the time spent studying per week has decreased while the level of boredom in class has increased. Although this evidence is true, it's only part of the report and even Leo admits that it, "should come with many asterisks attached." He mentions that students are "less elite" today and have jobs and families to contend with. If he had read beyond the section he has quoted from he would realize how very true that statement is. According to Alexander W. Astin, director of the same UCLA survey report, in order to pay for rising tuition fees, "increasing numbers [of students] expect to work while going to school to help pay college expenses (41.1 percent compared to a low of 34.7 percent in 1989)." The number of students working full-time at off-campus jobs also continues to rise. I myself work twenty hours a week, mostly at night, at a retail store and carry a full load of classes during the day. I don't think it would come as a surprise to anyone when I say that I spend less time studying than I probably should. But it's not because I'm lazy, it's because I'm tired. Like many students, I have to work to pay for college expenses that decreasing financial-aid does not.

When you include the increasing number of non-traditional students, those returning to school who are typically older with wife and/or kids, it becomes easier to understand why students might miss class. One Virginia Tech teacher quoted by Leo said that students, "have not read the [assigned] material and have scant interest in learning it." This negative sentiment is expressed by all of the teachers Leo quotes and begs the question: Are they interested in teaching it?

Bauer of Virginia Tech is quoted as saying that students "carry a chip on their shoulder and expect good grades without attending class or studying." He holds up charts he has created showing how students "have done progressively worse on final exams" even though they knew the questions came from the quizzes they seemed to do well. Bauer thinks the final exams should be easy especially when the students knew what the questions would be. He's right, it does sound easy, but not very challenging. Here's an idea—how about asking them questions they haven't been asked before in order to stimulate some interest in studying for the final exam. Leo quotes a retired professor from Southern Connecticut State who said, "I found my students progressively more ignorant, inattentive, inarticulate." It's a good thing he is retired because I certainly wouldn't want to take a class from someone with such pre-conceived notions of students. Maybe it's teachers like this who have a chip on their shoulder, not the students.

Leo relies heavily on Peter Sacks's book, *Generation X Goes to College,* to support his argument. Sacks wrote his book based on his time teaching (we're not told how long) at one small, suburban community college. From his limited experience he draws the con-clusion that students now have a "disengaged rudeness" in their attitude towards school. He says that students would sometimes, but not all of the time, "chat loudly, sleep . . . paying attention only when something amusing or entertaining occurred." Evidently, this is a new attitude in students and has never happened in class-rooms before Generation X hit them. I suppose we also developed the art of note passing, the spit-ball, and crib notes—cheat sheets to you laymen out there.

Sacks relates the decline in the work ethic to the dumbing-down of courses in order to "accommodate a generation of stu-dents who had become increasingly disengaged from anything resembling an intellectual life." If Sacks would join Leo in reading through the rest of the UCLA survey, they would find that, contrary to their opinion, students are actively pursuing the intellectual life earlier than ever before in the form of college preparatory classes in high school. The survey states that a record number of students are taking more math, foreign language, biological science, phys-ical science, and computer science than ever before. Linda J. Sax, a professor of Education at UCLA, agrees in the report that, "teach-ers are feeling more pressured to be lenient in their grading," but that students are also feeling greater pressure to succeed. This becomes apparent when 66.3 percent of incoming freshman, when questioned, respond that they plan to earn graduate or advanced professional degrees. Perhaps the reason students are getting higher grades is because they have to know more coming into college than students did 10 years earlier in order to succeed.

Not only are students actively engaging in an intellectual life, more of them want to teach and encourage others to do it also. The UCLA survey reports that the "interest in elementary and secondary teaching careers rose again, to its highest point in 23 years," while "interest in business careers hit a 20-year low at 14 percent, compared with the all-time high in 1987 of 24.6 percent."

Leo summarizes more of Sacks's opinion when he says that students, "now have a postmodern sensibility—distrustful of reason, authority, facts, objectivity, all values not generated by the self," and that they, "distrust anything that purports to be a source of knowledge and authority." Challenging authority? Is this unique to the students of Generation X? Has it never happened before? If not then I am glad to be a part of the group who invented it. Sacks thinks that we shouldn't question any "source of knowledge and authority" and that we should simply believe everything our teachers tell us, soaking it up like a brainless sponge. This runs counter to what I thought school was about, to learn by questioning, to discover the truth for ourselves in the information given to us rather than having it spoon-fed.

Leo utilizes minimal evidence and selectively cites biased teachers to argue that incoming freshman students are worse off now, academically and attitudinally, than they were a decade earlier. Had Leo included the entire UCLA freshmen survey he would have been forced to conclude that incoming freshmen are not only better prepared academically, but in fact work harder inside and outside of the classroom than ever before with aspirations of continuing in higher education. He quotes Sacks and some fellow teachers as saying that they were "in the midst of a profound cultural upheaval that had completely changed the students and the collegiate enterprise from just 10 years earlier." I believe that every generation, whether it is the Gen X's, the baby boomers, or the hippies, has a "cultural upheaval" and that, as Leo says, "we can expect greater campus conflict and upheaval in the years ahead." However, I don't agree with him that this is necessarily a bad thing. He quotes Bauer as saying, "college students have changed for the worst." I don't think we have changed for the worst, but I agree that we have definitely changed.

Chapter 6:
Understanding Comparisons, Embracing Contraries

Chapter 5 spoke briefly about analogies as a persuasive technique—often a dismissive one. We'd like to conclude ASKING QUESTIONS by asking you to reflect further on the simple act of comparing and contrasting.

We compare and contrast all the time. McDonald's tonight, or Chinese? The new Toyota pickup or the used Camry? Anthropology at 9 o'clock Monday-Wednesday-Friday or Women in the Novel? We have to make choices every day and that means comparing and contrasting options, on paper, in conversation, or in our minds, until we've arrived at a decision.

❖ *Solo Activity 6.1* Think back to a recent decision you made between two different options. How did that decision happen? Did you write lists? Consult others? Lose a night's sleep? Wake up one day and just know what to do? Roll dice?

Draw one line down the center of a piece of paper and another line horizontally across the middle so you have four squares. In the left two squares, list the advantages and disadvantages of the one option; and on the right, list the other option.

Now, turn over the paper and do a brief freewrite on any second thoughts. Having already experienced the choice you made, what do you know now that you didn't know before? Were you right? Is there any way you could have anticipated what you learned? ❖

At a deeper level, comparing and contrasting is the key way we learn things. We interpret unfamiliar territory by relating it to places we've already been. *This* is a little like *that*—and so a bridge gets built so we can cross into the differences and complexities of the unknown.

Say you're trying to describe the feeling you have as you consider your new textbooks. It may be so unique that it compares to nothing you've experienced before: "I can't believe I'm going to actually learn all of this!" Or say you're trying to teach a new employee at the restaurant where you work how to get along in the huge kitchen in back. "Just pretend you're the water boy on the football team." Or "Remember that you're at the bottom of the totem pole—when someone asks for help, give it." Or "We're a well-programmed computer here, and you better learn your part in the program." As you try to explain yourself, you naturally draw on common frames of reference.

Maybe you're taking a Literature of Western Civilization course. Suddenly you realize that Achilles in Homer's *Iliad* is a lot like Michael Jordan, at least in his physical ability—or that Arnold Schwarzenegger could play Achilles in the movies. Come to think of it, though, Achilles is more open emotionally than the Terminator. He's more well-rounded than Michael Jordan, and certainly more articulate. There are differences, too, and that's part of the usefulness of the comparison. You're starting to understand the story a little better.

One key to appreciating any of the literature of the past is to think about likenessness and differences. In some way, the people in these stories must have something to do with us. In some way, we must be able to put ourselves in their shoes, or the literature wouldn't have lasted so long. And yet at the same time, the people who wrote and star in the ancient epics weren't from around here. They came from a different culture and landscape, and so thought differently than we do.

❖ **Solo Activity 6.2** Think of a literature, history, or philosophy class you've had at the university that involved ideas or figures from the past. Take one example—a particular figure or moment—and do a brief one-page screenplay that somehow brings it to life. Who would play the main character in the movie, and why? What music would be playing in the background? What other movie or television show comes closest to describing what this one will be like?

Or do the same exercise about the professor and the class itself. What movie or television show comes closest to describing Introduction to Philosophy? *Jeopardy*? *Star Trek: The Next Generation*®? *The English Patient*? ❖

COMPARISONS AND SCIENCE

Comparisons always work on the basis of similarities and differences. And useful comparisons abound in the sciences, too, though the comparisons in science are sometimes drawn based primarily on data. Thus, the frequency of heads versus tails in one hundred flips of a quarter may be compared to the frequency of female births versus male births. Such comparisons are useful not because their equivalence can be guaranteed, but because they can help people understand. In truth, the ratio of female births to male births worldwide is *not* equivalent, despite what we might guess. Another example: in a vaccuum, a feather and a bowling ball fall at the same rate. Seeing this comparison can lead to a better understanding of the nature of a vaccuum and the effects of friction.

❖ *Group Activity 6.3* Consider some aspect of scientific knowledge—any natural or social science, from physics to economics will work. Use a comparison to help explain or illustrate a principle or concept. Some possibilities include the law of supply and demand; the principle showing that as substances rise in temperature, their atomic and molecular activity increases; the assertion that a sport mirrors some aspect of society; or why the stock market rises or falls. Whatever you choose as your principle or concept, use comparison(s) to help people understand it. ❖

COMPARISON AND METAPHOR

The act of comparing is embedded in our language. We can't speak without comparing one thing to something else. In other words, we can't speak without metaphor.

As we saw in Chapter 3, a metaphor uses a familiar image—something concrete and available—to convey a sense of the mystery and complexity of a feeling or idea that may be present only in our own heads. "My love is a red, red rose," the Scottish poet Robert Burns wrote. We all know a little about roses—they're beautiful, they have thorns, and they have a lovely smell. Maybe, then, we know a little about the person the poet loves and how the poet feels about her.

Metaphors like this aren't just the work of poets. They're natural to the way the mind works. Millions of metaphors are involved in the very structure of our language. Every sentence we utter contains some sort of metaphor that we've used so much, we no longer think of it as a metaphor. "Structure," for example, in the phrase "the very structure of our language," is a metaphor from the building or shape of physical things, used here to describe something conceptual. We described comparison earlier as a kind of "bridge" into new material and then compared different realms of thought to "territories."

Or look at the last sentence itself: "material," "realms." Almost every word we use to position concepts or establish frames of reference involves an implicit comparison we've come to take for granted. "Position," for that matter, literally means where something is put; and "frames" means something that surrounds something else—such as window frames or frames of glasses.

In this sense, all thinking requires a particular kind of comparing and contrasting between an object in the physical world and an idea in the intellectual world. All thinking at root involves using nature and experience—what can be touched and tasted and felt—to negotiate the conceptual.

(Note all the metaphors in that last paragraph: "world," "root," "negotiate.")

❖ *Solo Activity 6.4* Refer to some previous writing you did for this or another class, or take a page from a book you're reading. Underline five of the "buried" or "hidden" metaphors. Then pick out two that seem particularly accurate or useful to your understanding. Write at least four sentences for each that explain why you found that metaphor particularly good. ❖

COMPARISON AND DIFFERENCE

By linking something we know to something we don't know—such as a shark's skin feels like sandpaper—we expand our knowledge. But comparisons are never fully accurate either—a shark's skin is *not* exactly the same thing as sandpaper. And the differences often tell us as much as the similarities.

❖ *Group/Solo Activity 6.5* Think about the metaphor, "My love is a red, red rose." In one column, list as many qualities of roses that you can think of—at least ten. In another column, list any of those qualities that might actually apply to a human being. In a third column, list all the ways—all the differences, however obvious or silly—a rose certainly isn't like a human being. For example, roses wouldn't be impressed by metaphors. ❖

❖ *Group Activity 6.6* Explain how studying in classes is *and* is not like working a job. ❖

❖ *Group/Solo Activity 6.7* Take a complicated class you've had or are taking right now—or take an idea or procedure from that class—and list as many similes that describe it. Do at least five. For example:

- Reading the Homeric epics is like climbing a beautiful mountain of white stone without many trees.
- It's like shifting from rock and roll to the sound of trumpets echoing against the hills.
- It's like beaming down to a planet, where the aliens are acting very strange and you don't understand what's going on at first.
- It's like walking into a big family reunion, where everyone is telling stories about people you never heard of and whole family histories everyone else seems to understand but you.

Remember, a simile is a metaphor that uses the word "like" or "as." "My love is *like* a red, red rose" is a simile. ❖

EITHER-OR PROPOSITIONING

To all this affirmative talk about comparisons, we add this important caution: our innate capacity for comparison also leads to the habit of either-or propositioning—of assuming that there is a clear right and wrong answer in every situation, and that every issue can be resolved into black-and-white, once-and-for-all categories.

We can't buy both the pickup and the Camry. We have to choose. We can't go to McDonald's and China Blue at the same time, though we might go to one on Tuesday and the other on Wednesday. When we buy something, we've got to choose one thing over the other—a fact that big multinational companies continually exploit in advertisement after advertisement, pitting Coke against Pepsi, Nike against Reebok, and Toyota against Ford. And our American political and judicial systems depend on either-or—yes or no, guilty or not guilty.

But however efficient this sort of polarizing can be, it has a dumbing-down effect over time. And that dumbing-down seems to have spread to all parts of our public discussion—either-or advertising reflects or has helped create a deep-seated and disturbing trend. We can vote for only one presidential candidate, but campaign strategists want us believe that there's a good person and a bad one, and that the candidates represent unambiguous and mutually exclusive choices. In complicated moral questions—such as abortion, minority rights, or even who to marry—hard decisions have to be made. But the debate about some public issues typically shrinks to the size of bumper-stickers—pro-choice or pro-life—as if those are the only two choices available, or as if those choices could be expressed in such abbreviated terms in the first place.

Environmental questions have been reduced in the same increasingly mindless ways, pat phrases like "spotted owls" versus "loggers" or "environment" versus "economy" substituted for the hard work of thinking about a very complicated problem. More and more it seems that we've let slogans and abbreviations do our thinking for us to the point that we've all but forgotten the shifting sands and nuanced realities of the concrete experience those labels originally described.

Maybe sports have taken over our national metaphors and, therefore, our national thinking, too. It's either the Packers or the Broncos. No ties. Sudden death. There have to be winners or losers. The allure here is quite real—at the end of the game, ambiguity has been resolved. The winners celebrate, while the losers console each other and make plans for improvement. Watching or playing a sport yields a focus and simplicity that often seems both pure and rare, hence valuable for its purity.

The danger comes in deciding or partially deciding that the purity and simplicity of sports can and should be transferred to other areas of human consideration. We can easily decide that intellectual life has to be imagined as a contest or battle, too.

❖ *Group/Solo Activity 6.8* Read the front page and the editorial page of your local newspaper for several days, and write down every headline or phrase that relies on "pro and con" and oppositional language. Or do the same exercise with television or radio news. Write down every use of an "us versus them" device. In the same way, watch a television talk show or listen to a radio talk show, and keep track of phrases from hosts, commentators, the audience, or callers to see how either-or propositioning, or black-and-white thinking, dominates our discussion.

After you gather these phrases, try to group them by issue. What are the major issues that seem to be polarizing the culture and your community right now? Share these in groups. ❖

❖ *Group/Solo Activity 6.9* Watch a popular sitcom or television drama for several weeks, and briefly summarize the plots. How many revolve around easy dualisms—the characters have clear choices between right and wrong, or the good and the bad? How often is there any doubt about the outcome? Are there clear heroes, and what do they look like, talk like, and act like? The villains? Are there always heroes and villains? Try this exercise with two different contemporary movies. Share your findings. ❖

EMBRACING CONTRARIES

The premise of the intellectual life is that things are rarely this easy. That's been the point of ASKING QUESTIONS from the beginning, when we asked you to challenge commonplace assumptions. Research and reflection often show that beneath the slogans and the easy oppositions are areas of terrific tension or overlap. It's not that one thing is always right and the other is always wrong, but that there are two or more conflicting areas of concern, all of which have validity. And it's not that we can simply say, "let's do both, like having our cake and eating it, too," because the two positions exist in tension. It's not possible to blend them together easily and naturally, no headaches forever after.

Writing teacher and theorist Peter Elbow uses the term "contrary" to describe this kind of dynamic tension. A contrary exists when two things are equally true and valid but somehow conflict with each other. A contrary exists when either-or propositioning doesn't work—if we choose one side over the other, or we lose too much of the complicated and messy truth.

The following essay applies this idea of contraries to an understanding of the teaching process.

❖ *Solo Activity 6.10* Read "Embracing Contraries in the Teaching Process."

- Mark it up, write heavily in the margins, and underline everything that seems important.
- Keep audience in mind. The author isn't writing to students, but to other teachers of college writing—the sort of people who read *College English,* where the essay was first published. In a sense, you're eavesdropping on a conversation that is not intended for you.
- There's nothing secret or that hard to understand in this essay. Part of what makes the essay valuable as a model is its directness and clarity.

- Note its structure, and how the author begins, uses transitions, and moves from section to section.
- As you read and write in the margins, jot down any ideas for a topic that might come to you on a piece of paper. Write them down quickly, without censoring, by listing whatever comes to mind. In other words, use the reading as a way of brainstorming. ❖

PETER ELBOW

Embracing Contraries in the Teaching Process

My argument is that good teaching seems a struggle because it calls on skills or mentalities that are actually contrary to each other and thus tend to interfere with each other. It was exploration of writing that led me to look for contraries in difficult or complex processes. I concluded that good writing requires on the one hand the ability to conceive copiously of many possibilities, an ability which is enhanced by a spirit of open, accepting generativity; but on the other hand good writing also requires an ability to criticize and reject everything but the best, a very different ability which is enhanced by a tough-minded critical spirit. I end up seeing in good writers the ability somehow to be extremely creative and extremely critical, without letting one mentality prosper at the expense of the other or being halfhearted in both. (For more about this idea see my *Writing With Power* [Oxford University Press, 1981], especially Chapter 1.)

In this frame of mind I began to see a paradoxical coherence in teaching where formerly I was perplexed. I think the two conflicting mentalities needed for good teaching stem from the two conflicting obligations inherent in the job: we have an obligation to students but we also have an obligation to knowledge and society. Surely we are incomplete as teachers if we are committed only to what we are teaching but not to our students, or only to our students but not to what we are teaching, or halfhearted in our commitment to both.

We like to think that these two commitments coincide, and often they do. It happens often enough, for example, that our commitment to standards leads us to give a low grade or tough comments, and it is just what the student needs to hear. But just as often we see that a student needs praise and support rather than a tough grade, even for her weak performance, if she is really to prosper as a student and a person—if we are really to nurture her fragile investment in her studies. Perhaps we can finesse this conflict between a "hard" and "soft" stance if it is early in the semester or we are only dealing with a rough draft; for the time being we can give the praise and support we sense is humanly appropriate and hold off strict judgment and standards till later. But what about when it is the end of the course or a final draft needs a grade? It is comforting to take as our paradigm that first situation where the tough grade was just right, and to consider the trickier situation as somehow anomalous, and thus to assume that we always serve students best by serving knowledge, and vice versa. But I now think I can throw more light on the nature of teaching by taking our conflicting loyalties as paradigmatic.

Our loyalty to students asks us to be their allies and hosts as we instruct and share: to invite all students to enter in and join us as members of a learning community—even if they have difficulty. Our commitment to students asks us to assume they are all capable of learning, to see things through their eyes, to help bring out their best rather than their worst when it comes to tests and grades. By taking this inviting stance we will help more of them learn.

But our commitment to knowledge and society asks us to be guardians or bouncers: we must discriminate, evaluate, test, grade, certify. We are invited to stay true to the inherent standards of what we teach, whether or not that stance fits the particular students before us. We have a responsibility to society—that is, to our discipline, our college or university, and to other learning communities of which we are members—to see that the students we certify really understand or can do what we teach, to see that the grades and credits and degrees we give really have the meaning or currency they are supposed to have.[1]

---

1. I lump "knowledge and society" together in one phrase but I acknowledge the importance of the potential conflict. For example, we may feel *society* asking us to adapt our students to it, while we feel *knowledge*—our vision of the truth—asking us to unfit our students for that society. Socrates was convicted of corrupting the youth. To take a more homely example. I feel institutions asking me to teach students one kind of writing and yet feel impelled by my understanding of writing to teach them another kind. Thus where this paper paints a picture of teachers pulled in two directions, sometimes we may indeed be pulled in three.

A pause for scruples. Can we give up so easily the paradigm of teaching as harmonious? Isn't there something misguided in the very idea that these loyalties are conflicting? After all, if we think we are being loyal to students by being extreme in our solicitude for them, won't we undermine the integrity of the subject matter or the currency of the credit and thereby drain value from the very thing we are supposedly giving them? And if we think we are being loyal to society by being extreme in our ferocity—keeping out *any* student with substantial misunderstanding—won't we deprive subject matter and society of the vitality and reconceptualizations they need to survive and grow? Knowledge and society only exist embodied—that is, flawed.

This sounds plausible. But even if we choose a middle course and go only so far as fairness toward subject matter and society, the very fact that we grade and certify at all—the very fact that we must sometimes flunk students—tempts many of them to behave defensively with us. Our mere fairness to subject matter and society tempts students to try to hide weaknesses from us, "psych us out," or "con us." It is as though we are doctors trying to treat patients who hide their symptoms from us for fear we will put them in the hospital.

Student defensiveness makes our teaching harder. We say, "Don't be afraid to ask questions," or even, "It's a sign of intelligence to be willing to ask naive questions." But when we are testers and graders, students too often fear to ask. Towards examiners they must play it safe, drive defensively, not risk themselves. This stunts learning. When they trust the teacher to be wholly an ally, students are more willing to take risks, connect the self to the material, and experiment. Here is the source not just of learning but also of genuine development of growth.

Let me bring this conflict closer to home. A department chair or dean who talks with us about our teaching and who sits in on our classes is our ally insofar as she is trying to help us teach better; and we can get more help from her to the degree that we openly share with her our fears, difficulties, and failures. Yet insofar as she makes promotion or tenure decisions about us or even participates in those decisions, we will be tempted not to reveal our weaknesses and failures. If we want the best help for our shortcomings, someone who is merely fair is not enough. We need an ally, not a judge.

Thus we can take a merely judicious, compromise position toward our students only if we are willing to settle for being sort of committed to students and sort of committed to subject matter and society. This middling or fair stance, in fact, is characteristic of many teachers who lack investment in teaching or who have lost it.

Most invested teachers, on the other hand, tend to be a bit passionate about supporting students or else passionate about serving and protecting the subject matter they love—and thus they tend to live more on one side or the other of some allegedly golden mean.

But supposing you reply, "Yes, I agree that a compromise is not right. Just middling. Muddling. Not excellence or passion in either direction. But that's not what I'm after. My scruple had to do with your very notion of *two directions*. There is only one direction. Excellence. Quality. The very conception of conflict between loyalties is wrong. An inch of progress in one direction, whether toward knowledge or toward students, is always an inch in the direction of the other. The needs of students and of knowledge or society are in essential harmony."

To assert this harmony is, in a sense, to agree with what I am getting at in this paper. But it is no good just asserting it. It is like asserting, "Someday you'll thank me for this," or, "This is going to hurt me worse than it hurts you." I may say to students, "My fierce grading and extreme loyalty to subject matter and society are really in your interests," but students will still tend to experience me as adversary and undermine much of my teaching. I may say to knowledge and society, "My extreme support and loyalty to all students is really in your interests," but society will tend to view me as a soft teacher who lets standards down.

It is the burden of this paper to say that a contradictory stance is possible—not just in theory but in practice—but not by pretending there is no tension or conflict. And certainly not by affirming only one version of the paradox, the "paternal" version, which is to stick up for standards and firmness by insisting that to do is good for students in the long run, forgetting the "maternal" version which is to stick up for students by insisting that to do so is good for knowledge and society in the long run. *There is a genuine paradox here. The positions are conflicting and they are true.*

Let me turn this structural analysis into a narrative about the two basic urges at the root of teaching. We often think best by telling stories. I am reading a novel and I interrupt my wife to say, "Listen to this, isn't this wonderful!" and I read a passage out loud. Or we are walking in the woods and I say to her, "Look at that tree!" I am enacting the pervasive human itch to share. It feels lonely, painful, or incomplete to appreciate something and not share it with others.[2]

2. Late in life, I realize I must apologize and pay my respects to that form of literary criticism that I learned in college to scorn in callow fashion as the "Ah lovely!" school: criticism which tries frankly to share a perception and appreciation of the work rather than insist that there is some problem to solve or some complexity to analyze.

But this urge can lead to its contrary. Suppose I say, "Listen to this passage," and my wife yawns or says, "Don't interrupt me." Suppose I say, "Look at that beautiful sunset on the lake," and she laughs at me for being so sentimental and reminds me that Detroit is right there just below the horizon—creating half the beauty with its pollution. Suppose I say, "Listen to this delicate irony," and she can't see it and thinks I am neurotic to enjoy such bloodless stuff. What happens then? I end up *not* wanting to share it with her. I hug it to myself. I become a lone connoisseur. Here is the equally deep human urge to protect what I appreciate from harm. Perhaps I share what I love with a few select others but only after I find a way somehow to extract from them beforehand assurance that they will understand and appreciate what I appreciate. And with them I can even sneer at worldly ones who lack our taste or intelligence or sensibility.

Many of us went into teaching out of just such an urge to share things with others, but we find students turn us down or ignore us in our efforts to give gifts. Sometimes they even laugh at us for our very enthusiasm in sharing. We try to show them what we under-stand and love, but they yawn and turn away. They put their feet up on our delicate structures; they chew bubble gum during the slow movement; they listen to hard rock while reading *Lear* and say, "What's so great about Shakespeare?"

Sometimes even success in sharing can be a problem. We manage to share with students what we know and appreciate, and they love it and eagerly grasp it. But their hands are dirty or their fingers are rough. We overhear them saying, "Listen to this neat thing I learned," yet we cringe because they got it all wrong. Best not to share.

I think of the medieval doctrine of poetry that likens it to a nut with a tough husk protecting a sweet kernel. The function of the poem is not to disclose but rather to conceal the kernel from the many, the unworthy, and to disclose it only to the few worthy (D. W. Robertson, *A Preface to Chaucer* [Princeton, N.J.: Princeton University Press, 1963], pp. 61 ff.). I have caught myself more than a few times explaining something I know or love in this tricky double-edged way: encoding my meaning with a kind of com-plexity or irony such that only those who have the right sensibility will hear what I have to say—others will not understand at all. Surely this is the source of much obscurity in learned discourse. We would rather have readers miss entirely what we say or turn away in boredom or frustration than reply, "Oh, I see what you mean. How ridiculous!" or, "How naive!" It is marvelous, actually, that we can make one utterance do so many things: communicate with the right people, stymie the wrong people, and thereby help us decide who *are* the right and the wrong people.

I have drifted into an unflattering portrait of the urge to protect one's subject, a defensive urge that stems from hurt. Surely much bad teaching and academic foolishness derive from this immature reaction to students or colleagues who will not accept a gift we tried generously to give (generously, but sometimes ineffectually or condescendingly or autocratically). Surely I must learn not to pout just because I can't get a bunch of adolescents as excited as I am about late Henry James. Late Henry James may be pearls, but when students yawn, that doesn't make them swine.

But it is not immature to protect the integrity of my subject in a positive way, to uphold standards, to insist that students stretch themselves till they can do justice to the material. Surely these impulses are at the root of much good teaching. And there is nothing wrong with these impulses in themselves—only *by themselves.* That is, there is nothing wrong with the impulse to guard or protect the purity of what we cherish so long as that act is redeemed by the presence of the opposite impulse also to give it away.

In Piaget's terms learning involves both assimilation and accommodation. Part of the job is to get the subject matter to bend and deform so that it fits inside the learner (that is, so it can fit or relate to the learner's experiences). But that's only half the job. Just as important is the necessity for the learner to bend and deform himself so that he can fit himself around the subject without doing violence to it. Good learning is not a matter of finding a happy medium where both parties are transformed as little as possible. Rather both parties must be maximally transformed—in a sense deformed. There is violence in learning. We can not learn something without eating it, yet we can not really learn it either without letting it eat us.

Look at Socrates and Christ as archetypal good teachers— archetypal in being so paradoxical. They are extreme on the one hand in their impulse to share with everyone and to support all learners, in their sense that everyone can take and get what they are offering; but they are extreme on the other hand in their fierce high standards for what will pass muster. They did not teach gut courses, they flunked "gentleman C" performances, they insisted that only "too much" was sufficient in their protectiveness toward their "subject matter." I am struck also with how much they both relied on irony, parable, myth, and other forms of subtle utterance that hide while they communicate. These two teachers were willing in some respects to bend and disfigure and in the eyes of many to profane what they taught, yet on the other hand they were equally

extreme in their insistence that learners bend or transform themselves in order to become fit receptacles.

It is as though Christ, by stressing the extreme of sharing and
being an ally—saying "suffer the little children to come unto me"
and praising the widow with her mite—could be more extreme in
his sternness: "unless you sell all you have," and, "I speak to them
in parables, because seeing they do not see and hearing they do
not hear, nor do they understand" (saying in effect, "I am making
this a tough course *because* so many of you are poor students").
Christ embeds the two themes of giving away and guarding—commitment to "students" and to "subject matter"—in the one wedding
feast story: the host invites in guests from the highways and
byways, anybody, but then angrily ejects one into outer darkness
because he lacks the proper garment.

Let me sum up the conflict in two lists of teaching skills. If on
the one hand we want to help more students learn more, I submit
we should behave in the following four ways:

1. We should see our students as smart and capable. We should
   assume that they *can* learn what we teach—all of them. We
   should look through their mistakes or ignorance to the intelligence that lies behind. There is ample documentation that this
   "teacher expectation" increases student learning (Robert
   Rosenthal, "Teacher Expectation and Pupil Learning," in R. D.
   Strom, ed., *Teachers and the Learning Process* [Englewood
   Cliffs, N.J.: Prentice-Hall, 1971], pp. 33–60).

2. We should show students that we are on their side. This
   means, for example, showing them that the perplexity or
   ignorance they reveal to us will not be used against them in
   tests, grading, or certifying. If they hide their questions or
   guard against us they undermine our efforts to teach them.

3. Indeed, so far from letting their revelations hurt them in
   grading, we should be as it were lawyers for the defense,
   explicitly trying to help students to do better against the
   judge and prosecuting attorney when it comes to the "trial"
   of testing and grading. ("I may be able to get you off this
   charge but only if you tell me what you really were doing
   that night.") If we take this advocate stance students can
   learn more from us, even if they are guilty of the worst
   crimes in the book: not having done the homework, not having learned last semester, not *wanting* to learn. And by
   learning more—even if not learning perfectly—they will per-
   form better, which in turn will usually lead to even better
   learning in the future.

4. Rather than try to be perfectly fair and perfectly in command of what we teach—as good examiners ought to be—we should reveal our own position, particularly our doubts, ambivalences, and biases. We should show we are still learning, still willing to look at things in new ways, still sometimes uncertain or even stuck, still willing to ask naive questions, still engaged in the interminable process of working out the relationship between what we teach and the rest of our lives. Even though we are not wholly peer with our students, we can still be peer in this crucial sense of also being engaged in learning, seeking, and being incomplete. Significant learning requires change, inner readjustments, willingness to let go. We can increase the chances of our students being willing to undergo the necessary anxiety involved in change if they see we are also willing to undergo it.

Yet if, on the other hand, we want to increase our chances of success in serving knowledge, culture, and institutions I submit that we need skill at behaving in four very different ways:

1. We should insist on standards that are high—in the sense of standards that are absolute. That is, we should take what is almost a kind of Platonic position that there exits a "real world" of truth, of good reasoning, of good writing, of knowledge of biology, whatever—and insist that anything less than the real thing is not good enough.
2. We should be critical-minded and look at students and student performances with a skeptical eye. We should assume that some students cannot learn and others will not, even if they can. This attitude will increase our chances of detecting baloney and surface skill masquerading as competence or understanding.
3. We should not get attached to students or take their part or share their view of things; otherwise we will find it hard to exercise the critical spirit needed to say, "No, you do not pass," "No, you cannot enter in with the rest of us," "Out you go into the weeping and gnashing of teeth."
4. Thus we should identify ourselves primarily with knowledge or subject matter and care more about the survival of culture and institutions than about individual students—even when that means students are rejected who are basically smart or who tried as hard as they could. We should keep our minds on the harm that can come to knowledge and society if standards break down or if someone is certified who is not competent, rather than on the harm that comes to individual students by hard treatment.

Because of this need for conflicting mentalities I think I see a distinctive distribution of success in teaching. At one extreme we see a few master or genius teachers, but they are striking for how differently they go about it and how variously and sometimes surprisingly they explain what they do. At the other extreme are people who teach very badly, or who have given up trying, or who quit teaching altogether: they are debilitated by the conflict between trying to be an ally as they teach and an adversary as they grade. Between these two extremes teachers find the three natural ways of making peace between contraries: there are "hard" teachers in whom loyalty to knowledge or society has won out; "soft" teachers in whom loyalty to students has won out; and middling, mostly dispirited teachers who are sort of loyal to students and sort of loyal to knowledge or society. (A few of this last group are not dispirited at all but live on a kind of knife edge of almost palpable tension as they insist on trying to be scrupulously fair both to students and to what they teach.)

This need for conflicting mentalities is also reflected in what is actually the most traditional and venerable structure in education: a complete separation between teaching and official assessment. We see it in the Oxford and Cambridge structure that makes the tutor wholly an ally to help the student prepare for exams set and graded by independent examiners. We see something of the same arrangement in many European university lecture-and-exam systems which are sometimes mimicked by American PhD examinations. The separation of teaching and examining is found in many licensing systems and also in some new competence-based programs.

Even in conventional university curricula we see various attempts to strengthen assessment and improve the relationship between teacher and student by making the teacher more of an ally and coach. In large courses with many sections, teachers often give a common exam and grade each others' students. Occasionally, when two teachers teach different courses within each other's field of competence, they divide their roles and act as "outside examiner" for the other's students. (This approach, by the way, tends to help teachers clarify what they are trying to accomplish in a course since they must communicate their goals clearly to the examiner if there is to be any decent fit between the teaching and examining.) In writing centers, tutors commonly help students improve a piece of writing which another teacher will assess. We even see a hint of this separation of roles when teachers stress collaborative learning: they emphasize the students' role as mutual teachers and thereby emphasize their own pedagogic role as examiner and standard setter.

But though the complete separation of teacher and evaluator is hallowed and useful I am interested here in ways for teachers to take on both roles better. It is not just that most teachers are stuck with both; in addition I believe that opposite mentalities or processes can enhance each other rather than interfere with each other if we engage in them in the right spirit.

How can we manage to do contrary things? Christ said, "Be ye perfect," but I don't think it is good advice to try being immensely supportive and fierce in the same instant, as he and Socrates somehow managed to be. In writing, too, it doesn't usually help to try being immensely generative and critical-minded in the same instant as some great writers are—and as the rest of us sometimes are at moments of blessed inspiration. This is the way of transcendence and genius, but for most of us most of the time there is too much interference or paralysis when we try to do opposites at once.

But it is possible to make peace between opposites by alternating between them so that you are never trying to do contrary things at any one moment. One opposite leads naturally to the other; indeed, extremity in one enhances extremity in the other in a positive, reinforcing fashion. In the case of my own writing I find I can generate more and better when I consciously hold off critical-minded revising till later. Not only does it help to go whole hog with one mentality, but I am not afraid to make a fool of myself since I know I will soon be just as wholeheartedly critical. Similarly, I can be more fierce and discriminating in my critical revising because I have more and better material to work with through my earlier surrender to uncensored generating.

What would such an alternating approach look like in teaching? I will give a rough picture, but I do so hesitantly because if I am right about my theory of paradox, there will be widely different ways of putting it into practice.

In teaching we traditionally end with the critical or gatekeeper function: papers, exams, grades, or less institutionalized forms of looking back, taking stock, and evaluating. It is also traditional to start with the gatekeeper role: to begin a course by spelling out all the requirements and criteria as clearly as possible. We often begin a course by carefully explaining exactly what it will take to get an A, B, C, etc.

I used to be reluctant to start off on this foot. It felt so vulgar to start by emphasizing grades, and thus seemingly to reinforce a pragmatic preoccupation I want to squelch. But I have gradually changed my mind, and my present oppositional theory tells me I should exaggerate, or at least take more seriously than I often do, my gatekeeper functions rather than run away from them. The more I try to soft-pedal assessment, the more mysterious it will seem to students and the more likely they will be preoccupied and superstitious about it. The more I can make it clear to myself and to my students that I do have a commitment to knowledge and institutions, and the more I can make it specifically clear how I am going to fulfill that commitment, the easier it is for me to turn around and make a dialectical change of role into being an extreme ally to students.

Thus I start by trying to spell out requirements and criteria as clearly and concretely as possible. If I am going to use a midterm and final exam, it would help to pass out samples of these at the beginning of the course. Perhaps not a copy of precisely the test I will use but something close. And why not the real thing? If it feels as though I will ruin the effectiveness of my exam to "give it away" at the start, that means I must have a pretty poor exam—a simple-minded task that can be crammed for and that does not really test what is important. If the exam gets at the central substance of the course then surely it will help me if students see it right at the start. They will be more likely to learn what I want them to learn. It might be a matter of content: "Summarize the three main theories in this course and discuss their strengths and weaknesses by applying them to material we did not discuss." Or perhaps I am more interested in a process or skill: "Write an argumentative essay on this (new) topic." Or, "Show how the formal characteristics of this (new) poem do and do not reinforce the theme." I might want to give room for lots of choice and initiative: "Write a dialogue between the three main people we have studied that illustrates what you think are the most important things about their work." Passing out the exam at the start—and perhaps even samples of strong and weak answers—is an invitation to make a tougher exam that goes more to the heart of what the course is trying to teach. If I don't use an exam, then it is even more crucial that I say how I will determine the grade—even if I base it heavily on slippery factors: e.g., "I will count half your grade on my impression of how well you motivate and invest yourself," or "how well you work collaboratively with your peers." Of course this kind of announcement makes for a tricky situation, but if these are my goals, surely I want my students to wrestle with them all term—in all their slipperiness and even if it means arguments about how unfair it is to grade on such matters—rather than just think about them at the end.

When I assign papers I should similarly start by advertising my gatekeeper role, by clearly communicating standards and criteria. That means not just talking theoretically about what I am looking for in an A paper and what drags a paper down to B or C or F, but rather passing out a couple of samples of each grade and talking concretely about what makes me give each one the grade I give it. Examples help because our actual grading sometimes reflects criteria we do not talk about, perhaps even that we are not aware of. (For example, I have finally come to admit that neatness counts.) Even if our practice fits our preaching, sometimes students do not really understand preaching without examples. Terms like "coherent" and even "specific" are notoriously hard for students to grasp because they do not read stacks of student writing. Students often learn more about well-connected and poorly-connected paragraphs or specificity or the lack of it in examples from the writing of each other than they learn from instruction alone, or from examples of published writing.

I suspect there is something particularly valuable here about embodying our commitment to knowledge and society in the form of documents or handouts: words on palpable sheets of paper rather than just spoken words-in-the-air. Documents heighten the sense that I do indeed take responsibility for these standards; writing them forces me to try to make them as concrete, explicit, and objective as possible (if not necessarily fair). But most of all, having put all this on paper I can more easily go on to separate myself from them in some way—leave them standing—and turn around and schizophrenically start being a complete ally of students. I have been wholehearted and enthusiastic in making tough standards, but now I can say, "Those are the specific criteria I will use in grading; that's what you are up against, that's really me. But now we have most of the semester for me to help you attain those standards, do well on those tests and papers. They are high standards but I suspect all of you can attain them if you work hard. I will function as your ally. I'll be a kind of lawyer for the defense, helping you bring out your best in your battles with the other me, the prosecuting-attorney me when he emerges at the end. And if you really think you are too poorly prepared to do well in one semester, I can help you decide whether to trust that negative judgment and decide now whether to drop the course or stay and learn what you can."

What is pleasing about this alternating approach is the way it naturally leads a teacher to higher standards yet greater supportiveness. That is, I feel better about being really tough if I know I am going to turn around and be more on the student's side than usual. And contrarily I do not have to hold back from being an ally of students when I know I have set really high standards. Having done so, there is now no such thing as being "too soft," supportive, helpful, or sympathetic—no reason to hold back from seeing things entirely from their side, worrying about their problems. I can't be "cheated" or taken advantage of.

In addition, the more clearly I can say what I want them to know or be able to do, the better I can figure out what I must provide to help them attain those goals. As I make progress in this cycle, it means I can set my goals even higher—ask for the deep knowledge and skills that are really at the center of the enterprise.

But how, concretely, can we best function as allies? One of the best ways is to be a kind of coach. One has set up the hurdle for practice jumping, one has described the strengths and tactics of the enemy, one has warned them about what the prosecuting attorney will probably do: now the coach can prepare them for these rigors. Being an ally is probably more a matter of stance and relationship than of specific behaviors. Where a professor of jumping might say, in effect, "I will explain the principles of jumping," a jumping coach might say, in effect, "Let's work on learning to jump over those hurdles; in doing so I'll explain the principles of jumping." If we try to make these changes in stance, I sense we will discover some of the resistances, annoyances, and angers that make us indeed reluctant genuinely to be on the student's side. How can we be teachers for long without piling up resentment at having been misunderstood and taken advantage of? But the dialectical need to be in addition an extreme adversary of students will give us a legitimate medium for this hunger to dig in one's heels even in a kind of anger.

This stance provides a refreshingly blunt but supportive way to talk to students about weaknesses. "You're strong here, you're weak there, and over here you are really out of it. We've got to find ways to work on these things so you can succeed on these essays or exams." And this stance helps reward students for volunteering weaknesses. The teacher can ask, "What don't you understand? What skills are hard for you? I need to decide how to spend our time here and I want it to be the most useful for your learning."

One of the best ways to function as ally or coach is to role-play the enemy in a supportive setting. For example, one can give practice tests where the grade doesn't count, or give feedback on papers which the student can revise before they count for credit. This gets us out of the typically counterproductive situation where much of our commentary on papers and exams is really justification for the grade—or is seen that way. Our attempt to help is experienced by students as a slap on the wrist by an adversary for what they have done wrong. No wonder students so often fail to heed or learn from our commentary. But when we comment on practice tests or revisable papers we are not saying, "Here's why you got this grade." We are saying, "Here's how you can get a better grade." When later we read final versions as evaluator we can read faster and not bother with much commentary.[3]

It is the spirit or principle of serving contraries that I want to emphasize here, not any particular fleshing out in practice such as above. For one of the main attractions of this theory is that it helps explain why people are able to be terrific teachers in such diverse ways. If someone is managing to do two things that conflict with each other, he is probably doing something mysterious: it's altogether natural if his success involves slipperiness, irony, or paradox. For example, some good teachers look like they are nothing but fierce gate-keepers, cultural bouncers, and yet in some mysterious way—perhaps ironically or subliminally—they are supportive. I think of the ferocious Marine sergeant who is always cussing out the troops but who somehow shows them he is on their side and believes in their ability. Other good teachers look like creampuffs and yet in some equally subtle way they embody the highest standards of excellence and manage to make students exert and stretch themselves as never before.

For it is one's spirit or stance that is at issue here, not the mechanics of how to organize a course in semester units or how to deal in tests, grading, or credits. I do not mean to suggest that the best way to serve knowledge and society is by having tough exams or hard grading—or even by having exams or grades at all. Some teachers do it just by talking, whether in lectures or discussions or conversation. Even though there is no evaluation or grading, the teacher can still demonstrate her ability to be wholehearted in her commitment to what she teaches and wholehearted also in her commitment to her students. Thus her talk itself might in fact alternate between attention to the needs of students and flights where

---

3. Since it takes more time for us to read drafts and final versions too, no matter how quickly we read final versions, it is reasonable to conserve time in other ways—indeed I see independent merits. Don't require students to revise every draft. This permits you to grade students on their best work and thus again to have higher standards, and it is easier for students to invest themselves in revising if it is on a piece they care more about. And in giving feedback on drafts, wait till you have two drafts in hand and thus give feedback only half as often. When I have only one paper in hand I often feel, "Oh dear, everything is weak here; nothing works right; where can I start?" When I have two drafts in hand I can easily say, "This one is better for the following reasons; it's the one I'd choose to revise; see if you can fix the following problems." With two drafts it is easier to find genuine strengths and point to them and help students consolidate or gain control over them. Yet I can make a positive utterance out of talking about what *didn't* work in the better draft and how to improve it.

she forgets entirely about students and talks over their head, to truth, to her wisest colleagues, to herself.[4]

The teacher who is really in love with Yeats or with poetry will push harder, and yet be more tolerant of students' difficulties because his love provides the serenity he needs in teaching: he knows that students cannot hurt Yeats or his relationship with Yeats. It is a different story when we are ambivalent about Yeats or poetry. The piano teacher who mean-spiritedly raps the fingers of pupils who play wrong notes usually harbors some inner ambivalence in his love of music or some disappointment about his own talent.

In short, there is obviously no one right way to teach, yet I argue that in order to teach well we must find *some* way to be loyal both to students and to knowledge or society. Any way we can pull it off is fine. But if we are teaching less well than we should, we might be suffering from the natural tendency for these two loyalties to conflict with each other. In such a case we can usually improve matters by making what might seem an artificial separation of focus so as to give each loyalty and its attendant skills and mentality more room in which to flourish. That is, we can spend part of our teaching time saying in some fashion or other, "Now I'm being a tough-minded gatekeeper, standing up for high critical standards in my loyalty to what I teach"; and part of our time giving a contrary message: "Now my attention is wholeheartedly on trying to be your ally and to help you learn, and I am not worrying about the purity of standards or grades or the need of society or institutions."

It is not that this approach makes things simple. It confuses students at first because they are accustomed to teachers being either "hard" or "soft" or in the middle—not both. The approach does not take away any of the conflict between trying to fulfill two conflicting functions. It merely gives a context and suggests a structure for doing so. Most of all it helps me understand better the demands on me and helps me stop feeling as though there is something wrong with me for feeling pulled in two directions at once.

---

4. Though my argument does not imply that we need to use grades at all, surely it implies that if we do use them we should learn to improve the way we do so. I used to think that conventional grading reflected too much concern with standards for knowledge and society but now I think it reflects too little. Conventional grading reflects such a single-minded hunger to *rank* people along a single scale or dimension that it is willing to forego any communication of what the student really knows or can do. The competence-based movement, whatever its problems, represents a genuine attempt to make grades and credits do justice to knowledge and society. (See Gerald Grant, et al., *On Competence. A Critical Analysis of Competence-Based Reform in Higher Education* [San Francisco: Jossey-Bass, 1979]. See also my "More Accurate Evaluation of Student Performance," *Journal of Higher Education*, 40[1969], 219–230.)

I have more confidence that this conscious alternation or separation of mentalities makes sense because I think I see the same strategy to be effective with writing. Here too there is obviously no one right way to write, but it seems as though any good writer must find some way to be both abundantly inventive yet tough-mindedly critical. Again, any way we can pull it off is fine, but if we are not writing as well as we should—if our writing is weak in generativity or weak in tough-minded scrutiny (not to mention downright dismal or blocked)—it may well be that we are hampered by a conflict between the accepting mentality needed for abundant invention and the rejecting mentality needed for tough-minded criticism. In such a case too, it helps to move back and forth between sustained stretches of wholehearted, uncensored generating and wholehearted critical revising to allow each mentality and set of skills to flourish unimpeded.

Even though this theory encourages a separation that could be called artificial, it also points to models of the teaching and writing process that are traditional and reinforced by common sense: teaching that begins and ends with attention to standards and assessment and puts lots of student-directed supportive instruction in the middle; writing that begins with exploratory invention and ends with critical revising. But I hope that my train of thought rejuvenates these traditional models by emphasizing the underlying structure of contrasting mentalities which is central rather than merely a mechanical sequence of external stages which is not necessary at all.

In the end, I do not think I am just talking about how to serve students and serve knowledge or society. I am also talking about developing opposite and complementary sides of our character or personality: the supportive and nurturant side and the tough, demanding side. I submit that we all have instincts and needs of both sorts. The gentlest, softest, and most flexible among us really need a chance to stick up for our latent high standards, and the most hawk-eyed, critical-minded bouncers at the bar of civilization among us really need a chance to use our nurturant and supportive muscles instead of always being adversary.

Essay Option 6A

Imitating the idea and the structure of "Embracing Contraries in the Teaching Process," write an essay to an audience of classmates and an instructor that shows how two things you think are equally true and important exist in some kind of creative tension or opposition. One useful possibility: "Embracing Contraries in the *Learning* Process." In other words, adapt Elbow's idea by shifting from his perspective as a teacher to your perspective as a student. How much of the same kind of creative tension applies? Assume you're writing for yourself and to other members of the class. Your claim here is that these two things are in creative tension or opposition—that, in some sense, they are both contradictory and true. Your support will be your own experience and your own analysis of that experience.

MORE ON THE EXAMPLE OF THE ENVIRONMENTAL DEBATE

In light of the "Embracing Contraries" essay, think again about the environmental discussion. Even a moment's reflection will show that people need raw materials, like wood and water, to survive. We all have economic needs, and small timber communities have suffered because mills have shut down and the use of the land is being disputed in the courts. But just a moment's reflection also makes it obvious that forests are beautiful and inspiring, and are necessary places of refuge and release—if not intrinsically worthwhile even apart from human needs. Loggers are moved by a sunrise in the trees; the operator of sawmill can love the sound of birds—just as "environmentalists" (of which there are many, many types, of course), drive cars and live in wooden houses, and wouldn't deny that they do. The sitcom caricatures simply don't do justice to the real messiness of the concrete situation.

For example, suppose a population of people earn their living fishing for a particular species of fish. It could be cod on the east coast, salmon on the west coast, or various fresh-water species in the Great Lakes. The waters these fish live in also are the waters that receive various sorts of polluted run-off from cities, towns, and farm fields. The people in the cities and towns, as well as the farmers in rural areas, want to make good livings. And those who fish want to make good livings. All of these people further agree that the fish being caught have some natural right to survive as a species.

Comparing "the right to make a living by fishing" with "the right to a manufacturing job that results in some pollution" is not as simple as either-or. Both rights make good sense.

And simple compromise may not work either. Suppose the proposed solution imposes some costs on manufacturers to work toward cleaner water, and it asks city dwellers to reduce the amount of pesticides they put on lawns, and it also requests a fishing level that's only three-quarters of the allowed catch from the previous five years. This sounds reasonable, but suppose the allowable catch in this compromise would cause a reduction in the fish population to unsustainable levels? Thus, the fish die out. The compromise looks reasonable, but its results are catastrophic for fish and for those who make their living fishing.

As Elbow puts it, "There is a genuine paradox here. The positions are conflicting and they are true."

❖   *Group Activity 6.11*   Reread the previous fishing example, and then work as a group to identify a local issue that seems similarly complex—even obvious compromise may not work or may require apparently unequal change or adjustments from one segment of those affected. As a group, write a paragraph of at least five sentences that explains why this issue must be seen in a more complex way than right versus wrong. ❖

❖   *Group Activity 6.12*   The following consensus-building exercise assumes that however subtle and difficult the issues involved, some kind of common ground can be found. Consensus-building begins and ends with the idea that whatever the creative tension between conflicting positions is, there's some place in the middle that people of both sides can occupy together.

This activity requires a common space—like your classroom, a group of people—like your class, a facilitator—like your instructor, and sufficient time—at least two hours. It begins with a statement about a controversy, problem, or issue that needs to be resolved or about some task that needs to be completed.

Assumption: The next election in your area will include a referendum vote to effectively ban all clearcutting on state and private lands.

1. Freewrite your first response. Do you think this is a good idea or not? Write what comes to you. (five minutes)
2. As you look over what you just wrote, where do you think that response came from? Write some sentences that talk about the origins of your response. (five minutes)
3. Reread what you've written so far, and boil it down to one sentence. Use this format: "I feel _____ because _____." (two minutes)
4. Now consider the proposal or issue again, but this time think of as many possible reasons to question, complicate, or

disagree with what you wrote earlier. Make a list of these things. (five minutes)

5. Considering all you've done so far, write one sentence that states your current position. (two minutes)

6. Find a partner, so you can work in pairs. Take turns reading the sentences you wrote for 5. Based on these two sentences, work together to arrive at one sentence that expresses your agreement on the issue, problem, or proposal. Here are your choices:
   a. You both agree to select one of the sentences written for 5.
   b. You decide to write a new position statement you both agree on.
   c. You write a sentence explaining that, though you cannot agree overall, as you consider this issue, you do agree on
   _____.

   Note: You cannot use cop-out agreements such as, "This is really hard" or "Clearcutting provokes more than one response." Stick with the clearcutting issue itself, and work to make your consensus genuine. When you finish this stage, volunteers will write their sentence on the board. (ten minutes)

7. Combine your pair with another pair by making a four-person group. Work together to write a single sentence that expresses your group agreement, following the same choices as in 6. When you complete this stage, volunteers will write their sentences on the board. (fifteen minutes)

8. Follow the same process one more time, but now combine your four-person group with another by making an eight-person group. Volunteers will then write their sentences on the board. (15 minutes)

9. Discuss the results. Among the possibilities on the board, how close to consensus is the whole group involved in this exercise? ❖

❖ *Group Activity 6.13* Is reaching a consensus a different intellectual act than "embracing contraries"? Are two different models involved, do they exist in contrary, or do they share a common ground? ❖

INTELLECTUAL MATURITY

Educational philosophers suggest that intellectual maturity requires us to move past the dualisms of childhood—Mom and Dad are always right or

Mom and Dad are always wrong—to a sense of complexity—Mom and Dad are real human beings. The goal of a university education should be to create what the nineteenth-century poet, John Keats, called "negative capability," or the capacity to live with unresolved contradictions.

What's so important about a negative capability like this is that it corresponds to the way the world really is—messy. Experience is not usually one way or the other, but lots of ways, simultaneously. This doesn't mean we spend the rest of our lives dithering. Commitments are necessary. Choices always have to be made. But choices made beyond an easy dualism are usually better choices, and they're usually made with some measure of charity, flexibility, and humility.

That's why we included a chapter on embracing contraries after the chapter on argument: because there is a stage beyond taking sides—the stage where we realize that all sides are often worth taking.

❖ *Group Activity 6.14* Discuss one or more of the following pairs of ideas as you've experienced them in your own reading and life. How are the values on either side of the slash related to each other? Is one value more important than the other? Or are they equally important? Is it possible to accommodate both values at the same time? Have you ever experienced a tension between such values?

- the need for freedom, creativity, and spontaneity/the need for discipline, order, and control
- the rights of the individual/the needs of society
- the truths of science/the truths of poetry
- the need for solitude/the need for community
- the obligation of the university to respect the rights and points of view of all people/the obligation of the university to instill in student democratic values ❖

❖ *Solo Activity 6.15* Freewrite for five minutes about the most important thing in your life—the thing you believe in most, care about most, and are the most committed to. No one else will read this. Freewrite for another five minutes about what opposing contrary, legitimate, and valid this commitment immediately calls to mind—what's the "evil twin" of this commitment, though the evil twin isn't really evil? Or would you argue that something deeply important in your life doesn't exist in creative tension with something else equally true and important? Freewrite by explaining and reflecting on this issue. ❖

Essay Option 6B

Compare the following two statements. Use your comparisons first to understand the two statements themselves—as separate from each other—and then draw conclusions about the values that underpin each of them. When you compare those values, do the values for the first overlap at any point with those for the second? If yes, to what extent? And how important or unimportant would you claim that overlap really is? End by explaining why you think students and teachers should see these two statements as very different, separate things, or as versions of one thing. Here are the two statements:

1. You go to college in order to get a high-paying job.
2. You go to college in order to learn about yourself in relationship to everything else there is and was.

Suggestion: Though you can write this essay for an audience of classmates and the instructor, consider writing it as a letter to a parent, sibling, or perhaps a dean or some other administrator at your school. In other words, imagine a real-world audience that may want or need to hear what you have to say. For example, maybe your parents want you to major in business so you can get a good job, but you're feeling pulled to major in dance, because you find it personally fulfilling. Write a letter to your parents that explores the relationship of these two possibilities. (Since this is a class assignment in the form of a letter, be sure to organize it around a single, clear thesis that you thoroughly and coherently illustrate.

THE ESSAY OPTIONS: GETTING STARTED

If you choose the first Essay Option, reading Elbow's essay is the first step in the writing process—the act of exploring the topic's question is the act of closely reading Elbow's argument. This may also may be useful as you begin to think about the second option.

❖ *Solo Activity 6.16* Drawing on the skills we discussed in Chapter 2, write a 250-word summary of Elbow's essay. Don't worry about the elegance of your language, just try to get the basic ideas down on paper. ❖

❖ *Group/Solo Activity 6.17* In a freewrite or a small group discussion, talk about several experiences from your life as a student at the university—experiences that either support or dispute one of the points Elbow makes from his perspective as a teacher. ❖

❖ *Group/Solo Activity 6.18* Make two lists to open up your thinking about the contrary or the paradox of your paper. One list should contain all the valid and good points that relate with one side of the tension, the other list should contain the valid and good points that relate to the opposite position. ❖

Invention and Imitation

An assignment like Essay Option 6A immediately involves you in the contraries of the writing process—contraries that Elbow also has written about extensively in articles and textbooks. For example, it's possible that as you read "Embracing Contraries," an idea will simply pop into your head, and some interest with gather. You're now ready to write.

❖ *Solo Activity 6.19* So write. Let it all come out quickly by discovering the order and shape of your essay in the act of writing—letting a rough draft develop spontaneously. That is, write an instant rough draft, all at once. ❖

The assignment also encourages close imitation of Elbow's own structure, a section-by-section mirroring. That, too, can be a way of stimulating your thinking in the beginning. Form, itself, can be a way of coming up with ideas.

❖ *Solo Activity 6.20* Outline "Embracing Contraries" by noting subtitles and other major indicators of structure. Compose your paper as a kind of filling-in-the-blanks that Elbow creates.

    a. Elbow begins his essay with a clear, straightforward thesis statement. Do the same by imitating the sentence as closely as possible.

        My argument is _____, which seems to be a struggle, because it calls on skills or mentalities that are contrary to, and tend to interfere with each other.

        If your idea doesn't fit the construction of this sentence, feel free to modify it further.

b. To help make your thesis statement clear, use a brief but significant quote from Elbow's essay. Use one to three sentences from early in the piece that capture his main idea about the contraries of the teaching process, such as:

> Peter Elbow says _____ about the teaching process. His statement is like what I'm talking about when I say _____.

In the final draft, you'll want to say this more elegantly. Also draw on any language from your earlier summary of this article.

Note: In the first section of his essay, Elbow talks about one side of the contrary for several sentences in the first half of a paragraph. Then he says "but," and spends the rest of the paragraph talking about the other side. Each paragraph is usually devoted to a particular point or subheading within the contrary, too. Later, he moves from one paragraph to the next—one paragraph talks about one side of the contrary, under a certain heading, then another paragraph talks about the other side. Make sure that the first part of your draft follows a similar pattern as it discusses both sides of the controversy you're discussing.

c. Conclude the first part of your paper by quoting these two important sentences exactly:

> There is a genuine paradox here. The positions are conflicting, and they are true.

Add several sentences to explain this in your own words.

d. Like Elbow, turn from this restatement and re-emphasis about the idea of paradox and the contrary, to some particular illustrations—both from your experience and from general knowledge. Elbow uses a hypothetical conversation with his wife, and then later talks about the figures of Jesus and Socrates.

e. Begin the next section with these sentences—or something along these lines that's been adapted for your purposes.

> Let me sum up the conflict in two lists of _____. If on the one hand we want to _____, I submit we should _____:

Follow these sentences, as Elbow does, with a numbered list of points that describe one part of your paradox. If they're workable, use the previous lists you first developed in your brainstorming. Both your lists can be much shorter than Elbow's—for example, use two or three points, if your paper will be shorter than Elbow's essay, which is about 25 manuscript pages.

Then adapt the sentence,

> If, on the other hand, we want to _____, then I submit the need _____.

Follow this sentence with a list of points that describe your thinking about the other part of your paradox.

   f. Conclude by suggesting a solution or by suggesting that there isn't one.

Note: Elbow concludes his essay by suggesting that the problem of the opposites in the teaching process can be solved "by alternating between them so that you are never trying to do contrary things at any one moment." He then gives a list of practical strategies for use in the classroom that make such alternation possible—though this list isn't represented graphically as a list, but is absorbed into a series of paragraphs.

Consider the possibility of alternation for your own contrary and practical strategies that might effect it. It's possible that your set of issues won't yield themselves to practical strategies. The way to conclude, then, is by acknowledging just that—by insisting on the complexity of these issues and the legitimate claims on both sides.

The final question for you to answer in this case is, so what? Given that these claims are in conflict, are there any mandates here for our attitude and our behavior at least? If we can't solve the problem, can we treat each other differently? Can we speak differently?

Academic Style

Compare these two paragraphs. The first is from Elbow's essay. The second is our deliberately abstract and wordy revision of this paragraph.

Many of us went into teaching out of an urge to share things with others, but we find students turn us down or ignore us in our efforts to give gifts. Sometimes they even laugh at us for our very enthusiasm in sharing. We try to show them what we understand and love, but they yawn and turn away. They put their feet up on our delicate structures; they chew bubble gum during the slow movement; they listen to hard rock while reading Lear and say, "What's so great about Shakespeare?"

not

The impulse to communication and expression that defines peda-
gogy exists in an ironic binary with the countercultural resistance of
the objects of instruction. Ridicule reverses the attempted privileg-
ing of some cultural products over others; or, by the same token,
apathy and indifference undermine the already debatable effects of
institutional coercion. . . .

The point is that Elbow avoids many of the common problems of
academic writing. Though he's dealing with complex ideas and staying
high on the level of abstraction, he manages to write directly, clearly, and
without affectation. Although his purpose is not to share his own experience but to make a philosophical argument, he feels free to use "I" and
to draw on illustrations from his own experience when they will serve to
make his point.

❖ *Group Activity 6.21*   Many of us heard in both high school and
recently in college that we should never use "I" in academic writing. Yet
here is Elbow, in an academic article, using "I."

Assume that the instruction to never use "I" isn't stupid and ignorant. What good purposes might be behind this "rule"? Why would a
teacher say such a thing?

Assume that Elbow is not a bad writer and that *College English*
didn't lapse or make an exception when it published his essay. What
would be a good reason for using "I" here? What does the use of "I"
suggest about the nature of academic writing?

Assume that the issue of using or not using "I" is a contrary or
paradox—or that the use of "I" is finally a trivial issue in itself, but one
that is symptomatic of something important about the intellectual life.
What would this be? ❖

Returning to the Preface

Contraries are everywhere in the intellectual life. They've been
present in every chapter of this book. Formulas can be good, but
there's a messiness that always exceeds them. Coherence is essential,
and it can be precisely described yet sometimes the best thing to do is
sit down and let it all come out freely—all at once, not worrying about
where the transitions should go. To succeed in college is to learn to
speak and write in another language, another voice. Yet in adopting that
voice and entering into that community, we somehow come to discover
who we really are.

❖ *Group/Solo Activity 6.22* Reread all your papers for this class, and take notes on any contraries you see as implicit—either in the things you wrote or in the comments of your teacher. Step back and reflect on the process of writing and rewriting these papers, and make another list of the contraries involved in that process for you. In groups, share your lists. How are these contraries related to the contraries of the teaching process that Peter Elbow explains in his essay? ❖

In the preface to this book, we quote two passages from the poet William Stafford on the "intellectual way, the university way." Here are those passages again:

> Suppose you start to write for some cause you believe in, and suddenly you're smitten with the recollection or a realization that there's something in that cause or some recent thing that's been done by people in that cause that would spoil your case. So you suppress it. That would be one way. It wouldn't be my way. I feel that the university way, the intellectual way, the way I want to promote here, is to face all the complexities of your thought as you go along. . . .

> As an intellectual I speak to you in a university. So let me appeal to you. What we have, the glimmer we have in front of us, the possibility that if we all key ourselves up enough and are alert enough, and are not satisfied with partial truths, partial information, we may find our way to some kind of betterment.

In a sense, every chapter of ASKING QUESTIONS has asked you the same set of questions, and those questions have to do with Stafford's sense of the university, which is our sense of the university, too: What is "the intellectual way"? What is "the university way"? What is the intellectual life, and why should anyone want to live it? How can anyone live it? Do the Stafford quotations make any sense in your own experience?

❖ *Group/Solo Activity 6.23* Your group is responsible for producing a one-page flier that introduces first-year students to the writing course you have just taken. Your task is to explain the course in a way that will prepare these people for the challenges and rewards of the intellectual life. Draft the flier. As you do, write brief sentences or phrases that answer the questions of this book—the questions we posed in the preface: How can we define the intellectual life? Why should anyone want to live that life? What practical tools do we need for living that life? The design of this flier could be based on the notion of contraries, although you can structure it in any way that makes sense to you.

Or, as Stafford put it in the conversation we quoted in Chapter 3, when we write it's as if we glimpse a little strip of the universe between the slats of a picket fence. "You are passing, and between the pickets you glimpse a little of what's beyond." This is the question of this book: what have you glimpsed through the slats of your fence? ❖

Essay Option 6C

Allyn & Bacon, the publisher of this book, has asked you to write a four- to six-page review of ASKING QUESTIONS to help the authors revise for a second edition. They want you to consider the following questions, among others:

- Is this book appropriate for college-level students? Is it too easy? Is it too hard?
- Is the tone of the book inviting and consistent?
- Is the sequence of chapters logical and effective?
- Are the writing assignments and in-class activities useful and effective?
- Does the emphasis on thesis and support serve the needs of college students, and is this emphasis effectively carried out?
- Does the book prepare students for the courses they will take in college?

You also are free to respond to anything that seems important. Write the review.

Essay Option 6D

Imagine that the papers you've written for this class will be published in a book. Write a four- to six-page preface to that book. Give the book a title, and explain what that title means in the preface. Your audience is other first-year writing students.

SAMPLE STUDENT ESSAY, OPTION 6A

As you work on your own essay for this chapter, consider the strengths and weaknesses of the following student essay. Does it follow the directions? Does it communicate clearly? Use the checklist in Chapter 1 as a guide while you read and evaluate.

Sarah Breeze

Finding Common Ground

My first question is this: what is the material on which this essay is printed? Don't answer right away—think about it. Paper is the obvious answer, but I ask you to dig deeper, think harder. Pulp may be your next response. Pulp, which has been squeezed dry of all water and laid on a screen to achieve the perfect condition in which it now exists. We could go on and describe every detail of the papermaking process, but let us just recognize that this paper started out as a tree.

Second question—what else is made of wood? Most likely the desk at which you are seated, the tissue you used or will use to blow your nose, the frames that hold up the structure you call home.

My point is that wood by-products are everywhere—and most people hardly pause to think of the process that brought it to them. Who held the saw that chopped the tree down in the forest? Who drove the truck of logs out of the forest to the mill where the bark was removed, and that tree—be it cedar, pine, or spruce—was sliced into perfect four feet by eight feet pieces and sent to the local paper mill or construction site or even all the way to Japan?

The timber industry, from start to finish, is a dangerous and complicated process. It involves many people in various communities, from CEOs to lobbyists to lumberjacks. Only recently (middle to late 20th century) has the concept of forest management been introduced to this industry. This idea sprouted from the gradual realization that the timber industry was clearing forests at an increasing rate, and they were not being replaced. Certain individuals, from members of Congress down to community locals, saw the need for reform.

As a result of the growing popularity of reform in the timber industry, two issues have sprung: the first being the salvation of the communities and industries dependant on the logging of forests; the second, the ever-increasing need for preservation and conservation of these very same forests. Two ideas, seemingly on opposite sides of the forest spectrum, yet it is my belief that these concepts are firmly embedded in the same root. The only way to recognize this sameness, however, is to identify and celebrate their differences, to examine the fundamentals, principles, and points of validity of each end of the spectrum. Only then can one realize that there is a common ground to start from—the overall commitment to and benefit of society.

The timber industry has been a central employer to most north-western rural areas for years. Small communities thrive on mills, which thrive on clearcutting, selective cutting, helicopter logging, and other practices. To impose an all-out ban on cutting down trees would wipe out these communities, one of them being the town in rural Idaho where I lived for 18 years. In this town there are 1500 people and four large mills—you do the math. Combine the total number of these towns and the total number of mills they depend on—that is more people than I care to see collecting unemployment checks.

As I stated before, the world in which we live uses numerous products every day that began as a tree. How do we even begin to replace these products with non-wood materials? It can be done, but is it cost-effective? What would be the economical impact of such a risky move? The timber industry and related industries have a commitment to consumers to provide inexpensive materials in order to enjoy the everyday products they use.

But to say that the timber industry can continue current logging practices for the sole benefit of society would be incorrect. From an environmental perspective, simply continuing to clear-cut and kill off species one by one would be to seal the fate of our survival on earth—and not in a positive way. How could forests possibly have that much of an effect on humans? In their process of photosynthesis, trees and other plants absorb carbon monoxide, a gas poisonous to humans, and release oxygen into the air. Fewer trees mean more poisonous gas for humans to breathe in. Want to breathe better in your home? Buy houseplants!

A less widely accepted reason is a concept that many have termed "Gaia," or, the idea that each species' chance of survival on this earth is directly related to other species' survival. You may have heard of the food chain once or twice in various classes. Starting with the smallest insect and working up to the largest mammal, we are all dependent on our food surviving. Rainforests are disappearing at alarming rates, taking with them undiscovered flora and fauna that will never return. No one knows if in these rainforests lie important vaccines, food alternatives—and no one ever will.

Some corporations, such as Weyerhaeuser, *are* implementing reforestation techniques. The short drive from Portland, Oregon to the Olympic National Forest in Washington is testimony to that. Oftentimes, though, they are nothing more than young tree plantations, monocultures, and certainly not places for wildlife to thrive. The simple truth is that nothing can replace the beauty and importance of an old growth forest.

And what about aesthetics? Have you ever woken up in the middle of a mist-covered forest with the lush green mountaintops blocking out even the vastness of the sky? Have you seen that same forest from an aerial view, the square patches of brown evidence of the human presence in that serene haven, broken roots and torn branches the only trace of the beauty that once existed? Conflicting views about the importance of aesthetics on the general health and well being of humans prevent this issue from becoming too important, but I ask you to at least *consider* your life with the absence of beauty, in any form.

Where, you may find yourself asking by now, is the common ground I spoke of before? It lies in the fact these issues, though opposing, are both valid. But it is not enough to simply realize this fact. They cannot continue in such opposing ways. To say it is a question of "the loggers versus the environmentalists" is to place society in conflict with its own well being. Better to say "I am a logger; therefore, I am an environmentalist." Where will the timber industry be when all the forests are gone?

It is not my place to provide suggestions as to how we can continue to support the timber industry while impacting the environment as little as possible. I will save this task for the experts. But as a functioning member of society, I have certain responsibilities. I must be willing to accept change in my life. I must listen to what the experts say and trust their commitment every step of the way.

I must accept that forest management is a contradiction in terms—that on the one hand is the struggle of small communities, including my hometown, to survive. There are entire industries dependent on the cutting down of trees, which in turn have a direct impact on the world economy. On the other hand is the fight for the earth, on which we all live, to survive. All species deserve a chance, down to the last spotted owl. There is the obligation to leave this earth much in the same way we entered it, so that generations to come can enjoy the comfort and the beauty we are all privy to. It is my belief that it is the task of the citizens to decide the fate of these two similar contraries. We are the voters, the laborers, the decision-makers. Only when we find a common ground, preferably a forest-covered ground, will we have gained as a society.

Index

215

Credits

Sarah Breeze, "Finding Common Ground." Used with permission.

Mona Charen, "Majoring in Sex" from *Corvalis Gazette-Times* (January 5, 1998). Copyright © 1998. Reprinted with the permission of Creators Syndicate, Inc.

David Denby, "Passion at Yale" from *The New Yorker* (September 22, 1997). Copyright © 1997 by The New Yorker Magazine, Inc. All rights reserved. Reprinted with permission.

Peter Elbow, "Embracing Contraries in the Teaching Process" from *College English* 45 (April 1983). Copyright © 1983 by the National Council of Teachers of English. Reprinted with permission.

Barbara Ehrenreich, "In Praise of 'Best Friends': The Revival of a Fine Old Institution" from *Ms.* (January 1987). Copyright © 1987. Reprinted with the permission of *Ms. Magazine*.

Shelley Fickes, "Where Have All the 'Best Friends' Gone?" Used with permission.

Scott Gallagher, "Address Unknown" and "But I Have a Question." Used with permission.

Langston Hughes, "Theme for English B" from *Collected Poems*. Copyright © 1951 by Langston Hughes. Reprinted with the permission of Alfred A. Knopf, Inc.

Isuzu advertisement "Outrun Civilization" courtesy of Isuzu.

Jim Beam advertisement "Get in touch with your masculine side" courtesy of Jim Beam.

Kate Lamont, "Reading Koi." Used with permission.
John Leo, "No Books, Please; We're Students" from *U.S. News & World Report* (September 16, 1996). Copyright © 1996 by *U.S. News & World Report*. Reprinted with the permission of *U.S. News & World Report*.
Adrienne Rich, "Claiming an Education" from *On Lies, Secrets and Silences: Selected Prose*. Copyright © 1979 by W. W. Norton & Company, Inc. Reprinted with the permission of W. W. Norton & Company, Inc.
Lex Runciman, "The Boat at Kelly's Lake" from Luck (Owl Bridge Press, 1981). Copyright © 1981 by Lex Runciman. Reprinted with the permission of the author.
Marjorie Sandor, "The Night Gardener" from *House Beautiful* (November 1997). Reprinted by special arrangement with The Lyons Press.
William Stafford, "Final Exam: American Renaissance" from *The Way It Is: New and Selected Poems*. Copyright © 1987, 1998 by the Estate of William Stafford. Reprinted with the permission of Graywolf Press. St. Paul, Minnesota.
William Stafford, "Learning How to Lose" from *An Oregon Message*. Copyright © 1987 by William Stafford. Reprinted with the permission of The Estate of William Stafford.
Deborah Tannen, "Intimacy and Independence" from *You Just Don't Understand*. Copyright © 1990 by Deborah Tannen. Reprinted with the permission of William Morrow & Company, Inc.
Marilyn vos Savant, "Good News for Poor Spellers" from *Parade Magazine* (September 27, 1998). Copyright © 1998. Reprinted with the permission of *Parade* and Marilyn vos Savant.
Tanya Williams, "Joe Camel and HIV Testing." Used with permission.